8/04

Encyclopedia OF Projects FOR *the Weekend Crafter®*

Encyclopedia
OF **Projects** FOR
the Weekend Crafter®

Terry Taylor ❧ Valerie Shrader ❧ Karol Kavaya & Vicki Skemp ❧
Jim Gentry ❧ Sheila Ennis ❧ Yolanda Carranza Valle

Sterling Publishing Co., Inc
New York

Material in this collection adapted from the following:
The Weekend Crafter® Paper Crafting © 2003 by Lark Books
The Weekend Crafter® Dried Flower Crafting © 2003 by Lark Books
The Weekend Crafter® Quilting © 2002 by Karol Kavaya and Vicki Skemp
The Weekend Crafter® Macrame © 2002 by Jim Gentry
The Weekend Crafter® Decorative Finishes © 2002 by Sheila Ennis
The Weekend Crafter® Metal Embossing © 2003 by Yolanda Carranza Valle

Every effort has been made to ensure that all the information in this book is accurate. However, due to differing conditions, tools, and individual skills, the publisher cannot be responsible for any injuries, losses, and other damages which may result from the use of the information in this book.

Library of Congress Cataloging-in-Publication Data
Encyclopedia of projects for the Weekend crafter/ Terry Taylor ... [et al.].
      p. cm. -- (The Weekend crafter)
    ISBN 1-4027-1266-9
     1. Handicraft. I. Taylor, Terry, 1952- II. Series

TT157.E497 2004
745.5--dc22

                            2003065732

10 9 8 7 6 5 4 3 2 1

© 2003 by Sterling Publishing Co., Inc.
Published by Sterling Publishing Co., Inc.
387 Park Avenue South, New York, NY 10016
Distributed in Canada by Sterling Publishing
c/o Canadian Manda Group, One Atlantic Avenue, Suite 105
Toronto, Ontario, Canada M6K 3E7
Distributed in Great Britain by Chrysalis Books
64 Brewery Road, London N7 9NT, England
Distributed in Australia by Capricorn Link (Australia) Pty. Ltd.
P.O. Box 704, Windsor, NSW 2756, Australia

Printed in China
All rights reserved

Sterling ISBN 1-4027-1266-9

CONTENTS

Paper Crafting

TERRY TAYLOR

INTRODUCTION

DO YOU REMEMBER the first craft material you ever used? Chances are pretty good that you were handed a pencil and a piece of paper to draw on. And such a piece of paper was given to you again and again throughout your school years when it was time to be "creative." Recently I found a manila envelope in my parents' attic filled with crayon drawings and a lovely get-well card I made in the first grade for my mother. The texture and color of the paper were just as I remembered them: slightly grainy and vaguely khaki. The red construction-paper vase on the front of the card still held its vivid color, and the attempt at creating dimensional petals was still evident, even after years of being packed in an envelope.

Those early school experiences were formative, and some of us became inordinately fond of paper and its possibilities. I know I did. I was the creative type in school, volunteering to make posters for special events, dioramas from cardboard boxes, seasonal bulletin boards, and the requisite prom decorations. Familiarity with construction paper, poster board, and crepe paper was essential.

Paper is considered by many to be an ephemeral, if not disposable, medium. However, ancient scrolls of papyrus are still unearthed on archeological digs, while paper flower vases and other examples of paper crafting are often found in our family attics. For me, that's part of the charm of paper: you can create useful or frivolous things for today and save them for posterity. And let's not forget the sensual charms of paper: its various textures, colors, and eye-engaging patterns.

The simple techniques you learned in school—how to paste, fold, tear, cut, and decorate paper—are a good foundation for your grown-up paper crafts. And you don't have to learn welding, buy elaborate power tools, or invest in expensive (and sometimes messy) materials to create beautiful things.

The projects in this book run the gamut from a functional place mat to a purely decorative (and impractical) floorcloth. Thankfully you don't have to complete these paper projects in the space of an hour's classroom lesson. Take your time—there's no better way to spend a weekend! If the directions tell you to let the project dry overnight, put your feet up and have a cup of tea. Then start again the next day. And there are no prohibitions preventing you from working during the week if you choose. By the time you return to the work-a-day world on Monday, you'll have created something substantial from a piece (sometimes literally) of paper.

PAPER CRAFTING BASICS

Papers

Have you shopped for paper lately? If you haven't, you're in for a pleasant surprise. You aren't limited to creating objects with grade-school construction paper or poster board these days. There's an infinite number of papers: from plain, stiff kraft boards to wildly patterned and colorful papers that mimic the pliability of soft, woven cloth. You'll find a wide variety of paper choices, not just in fine art supply and craft stores, but in home improvement stores and party and office supply stores, as well as from online suppliers.

ART PAPERS

A wide variety of fine papers are made for use with fine art techniques, such as drawing and sketching, painting, or printing. These papers are made in a variety of weights (thicknesses), with smooth or textured surfaces, and a range of colors. Use them in their natural state or embellished with whatever techniques you desire. The desk organizers on page 31 were made with a heavyweight paper artists use for printing etchings.

TISSUE PAPERS AND NAPKINS

Simple, white tissue paper has its everyday uses; green and red have their traditional holiday uses. Manufacturers also offer consumers stylish choices in a rainbow of solid colors that are paired with contemporary patterned tissue papers. You can also discover uses for the metallics, traditional patterns, faux prints, and lightly textured surfaces. Use them for decoupage (page 28) and as a decorative final layer for objects made of paper mache (page 60).

Decorative double-ply napkins can be used with decoupage techniques, too. You've no doubt seen the wide variety you can choose from in many stores. You can cut out individual motifs or use the broad colorful borders or the entire napkin in a variety of ways. They make great translucent embellishments on a window treatment (page 19).

PAPER BOARDS

Single-face cardboard, sometimes called corrugated paper, is available in a variety of colors and flute sizes (the rippled layer attached to or between the outer flat layers). Your color palette is not limited to the natural light-brown color (called kraft). Today's choices range from pure whites to metallics and bold colors. Crafters like their texture and versatility. You can play with their surfaces to create a striking soft book cover (page 34), or combine them with other papers in collage (page 43).

Double-wall cardboard, as used in the common brown cardboard box, is made of single-face cardboard with an additional face. It's the workhorse of paper crafting. Use it to form three-dimensional shapes to cover with paper mache (page 37) or as a substitute cutting surface if you don't wish to invest in a cutting mat.

Poster board (as every student and parent knows) is a useful single-ply board. It's lightweight, easily scored, inexpensive and readily available. Remember that midnight dash to complete the school project that's due tomorrow? Even grocery stores carry it. Manufacturers have responded to consumer tastes with fluorescent colors and metallic finishes, in addition to the traditional basic range of colors. Use it as a flat sheet or cut it into complex geometric shapes (page 46).

Illustration and mat boards are found in stores that stock fine art supplies. These strong, smooth-surfaced boards are available in a variety of thicknesses and colors. Store them flat at all times to prevent warping.

Foam-core board is made of two layers of smooth card stock laminated over a layer of polystyrene. White and black foam-core boards are commonly available in craft and office supply stores. You can't fold or crease this board, but it can be glued or pinned together to form three-dimensional shapes. It makes an excellent backing board for school projects and can give dimension to a flat project, such as a checkerboard (page 22).

VELLUM AND SCRAPBOOK PAPERS

Delicate, translucent sheets of vellum are popular crafting papers. They're somewhat stiff and hold a sharp crease when folded. Use them as accents in collages (page 39) or create whimsical shades for mini-lights (page 51). When you glue these papers, avoid using broad strokes of glue. Instead, apply tiny dots to prevent disfiguring stains and wrinkling.

Papers sold for scrapbook or memory album crafting are available in a mind-boggling profusion of patterns, finishes, and textures. To say they are infinitely useful and fun to use is stating the obvious. Their only limitation is that they are commonly available only in 12-inch-square (30.5 cm) sheets.

PRINTED PAPERS

Gift-wrap papers, both coated and uncoated, are available in flat or folded sheets, as well as rolled lengths. Machine-printed patterns imitate calligraphy, intricate fabric patterns, and hand-blocked patterns. Japanese washi papers are printed with intricate patterns on fine-grained paper, and they're great to work with. Other handmade Asian papers are often decorated with clean-lined stencilled patterns or hand-printed patterns from hand-carved wood blocks.

HANDMADE PAPERS

Admit it: you may like paper, but you truly lust after handmade papers. If you have yet to discover the joys of handmade papers, prepare yourself. Their textures and patterns are alluringly seductive. True paper junkies hoard sheets of papers with names like *unryu, sunomi, hosho,* and *momiji*—solid sheets formed with long, visible fibers and natural inclusions or sheets as delicate as handmade lace. Then there are crisp sheets; thick, textured sheets; and even rolls of fabric-like paper to delight the crafter's eye and touch. Be forewarned: they're a pleasure to work with and truly addictive. Use handmade papers to create a charming window treatment (page 58) or a decorative table accent (page 63).

Tools and Supplies

Most—but not all—of the tools and supplies needed for paper crafting you'll find you already have on hand. Tools like bone folders can be improvised with household items; cutting mats can be replaced by layers of recycled cardboard. Don't feel that you have to run out and purchase a specific tool or supply item. Use your common sense and ingenuity to create what you're missing.

HANDY TOOLS

Metal-edged rulers are indispensable. The metal edge ensures straight and accurate edges as you cut against them with sharp craft knives. You can also tear paper against the edge of the ruler to create a straight, softly torn appearance.

A bone folder is an excellent tool for creasing and scoring paper. If you don't happen to have a bone folder, the dull blade of a table knife is an acceptable substitute. In a pinch, your fingernail drawn across a folded line also will create a sharp crease.

Good quality drawing pencils and a small pencil sharpener should be in every crafter's tool box. A sharpened pencil marks a fine, well-defined line for cutting. Lightly penciled registration marks make it easy for you to place cut-paper motifs accurately on flat surfaces. A soft, kneaded eraser is also nice to have on hand.

A French curve and a compass are great for drawing fluid curved lines or creating circular shapes. In a pinch, use plates, drinking glasses, or saucers as templates to mark curves or circles.

Technically speaking, waxed paper is a material, but it's a useful tool as well. Use a sheet of waxed paper to protect glued surfaces when you press them with a weight.

Put your old textbooks or dictionary to good use as pressing tools. Glued surfaces dry with less wrinkling when weighted.

Keep a selection of brushes at hand for gluing, painting, and varnishing paper. A well-made glue brush with soft bristles is a wise investment. The flexible bristles make coating paper with an even coat of glue a snap. Take care of your brush and clean it in warm, soapy water after each and every use. A brush covered with dried glue is worthless. Period. Stencil brushes and other paintbrushes are valuable when working with paper.

Disposable latex gloves provide protection for your hands when you work with paper mache; unless you enjoy peeling a layer of dried glue from your fingers, you'll be wise to wear them.

Recycled materials such as food trays and plastic lids are excellent containers for glues, paints, and varnishes. Keep some on hand for a variety of crafting chores.

Pieces of soft cloth are also useful; use them to clean fingertips stained with glue and to wipe away excess glue from paper surfaces.

TAPES AND STAPLERS

Masking tapes in a variety of widths, types, and colors can always be put to good use by paper crafters. Black masking tape (purchased from an art supply store) has excellent adhesive qualities, in addition to having a decorative potential. Low-tack painting tapes, because they are less likely to mar paper surfaces, are a good choice when you wish to hold papers together temporarily. Good quality white artists' tape is a fine tape. Narrow, white drafting tape holds paper well and is not likely to mar paper surfaces. I like to use gummed paper tapes when constructing the basic structures for paper mache. Double-sided foam mounting tapes can be used to give layered papers dimension (page 49). Cellophane tapes, single- and double-face, come in handy, too.

The common office stapler can be employed to affix photocopied templates to your craft paper. The staples prevent the templates from moving while you score or cut out shapes (page 46).

GLUES

Every crafter has a favorite glue. It's also safe to assume that every crafter has an assortment of glues stored away for a variety of uses. If you look around your house, you'll probably find that you have two or more types of glue. Examine your stockpile and read the labels to determine if they can be used with paper.

Polyvinyl acetate (PVA) is one of the best glues to use with paper. It dries clear, and quickly, and is relatively inexpensive. Simple white craft glue is a PVA glue, and the terms can be used interchangeably. You can dilute the glue with water to make it more spreadable or to use for paper mache. Other glues, such as wallpaper paste and rice-based glues, can be used as well.

Rubber cement is good when you need a temporary bond. A single coat of cement is repositionable. A more permanent bond can be created by coating both surfaces to be joined, letting the cement dry, then pressing the surfaces together. Spray adhesives work in much the same way. They're handy when you have large surface areas to bond (page 72). Be sure to cover your work area to protect it from overspray, and work in a well-ventilated room when you use spray adhesives.

Semisolid glue sticks, epoxy glues, and hot glue can be used with paper, too. You can use a hot glue gun and glue sticks to join together and construct dimensional shapes from cardboard or foam-core board. Don't attempt to use hot glue as you would PVA glue. You won't be happy with the results. That said, there are times when hot glue is just the thing. Decoupage mediums, acrylic varnishes, and acrylic mediums can also be used to adhere papers. They are available in matte, satin, and gloss finishes.

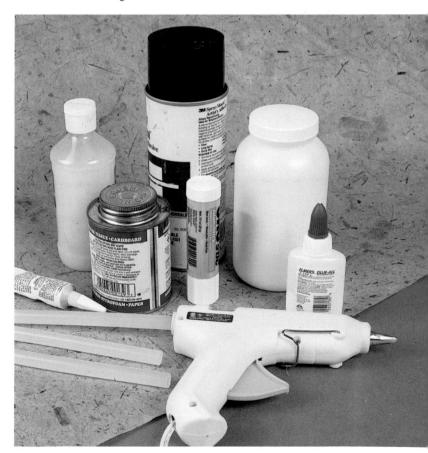

sizes, from small personal-size cutters for trimming photos to the heavy-duty cutters found in copy shops and offices.

PIERCING TOOLS

The humble, hand-held office hole punch is not the only choice for piercing holes. Manufacturers have created inexpensive hand punches that can pierce holes in a variety of sizes and shapes. And a hole doesn't have to be round anymore: stars, squares, rectangles, and hearts (just to name a few) can be punched in paper (page 49). Eyelet punches make holes into which decorative and functional eyelets can be set (page 27). The throat depth of your punch is the only limitation for its use. A hole punch can only be used around the edges of a sheet of paper. If you want a hole in the center of a sheet of paper, you'll need to cut it out with a sharp craft knife or scissors.

CUTTING TOOLS

A utility knife with breakaway blades is an ideal tool for cutting heavy cardboard. Craft knives with disposable blades are a must-have when you work with papers and lightweight board. Change the blades frequently: a dull blade will leave a ragged edge when you try to cut with it.

Keep your favorite pair of scissors close at hand when you work with paper. I have a small, black-handled pair of scissors purchased in a photo store that I use only with paper. Woe to anyone who mistakenly tries to cut something else with those scissors! Handle scissors with sharp, curved blades and fine points with care. If they are treated like fine tools, their cost will be repaid over the years. There are many inexpensive scissors used for cutting decorative edges: wavy, deckled, or geometric. Pinking shears are sewing scissors that create decorative edges.

Rotary cutters are packaged with circular blades made to cut straight-edged lines. They are useful when you need to make long, straight cuts. Manufacturers have created deckled and wavy-edged blades for rotary cutters.

A self-healing cutting mat is a necessity when using a craft knife, utility knife, or rotary cutter. If you don't have a self-healing mat, protect your work surface with a sheet of double-face cardboard or a thick magazine.

A paper cutter with a guillotine blade is great when you have to cut multiple sheets or many same-size pieces (page 52). You can find this type of cutter in a variety of

Techniques

DECOUPAGE

Decoupage, from the French verb *découper*, "to cut out," is the technique of cutting and pasting paper to a surface to create an image or pattern. Just about any type of surface can be used for decoupage: metal, glass, wood, cloth, and paper, too.

Simply adhere your cut paper shapes to a clean surface with PVA glue diluted with a little water or with commercially available decoupage mediums. Make sure the cut paper is laid smoothly on the surface without wrinkling or creating air bubbles. A sharp, straight pin is useful for puncturing air bubbles, which can then be smoothed into place with your fingers or a soft cloth. A final protective coat of acrylic varnish is brushed onto the entire surface to protect the applied papers.

WEAVING

Paper is composed of plant fibers, so it's only natural that it be used as a material for weaving. For weaving at its simplest, cut slits in a sheet of paper and weave strips of paper over and under the slits. Use flat or folded strips of paper to form the warp (vertical strips) and weft (horizontal strips) and to create the simple over-and-under pattern (or more complex patterns) of weaving.

FOLDING

One of the most useful properties of paper is that it can be folded to hold a sharp crease. A crease in paper, however, is almost impossible to eliminate. That said, store your papers flat and be very sure you make a fold where you want it.

A single fold or crease will give a flat sheet just a hint of dimension. Combining multiple folds can create truly three-dimensional forms from a flat sheet. The Japanese art of origami is the most widely known technique for creating a three-dimensional form from a sheet of paper. Multiple folds can also be used to create simple forms that in turn can be joined to make sculptural shapes (page 46).

Folded paper can also be used to create other forms.

Simply folding strips of paper in half for weaving will give you a double-sided mat (page 69). Folding small strips of paper and interlocking them (page 52) presents many possibilities.

STITCHING

Machine or hand stitching can be used to join sheets of paper much as you would fabric. Even more exciting are the possibilities for using stitchery as a decorative element with paper. Experiment with the variety of stitches you can create by hand or with a machine. Stitching is used to join sheets and embellish the Golden Temple Floor Cloth (page 72).

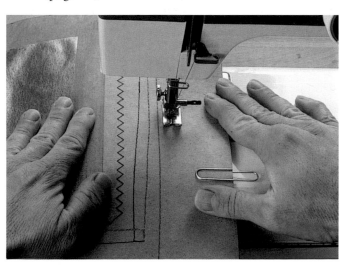

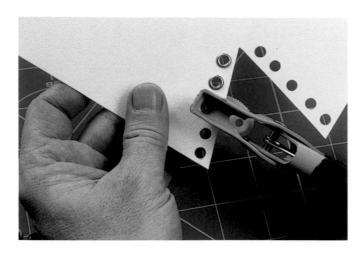

CUTTING AND PIERCING

Cutting a sheet of paper is not rocket science. You can make sharp, clean-edged straight cuts with scissors or a sharp knife drawn against a metal ruler. If you want a softer edge, tear the paper against a metal ruler or fold the paper and tear along the crease. Handmade papers and Oriental papers with long fibers can be cut with scissors, but they look best when torn.

When you want to cut out printed or traced shapes, first excise the unwanted internal sections with a craft knife or sharp, pointed scissors. Then cut out the external edge of the shape. You'll find that you can make a smoother cut by moving the paper towards the scissor blades rather than pushing the scissors forward.

You can pierce (make holes in) paper with a variety of punches, needles, or awls. Holes can be functional (page 25) or decorative (page 49).

PAPER MACHE

Paper mache is the craft of modeling three-dimensional shapes with pasted, torn paper strips. Useful and decorative objects can be created from this humble material.

The paper mache projects in this book are constructed with double-wall cardboard bases. The bases should always be coated with lightly diluted PVA glue and allowed to dry. This seals the cardboard and prevents it from absorbing excessive amounts of moisture during construction. Other bases can be used in creating paper mache objects: plates, bowls, modeling clay, or balloons. These bases should be coated with a thin layer of petroleum jelly before the paper mache mixture is applied to them.

Tear one-inch-wide (2.5 cm) or smaller strips of newspaper; do not cut them with scissors. A torn edge exposes the fibers and thus helps to blend the edges when they are pressed into place. Dip a strip in a 1:1 mixture of PVA glue and water. Resist the urge to throw a handful of paper strips in the mixture to soak: they'll dissolve and you'll have a mess on your hands. Dip them, one at a time, until they are well coated with the mixture. Hold the strip over your container of PVA mixture and pull it between two fingers to remove excess liquid. Then apply the strip to your form.

Paper mache is a gleefully messy business—there's no getting around it. Cover your work area with plastic sheeting or plastic trash bags. Wear a pair of disposable latex gloves, unless you don't mind tediously scrubbing your hands and peeling off layers of dried PVA glue. Kids of all ages love paper mache.

Rice Paper Blinds

Here's an easy way to transform white rice-paper blinds if you're the kind of person who likes a little color and pattern in your life. These blinds look great inside and out—light passing through the shades makes a colorful garden glow.

1 Measure your window before you purchase a rice paper blind. There's nothing worse than getting home after a shopping trip and finding you've bought the wrong size blind (comforter, lamp shade, or rug!).

2 Use sharp scissors to cut out the design elements you wish to use. Set them aside. The decorative napkins have two or more layers. (You probably discovered this while you were cutting out the design elements.) Peel the printed layer away from the white layer.

3 Unroll your blind onto a large, flat surface covered with plastic sheeting. A dining table, or even the floor, makes an excellent working surface. Move any cords to the side; you don't want them in the way while you work. Arrange the design elements you've cut out. When you're pleased with the way they look, draw light, pencil marks on the shade around the elements to guide you when you glue them down. This is especially important if your pattern is a repeating pattern, but not so important if it's a casual, unstructured arrangement.

5 Place the pattern element onto the shade. Use a stencil brush and a straight up-and-down pouncing motion to adhere the element to the shade. You may need to add a bit of medium around the edges of the pattern. Use a small brush to paint medium under the edges and a stencil brush to pounce them down. Allow the shade to dry flat overnight before replacing the cords and hanging it.

4 Pick up one shape and spread a thin coat of decoupage medium onto the shade in approximately the same size and shape you just picked up.

Chic Checkerboard

Red and black are the classic colors for a checkerboard, but who's to say that you can't make one in the colors of your choice? Anyone for a game of checkers played on an apple green and citron board?

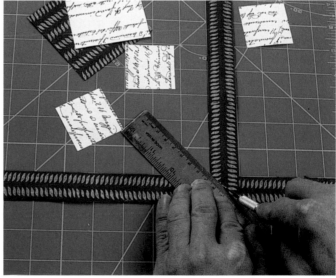

1 Measure and use a utility knife to cut out a 16-inch (40.6 cm) square of illustration board. Cut out a 15-inch (38.1 cm) square of foam-core board. Cut out a second square of illustration board, measuring $18\frac{1}{2}$ inches (47 cm) square. Set the largest board and the foam-core board to the side.

Using a metal-edge ruler and a sharp pencil, lightly draw a one-inch-wide (2.5 cm) border around the edge of the 16-inch (40.6 cm) square. Then mark a grid of $1\frac{3}{4}$-inch (4.4 cm) squares in the center of the board, as shown. You will need 64 squares in all for the playing surface.

2 Measure and cut $1\frac{3}{4}$-inch (4.4 cm) squares of the Florentine script paper. You will need 32 in all. Measure and cut four 1×18-inch (2.5×45.7 cm) strips of the kilim print paper. Lay two long strips at right angles to each other (a cutting mat marked with a grid helps you align them accurately). Cut a mitered corner with the craft knife and a metal-edge ruler. Lay another strip over the opposite end and cut another mitered corner. Miter all the corners and set them aside.

Cement together the largest board and the foam-core board. Then cement the playing surface onto the foam core. You may use spray adhesive if you wish. Cover the sandwiched playing board with waxed paper, weight it with books, and let it dry.

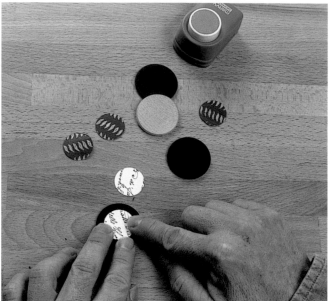

3 Spread a thin coat of rubber cement on the border strips. Then spread a thin coat of cement on the border area. Let the cement dry. It's hard to reposition surfaces that are coated with dried rubber cement, so work carefully as you place each border on the board.

Coat the squares with cement, as shown. Carefully position the alternating-colored squares on the board. Align the script right side up on four rows, then turn the board and position the remaining squares. Cover the board with waxed paper and weight it with books for an hour or so.

5 Use the circular paper punch to make 12 circles out of each of the two decorative papers. Set the circles aside. Paint both sides of the wooden craft circles with acrylic paint. Let each side dry before painting the opposite side. Use PVA glue to adhere the paper circles to the wooden circles.

4 Measure and cut four 3¼-inch (8.2 cm) squares of the border paper. Mark and cut out four 2½-inch (6.4 cm) squares of the Florentine script paper. Cement the larger squares just inside the four corners of the large illustration board. Center and cement the squares of Florentine script paper in the border paper squares. Let them dry.

Not Your Grandmother's Quilt

This wall piece is a tribute to the thrifty quilt makers of the past. They recycled bits of outgrown or worn clothing and traded scraps of cloth to create beautiful quilts for practical purposes. This paper quilt has no practical purpose, but it's a striking decorative use of recycled materials just the same.

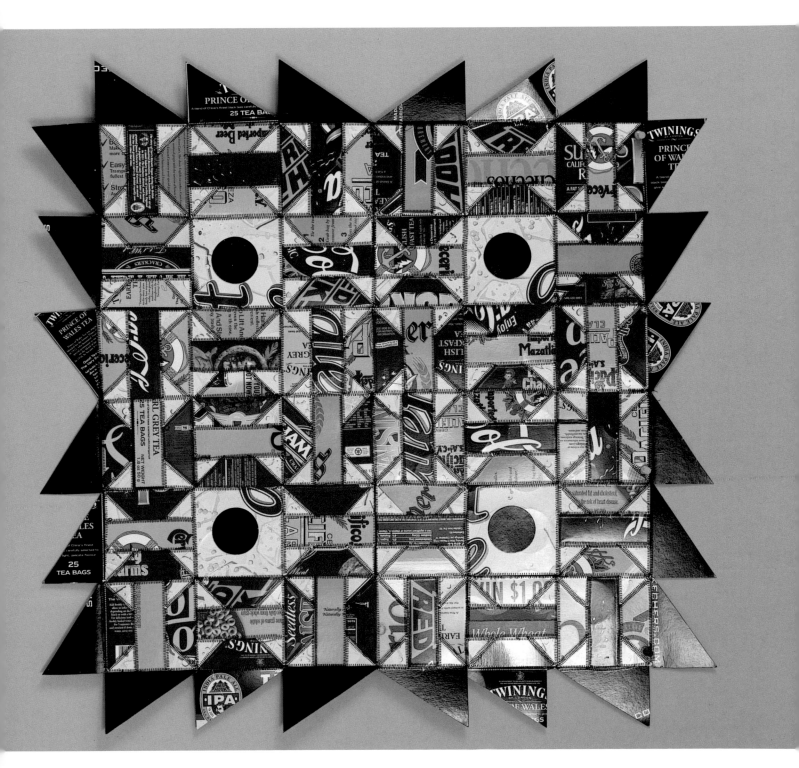

*It takes some ahead-of-time planning to amass the colors you'll want to use. Ask your friends to put aside cardboards of certain colors from their recycling bins. And feel free to make your family drink only that soda found in a pale-green carton or breakfast on the cereal that comes in bright blue boxes.

1 We used an adaptation of the Beggar Block pattern found in the 1931 edition of *101 Patchwork Patterns* by Ruby McKim. You can use the quilt block pattern on page 81 or consult any number of quilting books for pattern ideas of your own. Photocopy your quilt template patterns and mount them on thin cardboard with spray adhesive. Cut them out. Consult the pattern block illustration when you assemble your block.

2 Trace your pattern templates on the back of the cardboard. Doing so brings a bit of the unexpected into your pattern, and the outlines are easier to follow when you cut. That's not to say that you can't choose to include a specific trademark or word if you so desire. Trace and cut out a few more pieces than your pattern calls for.

3 Assemble the smallest pattern pieces to create larger pieces. In this case, two small triangles are attached to a rhombus to create a rectangle. Use short lengths of tape to join the pieces together on the back.

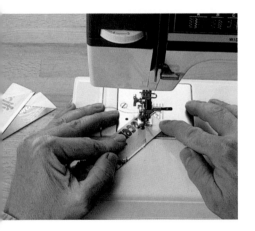

4 Join the small pieces with a decorative zigzag or satin stitch on your sewing machine. Trim the loose thread ends with scissors.

5 Assemble a square by taping together three rectangular units. Machine-stitch the units together after you have joined them with tape. Trim the thread ends.

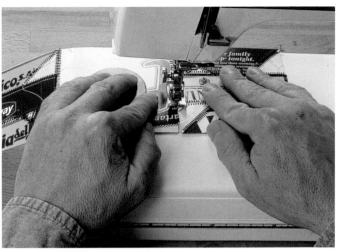

6 Join three squares together to create a row. Then join three rows together to create a complete block. You can stop with just one block or assemble and join four blocks to create a wall piece as in this project. (The circle in the center of each block was created with a paper punch and adhered with glue.)

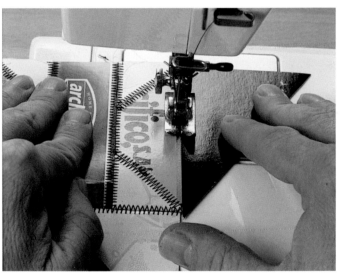

7 If desired, machine-stitch a border of right-angle triangles to the hanging. You may choose to finish the back of the piece with a glued sheet of decorative paper. Set eyelets into each corner of the quilt. Hang the quilt on the wall with small tacks.

Photo Storage Boxes

Do you have stacks of vacation photos stuffed into shoe boxes (or worse)? If the decorative storage boxes you find in the stores don't suit your fancy or fit into your decorating scheme, create your own stylish boxes.

Photo storage boxes in a solid color

Colored and patterned tissue paper

Scissors or rotary cutter

Plastic sheeting or trash bag

Decoupage medium

Small brush

1 Cut the folded tissue papers into strips of varying widths. A rotary cutter used on a cutting mat makes quick work of creating more than enough strips. Set the strips aside.

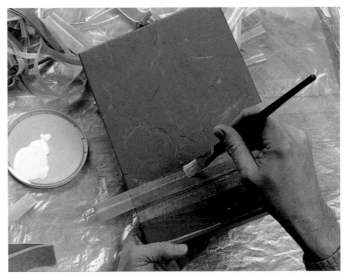

2 Cover your work surface with plastic. Start on the box lid by painting a wide line of decoupage medium across the width of the lid. Lay a strip of tissue on the medium. Paint the medium onto the exterior and interior sides of the lid. Fold each end of the strip over the sides and onto the inside of the lid. Use your brush to smooth each strip as you work, pressing out air bubbles and wrinkles.

3 When you have laid strips across the width of the lid, repeat the process with strips running lengthwise. Use the brush to smooth each strip as you work.

5 Give the box and the lid a final coat of decoupage medium. Let them dry.

4 Though it isn't absolutely critical, matching the stripes of the plaid on the base of the box creates a nice touch. Start work on the sides, matching each tissue stripe with the one on the box lid. Use decoupage medium to attach a strip of tissue to each side. Overlap a small amount of each strip into the interior and onto the bottom of the box. Then adhere lengthwise strips of tissue around the box.

Jute-Laced Desk Organizers

Simple materials and casual (but not sloppy) construction both aptly describe these organizers for the home office. Once you've mastered the construction steps it's easy to create different sizes and shapes to suit your storage needs.

YOU WILL NEED

140 lb. Fabriano murrillo paper*

Metal-edged ruler

Sharp pencil

Craft knife

Bone folder

Hole punch

Eyelets and eyelet punch

Jute

Cellophane tape (optional)

*Use any heavyweight paper you desire. Poster board and watercolor papers are excellent alternate choices.

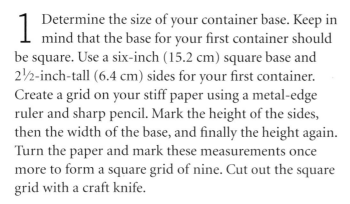

1 Determine the size of your container base. Keep in mind that the base for your first container should be square. Use a six-inch (15.2 cm) square base and 2½-inch-tall (6.4 cm) sides for your first container. Create a grid on your stiff paper using a metal-edge ruler and sharp pencil. Mark the height of the sides, then the width of the base, and finally the height again. Turn the paper and mark these measurements once more to form a square grid of nine. Cut out the square grid with a craft knife.

2 How wide do you wish the top of your container to be? This will determine the angle of the sides. For your first container, make a mark one inch (2.5 cm) from each side at the top, as shown. Use a metal-edge ruler to connect the marks from the top to the corner of the base. Use a bone folder to score the lines of the square base.

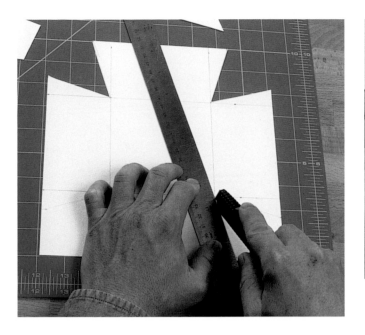

3 Cut out the angled shapes you marked in step 2.

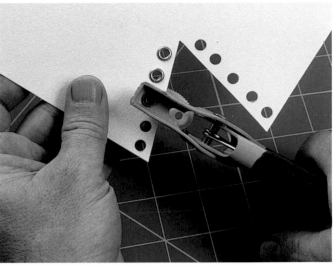

5 Use a handheld eyelet punch to set the eyelets along each side.

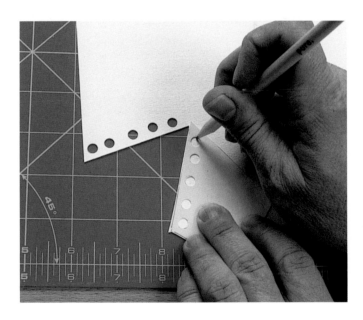

4 Use one of the cut-out shapes or another piece of paper to create a template for the spacing of the holes you will punch along each side. Use an odd number of holes. When you are satisfied with the spacing of the holes, use the template to mark each edge. This will ensure that the holes you punch are aligned with the holes on the adjacent edges. Punch the marked holes with a hole punch.

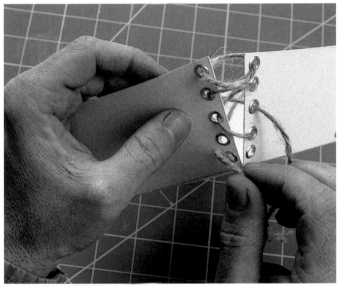

6 Cut four lengths of jute, each measuring four times the height of your sides. If you are lacing a tall shape, wind a bit of tape on each end of your jute to prevent raveling. Start lacing at the top of two adjacent sides. Bring the ends through the eyelets from the inside. Then cross the laces to opposite sides, just as you would when you lace your shoes. Pull the adjacent sides together gradually as you work your way to the base. End the lacing on the inside, knot the jute, and trim it closely. Lace all the sides this way.

Corrugated Marquetry Photo Album

*Are you a tourist who enjoys using the panoramic function on
your camera? Unfortunately, those panoramic photos don't fit neatly into
storage boxes and usually don't fit in the family photo album either.
Here you'll use corrugated papers to create your own specially
made album for those oversize photos.*

YOU WILL NEED

Panoramic photos

Corrugated paper in two or more colors

Metal-edged ruler

Pencil

Your choice of page papers

Thin rice paper

Metal screw posts*

Large paper punches

PVA glue

Waxed paper

Small hole punch

Photo corners

*You'll find these posts in craft stores and stores that carry bookbinding supplies. Purchase posts that are suitably sized for your album; we used $\frac{1}{2}$-inch (1.3 cm) posts for this project.

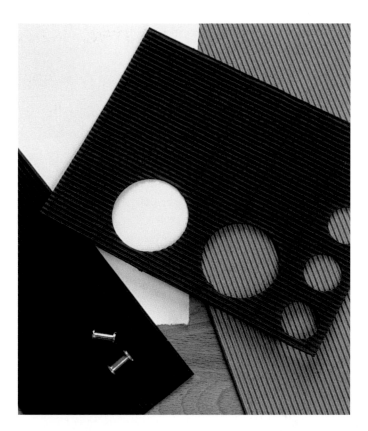

1 Measure your panoramic photo to determine the size of your album cover. Your cover should be slightly larger than the photo. The cover we created measures $14 \times 5\frac{1}{4}$ inches (35.6×13 cm). Measure and cut two covers. Be sure the flutes of the corrugated paper run vertically rather than horizontally.

2 Measure and cut the pages for your album. Our pages measure $14\frac{3}{4} \times 5$ inches (37.4×12.7 cm). Make a $\frac{3}{4}$-inch (1.9 cm) fold at one end of each page. The folded edge creates a spacer to allow the pages to lay flat when all the photos are mounted in the album. Set them aside.

3 Use a large paper punch to create circular negative shapes in your cover. Save the punched shapes for other projects. Use the same punch to create circular shapes in a different-colored corrugated paper. The punched shapes will fit snugly into the negative shapes on your cover. If desired, use smaller punches to create shapes within shapes, as shown. Rotate the shapes so that the corrugated lines contrast with the corrugated lines of the cover.

5 Use a small hole punch to make two holes in the front and back covers. Use the holes as templates to mark the pages. Punch holes in the marked pages. Use metal screw posts to assemble the album.

4 Measure and cut a piece of rice paper slightly smaller than your cover. Turn over your cover, repositioning the shapes as needed. Spread a light coat of PVA glue on the back of the cover and adhere the rice paper. Smooth the paper, cover it with waxed paper, and weight it with a book. Allow the glue to dry.

Thousand-and-One-Nights Vase

Delicate Arabic script and stylized floral motifs make this vase a stylish addition to any Scheherazade's decor. Who knew paper mache could be so easy?

YOU WILL NEED

Template on page 82

Double-wall corrugated cardboard*

Pencil

Utility knife

Metal-edged ruler

Paper tape

Newspaper

PVA glue

Flat container

Plastic sheeting or trash bag

Disposable latex gloves

Gesso or white acrylic paint

Paintbrush

Sandpaper (optional)

Scissors

Foreign language newspapers

Hand-printed paper

Thai *unryu* paper

Gold paint or imitation gold leaf (optional)

Acrylic varnish

*Use flattened portions of recycled boxes.

1 Enlarge the vase template on page 82. To make your own template for a vase shape, make a rough sketch of the shape you wish to create on a piece of paper as tall as you would like your vase to be. Fold the paper in half down the length of the vase shapes, and cut with scissors to form a template. Trace around the template to make four cardboard shapes. Cut out the shapes with a utility knife. Measure the base of your vase shape. Measure and mark a square on cardboard equal to the width of the vase. Cut it out. Coat each side of the cardboard pieces with a lightly diluted mixture of PVA glue and water. Let the pieces dry for at least four hours.

2 Gently curl the vase shapes against the edge of your work surface from the top to bottom. Join the sides with short lengths of paper tape. Take your time as you join the sides. Tape the cardboard square to the bottom to complete the vase form.

3 Cover the vase with a layer of newspaper strips dipped in a mixture of PVA diluted with water, as described on page 18. Add two additional layers. Let the layers dry overnight.

5 Cut headlines from the foreign language newspaper. Cut printed motifs from the handprinted paper. Adhere the headlines and patterns to the vase with the diluted PVA mixture. Use a brush to smooth the papers on the vase surface. Work carefully to avoid air bubbles.

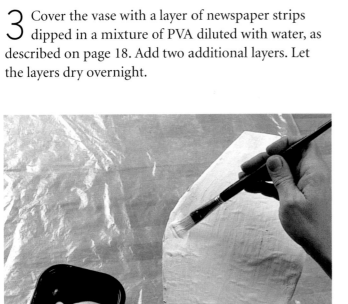

4 Brush the dried vase with two coats of gesso or white acrylic paint. When dry, lightly sand any rough places on the surface.

6 Tear hand-size pieces of the Thai *unryu* paper. Cover the surface of the vase with overlapping pieces of this paper dipped in the diluted PVA mixture. Let the vase dry. Add gold highlights to the vase with paint or imitation gold leaf. Brush or spray the vase with a coat of acrylic varnish, if desired.

Faux Mosaic Wall Clock

Roughly torn paper tesserae (tiles) create a surface that mimics unglazed ceramic mosaic. But this mosaic is far easier and less messy to make. You won't need a large nail, either—the clock is light enough to hang on the wall by a pin!

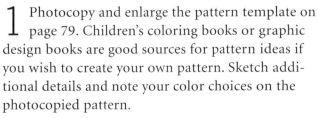

1 Photocopy and enlarge the pattern template on page 79. Children's coloring books or graphic design books are good sources for pattern ideas if you wish to create your own pattern. Sketch additional details and note your color choices on the photocopied pattern.

2 Tear long strips of your papers, using a metal-edge ruler to help keep the strips a uniform width. Then tear the long strips into smaller one-inch (2.5 cm) strips. Sort the short strips into piles of the same color. These are your mosaic "tiles."

3 It's helpful to arrange the small tiles on your pattern before you start. You can adjust their size if needed before you get involved in gluing them down.

Glue a background paper of your choice to the cardboard round. Trim it to fit. The background paper mimics the grout of traditional mosaic, so you just have to decide whether you want a light or dark colored "grout." Lightly sketch the central lines of your pattern onto the covered cardboard round.

5 Use an awl or craft knife to pierce a small hole in the center of the clock. Enlarge the hole as needed to accommodate the stem of your clockwork assembly. Follow the manufacturer's instructions for assembling the clockworks.

4 Adhere the paper tiles to the clock face with PVA glue. Leave a bit of the background paper exposed between tiles. Cover the entire surface with tiles, then cover the clock face with waxed paper and a heavy book. Allow the glued tiles to dry overnight.

Paper Quartet Collage Bottles

*Admit it: Somehow you've saved up a pile of too-pretty-to-toss scraps that just
don't appear to be useful. Here's an addictive little parlor game I like to play
with such scraps. Sort through your pile and pull out four (and only four!) papers.
Then use those four papers to create small collages to embellish glass bottles,
cards, scrapbooks, or even one-of-a-kind jewelry pieces. When you've used
your first selections, choose four more, and play again.*

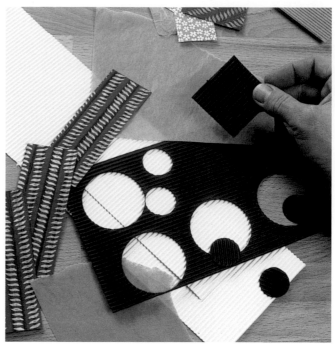

1 Select four different papers from your pile of scraps. We've chosen corrugated paper in two colors, translucent tissue, and a hand-printed paper.

2 Cut a central piece of corrugated paper to cover one side of your bottle. Use a paper punch to create holes in the paper.

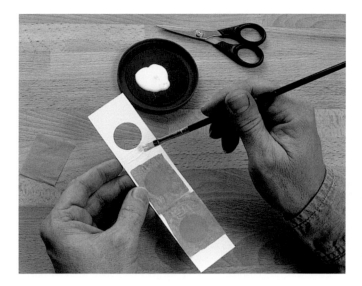

3 Cut or tear small pieces of tissue. Glue the pieces
to the back side of the corrugated paper.

5 Glue the collage to one side of the bottle. Cover
the collage with waxed paper and weight it with a
small book. Let the glue dry.

4 Embellish the front of the corrugated paper with
small shapes of printed paper and scraps of
corrugated paper. Use paper punches and decorative
scissors, or tear the papers to make decorative elements
for your collages.

Star-Bright Night-Light

*We don't suggest trying to read by the light of this
striking lamp. Instead, use it to ward off the
wild things that go bump in the night.*

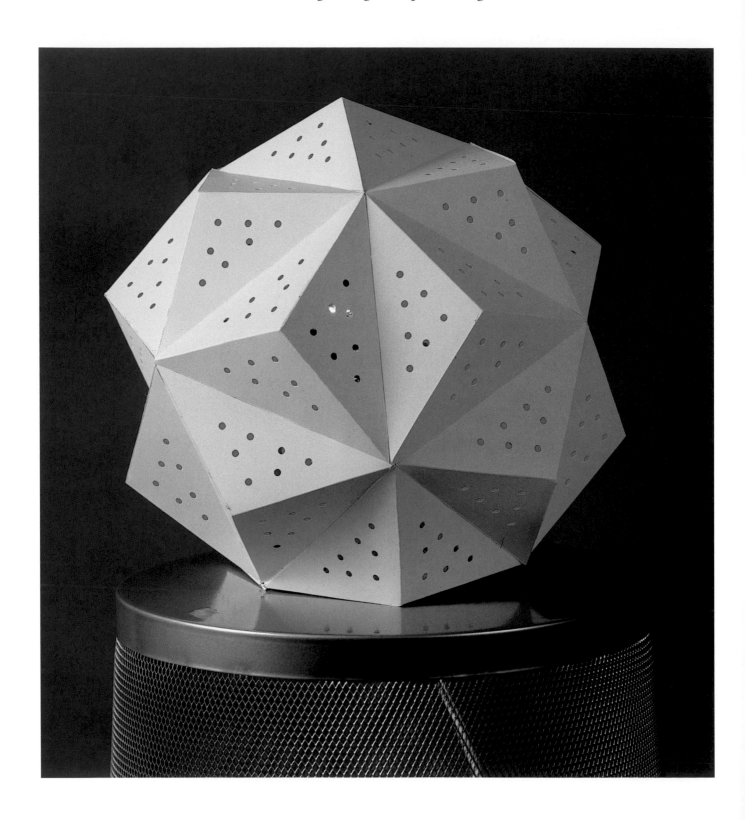

Pattern template on page 78

Brightly colored poster board

Scissors

Stapler

Metal-edged ruler

Bone folder

Sharp craft knife

Artists' or masking tape

Rubber cement

Hole punch

Low-wattage candle light

Mini-light strand (optional)

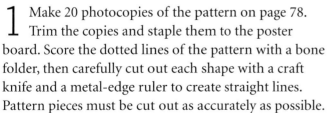

1 Make 20 photocopies of the pattern on page 78. Trim the copies and staple them to the poster board. Score the dotted lines of the pattern with a bone folder, then carefully cut out each shape with a craft knife and a metal-edge ruler to create straight lines. Pattern pieces must be cut out as accurately as possible.

2 Use a scrap piece of poster board to create a template for the placement of holes you'll punch in each portion of the pattern piece. The holes allow the light to shine through. Mark each piece and punch the holes. Set them aside.

3 Gently bend the scored lines to create a pyramid shape. Spread a thin coat of rubber cement on the flap and on the back edge of the adjacent triangle unit. Let the rubber cement dry. Fold the pattern to form a pyramid. Assemble all of the pyramids.

5 Join the groups of pyramids together with tape to form the star-like shape. You may remove one of the pyramids if you wish your star shape to sit flat on the table. Otherwise, don't tape the last two sides of the last pyramid together. Use a low-wattage single bulb or a small strand of mini-lights to illuminate the star.

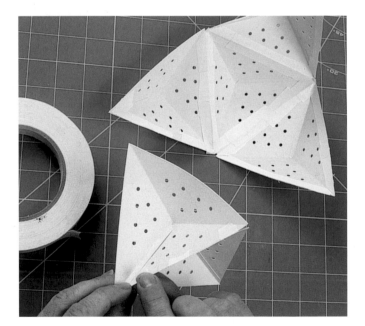

4 Work slowly and carefully to assemble the pyramids in groups of four. Use short lengths of tape to join them together. Pay attention, aligning the pyramids as precisely as possible. When you have them aligned, join them with longer lengths of tape.

Decorative Pierced Greeting Cards

The Victorians created intricate designs by pricking holes in paper items. The raised designs created texture on flat surfaces and allowed patterns of light to shine through as well. The modern crafter has a plethora of punches available to achieve similar, but contemporary, effects.

YOU WILL NEED

Scrap paper

Decorative hole punches

Sharp pencil

Blank greeting cards and envelope

Craft knife

Foam mounting strips

Translucent vellum (optional)

1 Experiment with your punches on a scrap piece of paper. Create designs that fit well in a corner and along the edges. Punches with simple, symmetrical shapes—circles, squares, rectangles, hearts, and teardrops—are easy to work with. Note the depth of your punch and how it relates to other punches you are using, especially when you are combining different shapes.

2 When you are happy with your pattern, use the punches to create a template of the pattern on a scrap piece of paper. You can punch patterns freehand, but if you are making a set of cards you'll find it easier to mark the pattern. That way, every card will look alike.

3 Position your pattern on the card and use a pencil to make lightly marked guides for your punches. Punch out your border.

5 You may simply mount the medallion on the card with small squares of foam mounting tape. Or, you can cut out a shape smaller than your medallion on the card and mount the medallion over the cutout shape. This allows light to pass through the medallion. Another colorful variation can be created by backing the medallion with a scrap of translucent vellum before you mount it.

4 If desired, you can create a central medallion for your card. Cut out a small square or rectangle from another card. Mark and punch your pattern on the piece of card.

Washi Paper Bracelets

Use elegantly patterned washi *papers to make these striking bracelets. The construction technique consists of creating an interlocked chain of folded paper strips. Perhaps you've seen similar items made of folded cigarette packs and gum wrappers in antique shops and books on folk art. Often called "joint" or prison work, it was a popular, folk craft in the early twentieth century.*

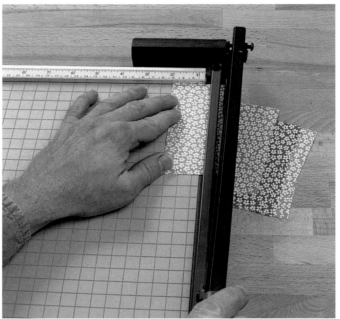

1 Measure and cut 2 × 4½-inch (5 × 11.4 cm) strips of paper. A paper cutter speeds up the task of accurately cutting the strips you'll need. An average-sized bracelet will be made up of 24 strips. Cut a few extra strips while you're at it.

2 Fold a strip in half along the length, and crease the fold with the bone folder or your fingernail. Open up the strip, and fold the two long edges into the center crease. Fold this strip in half again lengthwise and crease it with the bone folder. Fold and crease as many strips as you think you will need.

3 Fold and crease the strip in half at the center. Open the folded strip, then fold in each of the two ends to the center. Fold the strip in half, as shown. Fold and crease all strips.

5 Continue interlocking the strips until you have made a chain the length you will need in order to slip it over your wrist.

4 Take a minute to look carefully at a folded strip. You will see that one edge is a solid fold and the opposite edge is composed of two folded edges. Always look at the folded edges to determine where you are going to interlock a folded strip. Always insert your folded strips into the edge made of one solid fold. Begin by interlocking two strips at right angles to one another, as shown. Pull them together snugly.

6 Pick up one folded slip and unfold the ends. Insert the long ends into the first interlocked strip. Pull the chain together snugly. Take each end and fold them back over the first strip. Slip each end under the crossing strip. If desired, put a dot of PVA glue on the end before you slip it under.

Garden Mini-light Garland

Quickly transform a plain strand of mini-lights into a delicate floral garland. Festoon a wall or wind them onto tree branches or railings for a Midsummer's Eve party. Translucent vellum and soft light are an unbeatable (and dreamy!) combination.

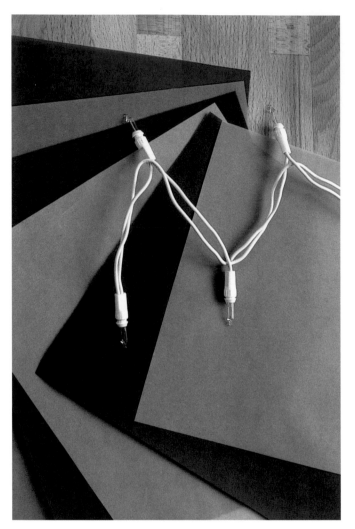

YOU WILL NEED

Templates on page 80

Cellophane tape

Translucent vellum

Scissors

Bone folder

Metal-edged ruler

Hole punch

Mini-light strand

1 Photocopy the templates on page 80. Enlarge or reduce the templates as desired. Make several copies. Cut out the templates and arrange them to fill a sheet of plain photocopy paper. Use cellophane tape to hold them in place. Make photocopies of this sheet.

2 Staple the photocopied sheet to a sheet of vellum. Score the dotted lines of each flower using a bone folder and metal-edge ruler. It is easier to do this before you cut out each flower. Then cut out the flowers.

3 Sharpen the creases in each flower with your fingers. The scored lines will show you where to crease.

4 Use a hole punch to make the center hole of each flower.

CAUTION: *Be sure that vellum flowers do not touch wire electrical contact on the bulb. For safety's sake, never leave illuminated strands unattended.*

5 Carefully remove a lightbulb from the mini-light strand. Slip one or two flower shapes onto the base of the bulb. Place the bulb back into the socket. The vellum flowers will be held between the outside rim of the socket and the base of the bulb. Fill the strand of mini-lights with alternating flower shapes and colors. Hang the garland of lights, and let the frivolities begin!

Soft-as-a-Breeze Cafe Curtain

Catch a breeze with these simple old-fashioned cafe curtains made from an unexpected material. Decorative-edge scissors and hole punches are used to imitate delicate eyelet embroidery without putting in hours of tedious stitching.

YOU WILL NEED

Thai soft *unryu* paper*	Decorative paper punches
Sharp quilting pins	Curtain rod
Sewing machine	
Sewing thread	*You can special order this luscious paper by the yard from most suppliers of fine paper.
Decorative-edge scissors	

3 Slip the curtain panels onto the rod. Determine where the bottom edge of the curtains fall on the windowsill. Mark this edge with a crease. Remove the curtains and lay them flat on your work surface. Use decorative-edge scissors to finish the bottom edge of each panel. Trim the overlapped edge as well.

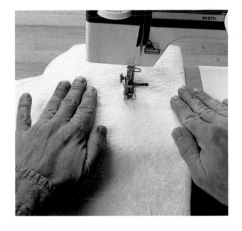

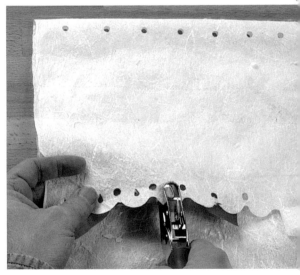

1 Measure the height and width of your window. Cut two lengths of soft *unryu*, each about 12 inches (30.5 cm) longer than the height of the window.

2 Fold over 10 inches (25.4 cm) of paper. Crease the fold. Use quilting pins to hold the folded-over paper in place. Sew a straight line of stitching approximately 2¼ inches (5.6 cm) from the fold. Then sew a second parallel line of stitching approximately 1¾ inches (4.4 cm) from the first line of stitching. This creates a channel for your curtain rod. Sew the second panel in the same way.

4 Remove the curtain panels from the rod. Use both handheld and larger paper punches to create faux embroidered eyelet along the edges of the curtains. You will find it easier to punch the paper if you back it with a sheet of stiffer paper as you punch. This is especially important if you are cutting shapes with large punches.

Caribbean Isles Frame

Random layers of pastels from the gentle color palette of the Caribbean islands evoke memories of sunny days, lush vegetation, and shimmering seas…even if you've only been there in your daydreams.

YOU WILL NEED

Double-wall cardboard*

Ruler

Pencil

Craft or utility knife

Hot glue gun and glue sticks

PVA glue

Newspaper

Gesso or white acrylic paint

Solid and colored tissue papers

Disposable latex gloves

Small paintbrush

Plastic sheeting or trash bag

Flat tray

*Use a recycled cardboard box.

1 Measure and mark two 9 × 11-inch (22.9 × 27.9 cm) rectangles on the cardboard. Cut them out with a craft knife. Mark a 5½ × 3¾ -inch (14 × 10 cm) rectangle in the center of one of the rectangles. Cut it out to create an opening for your photograph. Measure and mark two 2½ × 9-inch (6.4 × 22.9 cm) rectangles and one 2½ × 6-inch (6.4 × 15.2 cm) rectangle. Cut them out with a craft knife. Arrange the small rectangles in a U-shape on the uncut rectangle, aligning the edges. Hot glue them to the rectangle. Brush all pieces with a coat of PVA glue that has been thinned with water. Let them dry for at least four hours.

2 Tear newspaper into one-inch-wide (2.5 cm) strips. Make a large pile of the strips. Pour PVA glue into a flat container. Thin the glue with an equal amount of water and mix it well. Cover your work area with plastic sheeting. Dip the strips, one at a time, into the PVA mixture. Cover all sides and edges of both rectangles with two or three layers of newspaper strips. Let them dry flat overnight. Save any leftover PVA mixture in a covered container.

4 Use a brush to apply the PVA mixture to a small area of the frame. Apply random strips or squares of tissue paper. Pat them down with the brush to smooth out wrinkles. Layer the different colors and patterns as desired. Give the frame a final coat of the PVA mixture and let it dry.

3 Paint both pieces with two coats of gesso or white acrylic paint. Let them dry in between coats. Tear your tissue paper into short one-inch-wide (2.5 cm) strips. Dip the strips of tissue into the reserved PVA mixture. Cover the outside edges and the edges of the picture opening with tissue. Let them dry. Hot glue the two rectangles together. Cover the edges of the frame with tissue, leaving the top opening free.

Mon-Kiri Table Runner

*Creating family crests (mon-kiri) is a centuries-old
Japanese craft. The delicate, cutout shapes—just a few of
the many crest designs—are showcased on contrasting
unryu and corrugated papers. Once you learn the fold, try
designing your own family crest.*

Faithful Companion Silhouettes

Could there be any more elegant way to capture Floyd's
(Fluffy's or Spot's) noble profile for posterity?

YOU WILL NEED

Photograph of your pet's profile*

Pencil

Stapler

Black paper

Sharp craft knife

Sharp, pointed scissors

Background paper

Frame

*Use your trusty camera or digital camera to create your photograph.

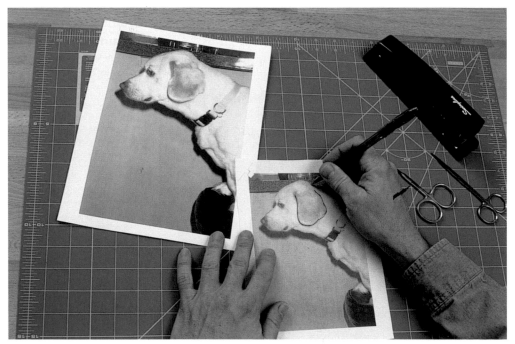

1 Fluffy may not take to posing at your command, so have your camera (digital or loaded with film) at hand. You'll never know when the mood may come upon her to elegantly crane her neck and turn her head...just so. If you're shooting digitally, you can enlarge and crop the photo with your computer's imaging program before you print it out. You'll need to photocopy and enlarge a film-based photograph to the size you wish.

Staple the photocopy or digital print to the black paper. Study the profile and outline it with pencil to define the lines, as shown. Outline any details (such as elegantly drooping ears) that you wish to stand out from the black profile.

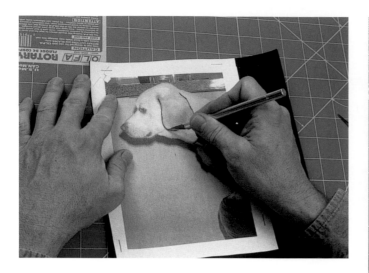

2 Cut along the outline of any interior detail with a very sharp craft knife. Make a second cutting line just a little bit away from the first cut. Use the tip of the knife to lift up the sliver of cut paper. If the cut doesn't show off that ear, then cut another sliver.

4 Adhere the silhouette to a bright-colored, patterned, or neutral background paper. Mount the silhouette in a frame.

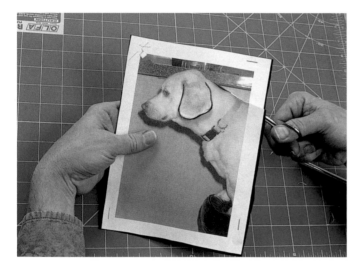

3 Use very sharp scissors to cut out the central profile. Move the paper, not the scissors, when you turn corners. (You'll get more clean-cut edges that way). Work slowly and carefully to capture the line of the profile.

Special Occasion Place Mat

Over, under; over, under. What could be simpler?
And what results you'll get when you weave
place mats for the family, or to
impress a swarm of dinner guests. Pull out
all the stops and create napkin rings to match.

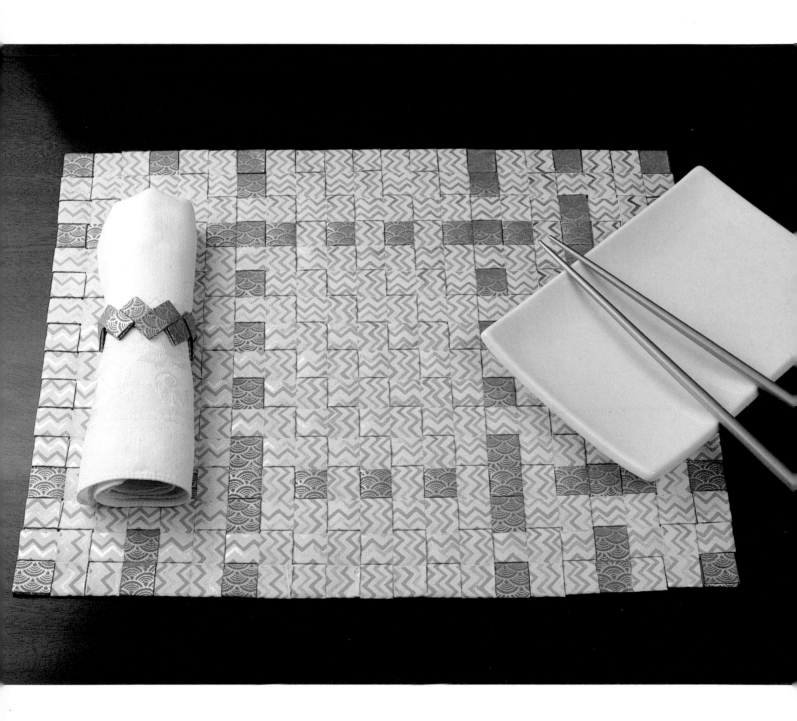

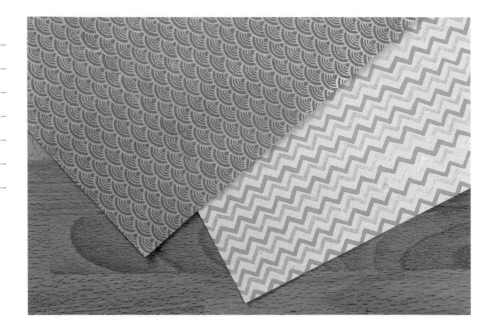

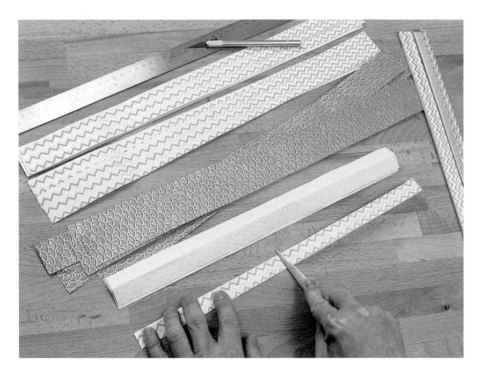

1 You can weave a place mat with just one type of paper, but using two complementary papers creates a more visually interesting weave. Measure and cut 1½-inch-wide (3.8 cm) strips of paper. You will need 21 strips that are 15 inches (38.1 cm) long and 16 strips that are 19 inches (48.3 cm) long. Fold all of your strips in half along their lengths. This gives your place mat a finished look on the reverse side. Crease each strip with a bone folder.

2 Create the warp with the 15-inch (38.1 cm) strips. Lay the strips on a flat work surface. Lay them close together but not touching. Secure them to the work surface with short lengths of tape. This prevents them from moving as you weave.

4 Fold the ends of the strips over and glue them down with a bit of PVA glue. Trim them as needed before you glue them. Turn over the mat, fold, and glue the ends as you did on the opposite side.

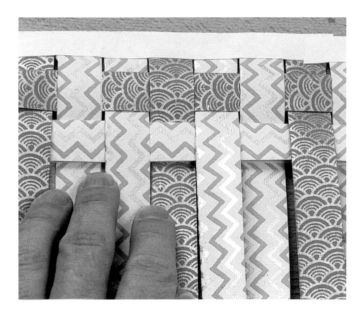

3 Weave the first row over and under each warp strip. Push it up close to, but not touching, the tape. Start the second row, weaving under and over. As you finish a row of weaving, push it up against the previous rows.

Weave all of the rows, pushing them tightly together as you work.

5 Create matching napkin rings with $\frac{1}{2} \times 4\frac{1}{2}$-inch (1.3 × 11.4 cm) strips of paper. Follow steps 3, 4, and 5 on page 54 to fold and link the strips.

Golden Temple Floorcloth

Definitely not a floorcloth for high traffic areas or muddy shoes.
But who cares? The dramatic impact this contemporary floorcloth has on
a room far outweighs its impracticality. Sometimes verve and elan
are all you want: Practicality be damned!

Brown kraft contractors' paper*

Oriental joss papers

PVA glue

Small brush

Napkin-size cloth

Waxed paper

Heavy books

Newspaper or plastic sheeting

Spray adhesive

Paper clips

Sewing machine

Various colors of sewing thread

Scissors

Acrylic sealer

*You'll find rolls of this paper in the flooring section of your local home improvement store. As an alternative, use brown kraft wrapping paper, but it isn't as durable as contractors' paper.

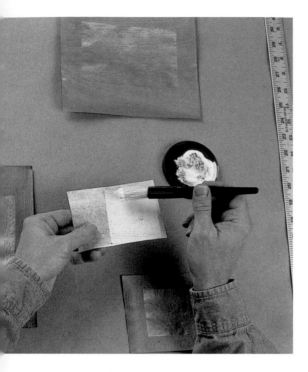

1 Decide how large a floorcloth you'd like to create. A 2 × 4-foot (60.9 cm × 1. 2 m) floorcloth is a manageable size to start with. A larger sized floorcloth can be created, but requires an extra set of hands and no small amount of contortion at the sewing machine (consider yourself forewarned). Measure and cut a length of contractors' paper to size. Lay it on a flat work surface (the floor is a good surface to work on). Arrange the joss papers in a pleasing pattern. Spread a coat of PVA glue on the back of one joss paper at a time. Place it on the contractors' paper and smooth out wrinkles with a small cloth. Adhere each of the papers, cover them with lengths of waxed paper, and weight them with books. Let them dry overnight.

2 Measure and cut four or five additional lengths of contractors' paper. Cover your work area with newspaper or plastic sheeting to protect it from overspray. Laminate the lengths together with light coats of spray adhesive.

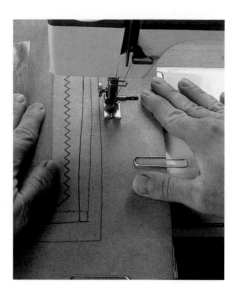

4 Machine-stitch around the perimeter of the rug. Use a variety of stitches and colors of thread. The stitched lines need not be straight, and you may wish to cross over previously stitched lines in some places.

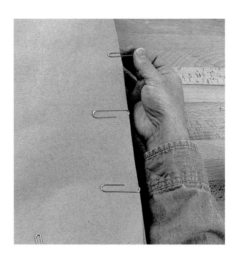

3 Spray a light coat of adhesive on the top sheet of the laminated stack. Carefully position the sheet decorated with joss paper on the stack. Hold the sheet in place with large paper clips.

5 If desired, spray a coat of clear acrylic finish on the completed floorcloth. Be sure you keep the rug safe from tiny (or adult-size) muddy shoes!

Nesting Collage Trays

Once you've painted the trays, the collages can change whenever you like. Create a set of painted nesting trays and present them as a gift with an assortment of printed papers and a sharp pair of scissors.

YOU WILL NEED

Unfinished wooden craft trays

Sandpaper (optional)

Acrylic paints

Painting tape

Paintbrush

Gift-wrapping papers

Patterned tissue paper

Sheets of single-strength glass

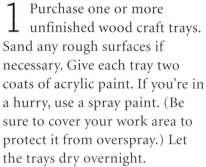

1 Purchase one or more unfinished wood craft trays. Sand any rough surfaces if necessary. Give each tray two coats of acrylic paint. If you're in a hurry, use a spray paint. (Be sure to cover your work area to protect it from overspray.) Let the trays dry overnight.

2 Use painting tape to create a grid on the surface of the tray. Paint the exposed squares with a contrasting color of acrylic paint. Let the paint dry. If you're in a hurry you can speed up the drying process by using your hair dryer. Apply an additional coat, if needed. Remove the painting tape when the paint is thoroughly dry.

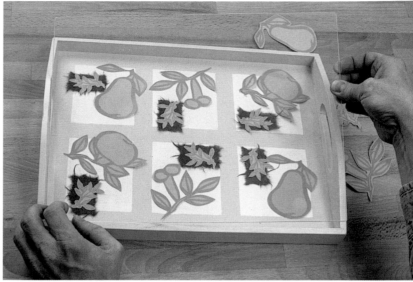

3 Cut out central motifs from your patterned papers. Tear small shapes of solid colors. Arrange the shapes and cutout motifs on the squares.

5 Have sheets of single-strength glass cut to fit your trays. Frame shops, glass shops, and home improvement stores will cut the glass for you inexpensively. Cover the collages with the glass. Simply remove the glass and the papers when you want to change the collage.

4 You may use a bit of glue to adhere the shapes to the tray if desired.

TEMPLATES

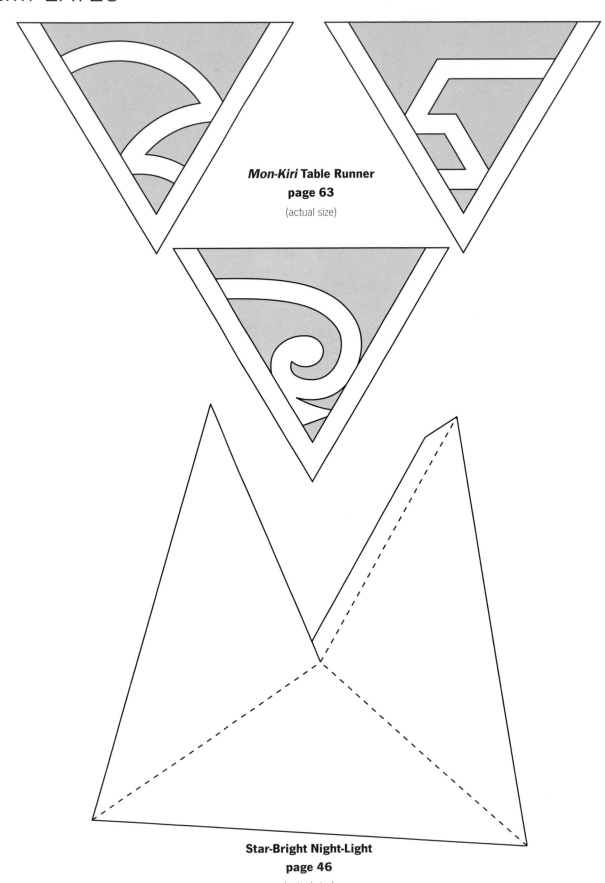

Mon-Kiri Table Runner
page 63

(actual size)

Star-Bright Night-Light
page 46

(actual size)

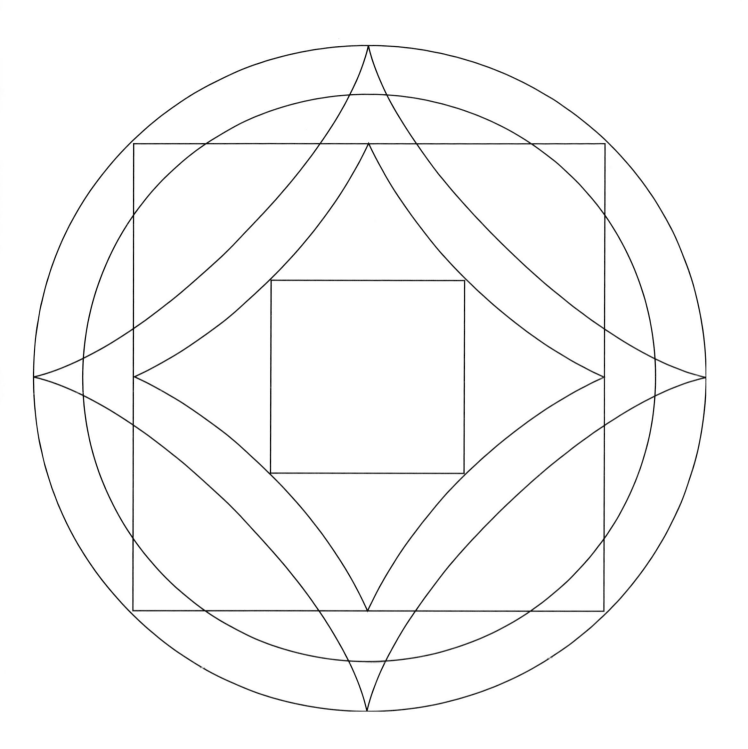

Faux Mosaic Wall Clock
page 40

(enlarge as desired)

Garden Mini-light Garland
page 55

(actual size)

Not Your Grandmother's Quilt
page 25

(actual size)

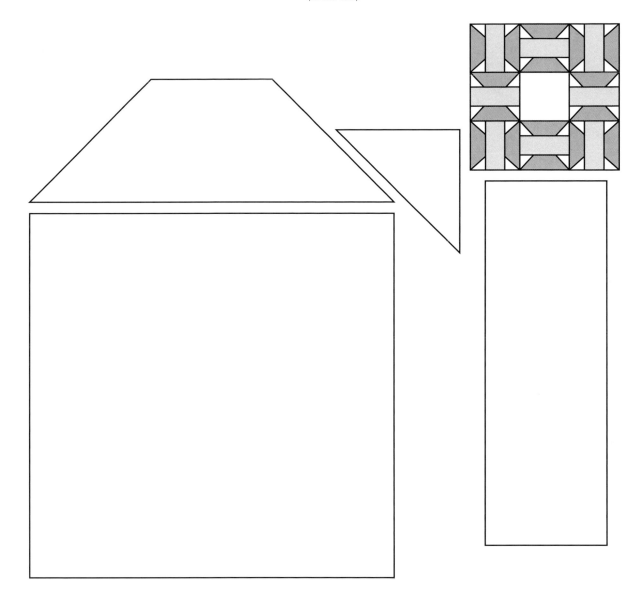

Thousand-and-One-Nights Vase
page 37

(enlarge as desired)

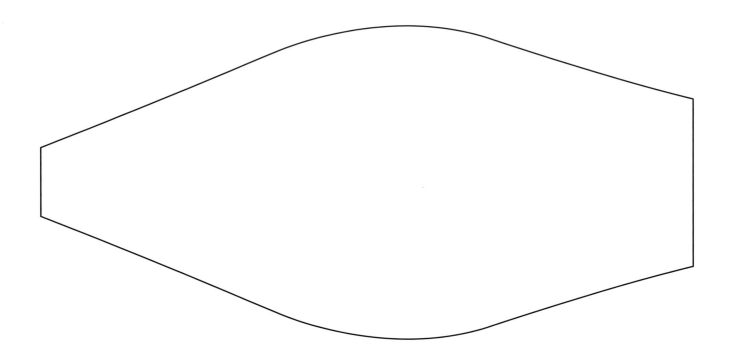

Dried Flower Crafting

VALERIE SHRADER

INTRODUCTION

WELCOME TO *Dried Flower Crafting,* a collection of new and unique ways to use dried flowers. Although it's true that the book includes a complete arrangement and a wreath or two (okay, three), you won't find page after page of flower displays that only a professional floral designer could assemble. Instead, you'll find curtains, cards, candles, lamps, drawer pulls, and other items that include dried and pressed flowers as a central design element. If you can wield a glue gun, hold a paintbrush, or thread a needle, there is a project here for you. No doubt, you'll discover what I have—that preserved flowers are remarkable, versatile, even breathtaking materials that can be easily incorporated into a variety of crafting processes.

If you're intimidated by the thought of working with dried flowers because they're fragile, you may be surprised to discover how resilient they can be; I know, because I've dropped a few! You only need treat them as you would a delicate sheet of vellum or fine piece of silk. You certainly can't argue with their exceptional beauty as a crafting element.

You'll also find information in the book for drying and pressing your own flowers, because it's far easier to do than many have imagined. I've gotten so much pleasure from experimenting with the materials from my own yard that you might want to give it a try, too. The first specimens I preserved in silica gel—a perfect iris and bud—were amazingly vivid. Read over the section on preserving flowers and find a method that appeals to you. You can begin this craft with little or no investment, and it will be with you for a lifetime.

This is much more than a list of preservation methods, though. The heart of this section is the projects, because they enable you to use preserved flowers in delightfully original ways. Several talented designers were inspired by this notion and created the exciting pieces in this book, like the set of stationery on page 149 and the mirror on page 131. Even those that are more traditional in nature, like the wreaths on page 146, have an updated, modern look. Glance over the project section and see how varied the uses of these materials can be; some common crafting skills are all that you'll need to start enjoying this book. And, these are projects that you can complete in a weekend, so you'll be able to explore the possibilities of using dried or pressed flowers quickly and easily.

It's very satisfying to nurture the plants that I later use in projects, and I also love to botanize in the mountains around my home. But most assuredly, you need not be a master gardener or even know much about flowers, for that matter, to create any of the projects in this book. Florists, craft and hobby stores, and even floral departments in large supermarkets stock dried or pressed flowers, so you can readily purchase these materials. There are also a number of vendors with websites, so you can now shop for dried flowers on your home computer if you wish. And, of course, you can buy fresh flowers and dry them yourself. How you obtain your materials isn't as important as how much pleasure they bring you while you work.

Be creative with the projects, too. Blue wreaths don't match your décor? Then investigate the other flowers that are available and find the perfect color for your home. Part of the real fun of working with preserved flowers is the discovery process, finding out how the materials and techniques best complement each other.

So, I encourage you to work with dried or pressed flowers. Walk around your garden, visit your florist, or browse through your craft store and find something beautiful. Since flowers bring such joy to our lives, take delight in crafting with dried flowers.

DRIED FLOWER CRAFTING BASICS

LET'S BEGIN by discussing the techniques you can use at home to preserve flowers. There are a number of different procedures you can try, depending on how you plan to craft with the finished product. Some projects may require dried flowers, like the tonal arrangement on page 115, while others need pressed flowers, like the lamp shade on page 104. If you want a rustic look, air drying is probably fine; if you want a truly lifelike product, try a desiccant like silica gel. Flower preservation is not an exact science, and there are many variables; often you have to match the process with the flower to achieve the most success, so have some patience as you begin. Here's a basic overview of drying techniques, starting with choosing fresh materials. Remember that you can use the preservation methods with purchased flowers, too.

Here's an assortment of flowers from my yard and garden that were dried or pressed, including iris, flame azalea, peony, daffodil, violet, dogwood, columbine, pansy, Jacob's ladder, and verbena.

CHOOSING FLOWERS

What kind of flowers can you preserve? The possibilities are as varied as nature itself, and even if some varieties don't lend themselves well to pressing, they may dry beautifully. I began looking for plants in my own yard, pressing the blooms of dogwood and native plants like azalea and columbine. A stroll through local nurseries and garden centers turned up a variety of species to experiment with—verbena, lisianthus, and Gerbera daisies, for example.

Practically everyone has let a rose hang to dry, so you probably know that is an excellent method for that species. The traditional everlasting varieties, such as statice and strawflower, are good candidates for this method, but other flowers, like blazing star, larkspur, and delphinium, dry quite nicely when left to hang.

Flowering spring bulbs, such as daffodils, tulips, and irises, dry with amazing realism in silica gel. Annuals like marigolds and zinnias work well in gel, too. Of course, you can get a good idea of which flowers you can use by glancing at the projects in this book.

Every flower has unique qualities that may affect your projects. Even though each of the varieties used in the projects shown in the photo at top right was pressed in the microwave, each reacts a little differently. For example, the marigold

Each of the flowers shown in the projects here, from left to right, marigold, osteospermum, and daisy, were pressed in the microwave, but each exhibit different characteristics when dried.

petals have to be pressed separately and reconstructed. The white osteospermum becomes infused with the purple from the underside of the flower when it is pressed. The daisy dries beautifully but quickly begins to reabsorb moisture, so it must be used (or sealed) immediately after pressing.

You will also find that certain colors or related species react differently to the preservation process. For instance, deep red roses tend to fade almost to black, but the lighter pinks remain lovely. Similarly, certain types of pansies require slightly different drying times; these examples reinforce the importance of keeping a journal or record as you work. If you become passionate about drying your own flowers, you will probably want to study the various species in more depth.

HARVESTING FLOWERS

It's best to harvest flowers late on a sunny morning when the morning dew has evaporated. As the day progresses, especially at the height of summer, the blooms will wilt from the midday heat, so gather them early when the plant itself is full of moisture, yet not wet. Likewise, you should avoid harvesting after a rain shower, with all the additional moisture that brings. If you absolutely can't avoid picking flowers when they are slightly wet, bring them inside and let them stand in a vase until they are dry.

If you plan to harvest lots of flowers and need to spend some time in the garden, you may want to bring along a container of water. Place the stems inside as you clip them, because you must begin the drying process with fresh blossoms. For just a brief trip, a basket will suffice to hold the blooms, as long as you plan to start working with the material immediately. In general, you should begin the preservation process as quickly as possible after harvesting.

These roses, which are being wired for air drying, are still lovely and fresh. Be sure that all the flowers you choose for drying and pressing are in pristine condition.

Here's some obvious advice: pick only perfect specimens. A flower damaged by insects or disease certainly won't improve during the drying process. Take a few more stems than you think you will need, for insurance against unsatisfactory results. Bear in mind that the flowers may shrink while drying, depending on which method you choose, so you may discover that you need a little more material than originally anticipated.

A flower's blooming cycle should also be taken into consideration when you're looking for material. You probably don't want a bloom that's been on the stem for a few days, because its beauty is beginning to fade. Look for fresh, unblemished blooms. With some species, you have to time your harvest perfectly, for its bloom may last only for a day.

Lastly, look out for insects. My peonies always seem to have an ant or two crawling around inside the petals. Remove the bugs before you bring the flowers into the house. An undetected insect can continue to munch on air-dried flowers, so be particularly vigilant if you use this method.

PREPARING FOR PRESERVATION

Generally, the greenery on a flower stem will not dry at the same rate as the bloom, and some stalks just won't dry well at all; you may have a beautiful blossom and an ugly brown stem. But don't be afraid to experiment. I harvested some peonies and kept just a leaf because

To wire the stems, insert the wire through the calyx and bend it down; then, wrap it around several times to form a stem or handle.

it framed the flower so nicely, and indeed it dried beautifully. Most authorities recommend removing all the foliage and stems before drying in silica gel, though there are some exceptions to this rule (some of the spring-flowering bulbs, for instance).

Depending on the intended use of the flowers after they are dried, you may find that it is helpful to wire the stems first, as shown in the photo at center below. This little handle of wire is very handy when you are removing the silica gel and helps if you want to seal the flowers afterward; you can insert the wire into floral foam while you spray the blossoms with the sealer. Of course, if you choose to use the microwave, you cannot wire the stem before drying.

DRYING TECHNIQUES

Now that you have prepared your flowers, which method will you choose to preserve them? Each species of flower will react differently to a specific preservation process, some with surprising results. Begin small, with just one or two specimens, to test the process. See how the flowers dried using that method work within the context of your craft project. Keep a record of your attempts. A little time and experimentation can be an investment in later success and satisfaction.

Compare these peonies: the specimen on the left was dried in silica gel, while the one on the right was left to hang dry.

Air Drying

This is the simplest method of drying—you just sit and wait! There are several different options to choose as you merely let nature take its course.

Hanging is really, really easy. Many perennials, like blazing star and larkspur, dry exceptionally well in this simple process. Roses, too, are well suited to this method. Merely bind the stems together (rubber bands work well) and hang them upside down. It's best to group together only the same type of flower, picked at a similar stage of blooming, since they will have approximately the same drying time. Pick a dry, warm location for drying, preferably out of the bright sunlight. The flowers will retain more of their natural color if they dry in a dark spot. Give them a peek every few days to check their progress.

Screen drying is another easy method. Here, simply spread the blooms on a wire screen and turn them every day or two to prevent curling. The screen allows ample ventilation during the drying cycle. This process works well for single flowers; if you want to dry the stems, too, use a screen with mesh that is wide enough to slip them through, and let the bloom rest flat on the screen.

Some flowers dry quite well in an upright position, too. Daffodils are often placed in a vase and allowed to dry naturally. They tend to better retain the gentle bend below the flower head if they sit upright as they dry. You should cut the stems at an angle and remove all the foliage before you place the flowers in just a bit of water in the vase; then leave them to dry.

Desiccant Drying

Desiccants are substances that absorb the moisture in plants. Sand, borax, cornmeal, and cat litter have been used to dry flowers, but silica gel crystals produce wondrous results. Although it is somewhat pricey, silica gel can be reused again and again, both as a normal drying agent and in the microwave; when it has absorbed all the moisture it can handle, silica gel crystals can be reactivated in the oven. Since the flowers have to be covered completely with the substance, you may need a fair amount to get started, maybe 10 pounds (4.5 kg) or so. But once you see how realistic the results are, you'll probably consider it a wise investment in your hobby.

USING SILICA GEL

To begin drying flowers with silica gel, try the traditional method of covering the flowers with the crystals and letting them sit in a closed container for several days. I've been able to achieve much more reliable results with this method, as opposed to using silica gel in the microwave. But you may love the latter method since it's so quick, so don't let me deter you! Rest assured, I'm not a microwave basher; flowers press beautifully in the microwave, and this method will be discussed on page 92.

Traditional Silica Gel Method

For this method, start with flowers that are completely dry. Use an airtight container with a tight-fitting lid, like a plastic food storage box. Put about 1 inch (2.5 cm) of crystals in the bottom of the container. Then, remove most of the stem, since the majority of the stems

Cover the fresh flowers completely with silica gel crystals, using a spoon to gently sprinkle the crystals over the blooms.

won't dry well, as stated previously. Add the flowers, making sure they don't touch each other. Some blooms, like many of the spring-flowering bulbs and tall flowers on spikes such as larkspur and delphinium, are best dried on their sides; a support of cardboard or other material is helpful to preserve the integrity of the bloom.

After you have placed the flowers in the container, add the silica gel crystals. Pour gently around the flowers first, so the crystals begin to fill in under the petals. Then, you may want to use a spoon to continue the process, as shown in the photo above. Lightly sprinkle crystals to cover the flower, yet be careful to retain the shape of the bloom. Completely envelop the flowers with crystals and cover the container.

When will your flowers be dry? In three or four days, probably, but some varieties could take up to a week. After a couple of days, gently pour off some of the crystals and check the blossoms. They should feel dry, crisp, and light to the touch—almost like a thin piece of paper. To remove all the silica gel, gently and carefully pour it off into another container, making sure a

Delicately remove the crystals from the dried blossom using a small paintbrush.

sudden cascade of crystals does not crush the flowers.

After you have uncovered the flowers, you will need to dust off the crystals that may be inside the petals. Holding the stem or wire, delicately shake the flower to remove the crystals. You can use a small paintbrush to brush off any stubborn silica gel, as shown in the photo at center below, but do this cautiously.

Microwave Silica Gel Method

The convenience and quickness of this method may appeal to you, although it will probably take some initial testing to arrive at the proper cooking times for the flowers you're drying. Thoroughly read the manufacturer's instructions before you begin, and be sure to let the gel cool before you remove the flowers.

Keep good records of your adventures with microwave drying. It does involve a little experimentation, partly because ovens vary, but of course flowers do, too. To use this technique, cover the flowers with silica gel as in the traditional method, but remember that you can't wire the stems. Be sure to use a microwave-safe container, and double-check the instructions on your silica gel for suggested drying times as well as the power settings for your microwave. Try 50 percent power for two minutes to dry marigolds, for instance, cooking them in one-minute increments. Don't forget—to avoid disappointment, let the crystals cool completely before you remove the flowers.

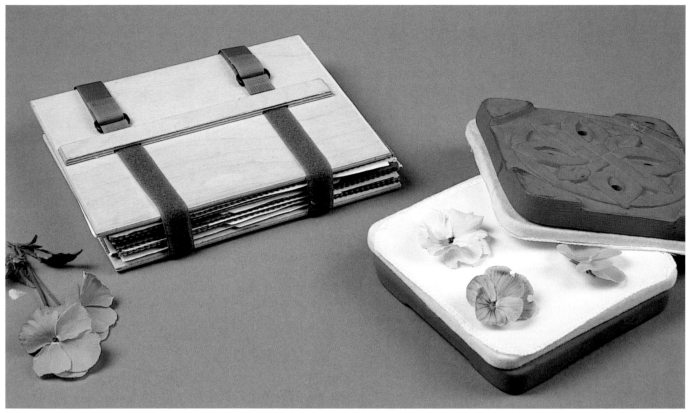

A traditional flower press, on the left, and a microwave press, on the right.

PRESSING TECHNIQUES

Pressed flowers can embellish many craft projects because of their two-dimensional nature; they can be glued or decoupaged onto just about anything, with a great deal of success. Like drying, there are several different methods you can utilize to press flowers. While I successfully dried some bleeding heart using the old-fashioned method of placing them in a heavy book, for instance, they did nothing but brown in the microwave, despite many attempts. It might take a couple of tries to get the results you want.

Preparation for pressing is pretty quick; remove as much of the stems and foliage as desired, and make certain that the petals are lying flat and open, with no creases or folds, before you begin. Be sure that the flowers aren't touching one another. Of course, the fresh material should be dry before you start.

Traditional Book Pressing

Tried and true, nothing could be easier than this ancient method. It's a very easy, satisfying method of preserving flowers, perfect to use when you're strolling around your yard and find just one little beauty you want to save. Place your specimens between sheets of porous paper and close them inside a heavy book, wait a few weeks, and *voilà*—pressed flowers. Wax paper will also produce pretty decent results, and some sources suggest using newspaper, though I'm not enamored of that material. If the ink transfers to your flowers, they'll be ruined.

Using a Flower Press

Another perfectly easy technique is the use of the flower press. These devices are generally made with two pieces of wood, with layers of blotting paper and cardboard in between. Closures can vary, from screws and wing nuts to hook-and-loop tape, but the idea is the same, which is to keep the material pressed tightly between the wooden cover pieces during the drying cycle. Pressing times of several weeks will vary according to the flowers, but you should check them for progress. If the material is damp or soft, leave it for a bit longer.

Using a Microwave Flower Press

You can obtain astonishing results with a microwave flower press, in only about two minutes or so. If you want to make a quick personalized card, or adorn a gift like the bags on page 108, this method will give you exquisite material with which to work.

I use a terracotta press, though the first generation of microwave presses were made of wood. The newer ceramic presses are generally sold with absorbent wool felt layers and thin sheets of tightly woven fabric. The flowers are placed between the layers of fabric, which are sandwiched between the felt and the press, as in the photo on page 91.

Then, place the press in the microwave for about two minutes or so, but here's the important part—*cook in 30-second intervals to avoid burning the flowers*. Let the flowers cool between the layers of fabric before you remove them; if you don't, they'll likely begin to curl.

Preparation for this technique varies little from the other pressing methods. However, some flower varieties press more successfully when the individual petals are dried. This is true for varieties that have a thick calyx like marigolds, or a bell-shaped structure, like the lisianthus. Gently remove the petals first, and place them in the press individually. Arrange them so that they lie flat and don't touch one another, as in the photo below.

Of course, not all flowers are suited to this method. Some colors just won't remain true with the microwave technique; my lovely deep rose pansies with delicate yellow centers faded to a rather depressing brown when pressed in the microwave. But the vibrancy of the lisianthus and the delicate, translucent quality of the poppies I've obtained with this method far overshadow the disappointments.

Be sure to keep a record of your pressing times, and include any other factors that may influence the outcome. If it usually takes two minutes to dry a pansy, you might discover that it takes a little bit longer if you've had a few rainy days, for instance. Jot down any information that may help your future efforts.

SEALING DRIED AND PRESSED FLOWERS

Most preserved materials need to be sealed in some fashion to prevent them from reabsorbing moisture. This can happen rather quickly and drastically; don't remove items from silica gel and then leave them sitting out overnight. You'll probably wake to discover melted lilies in the place of your picture-perfect specimens. So, be sure to factor in this important part of the preservation process.

There are many products for this purpose. Some are preservatives, which can be used before and after crafting or arranging. Other products are designed only for use on specific types of flowers. Surface

Some blossoms can't be pressed whole, but you can remove the petals and press them separately.

This peony was dried in silica gel and then sprayed with three coats of surface sealant.

sealants work very nicely on silica-dried flowers. Acrylic sprays can be used as a final coat, if desired. Visit your local craft store and investigate the different products, because you may need one specific to your flower as well as to your intended use. However, many of the sealants contain toxic ingredients, and should be used only with proper ventilation and protective gloves, if necessary.

Pressed flowers can be sealed prior to use. The edges of the flowers may want to curl, so sometimes this can be a bit frustrating. But it does produce a well-preserved blossom. Depending on how you will use them, though, it may

not be necessary to seal the flowers first; decoupage does a fine job of sealing most flowers in the course of the project.

A couple of notes about sealing: The level of humidity in the atmosphere has a big effect on the success of the sealing process. In general, try to seal only on sunny, calm days. If I have to remove some flowers from gel on a rainy day, I set them in foam, place them in a sealed container with a thin layer of gel on the bottom, and wait until the conditions are more favorable. You don't

want to seal moisture into the flowers; you want to seal it out.

Finally, though some sources recommend holding dried flowers and applying the sealant, I prefer to use the wire handles on the flowers and sink them into floral foam. Then place them on a work surface to be sprayed.

STORING PRESERVED MATERIALS

Make sure that your flowers are absolutely dry before you consider storing them. Air-dried materials can be wrapped in paper and stored in boxes; you may want to toss in a few mothballs for insurance. Silica-dried materials should be stored in an airtight container, in a dry location away from sunlight; leave some silica crystals in the box for additional protection. Pressed flowers can be stored in a variety of ways, in envelopes or plastic sandwich bags, but be sure that they remain flat to preserve their beauty. A sturdy box is good protection, too. You might want to consider labeling your storage containers, so you can quickly locate the items when you are ready to craft.

This trellis is a lovely way to display dried flowers and herbs. For project instructions, see page 111.

TOOLS AND TECHNIQUES

FLORAL TOOLS AND SUPPLIES

Okay, whether from your own garden or the craft store, you have dried flowers on hand and a project in mind. What else do you need? Probably not much more than you already have.

If you need to purchase any of these items, they are certainly on the inexpensive side and are readily available at craft stores or garden centers. Floral wire is helpful to secure flowers, as is floral tape.

(Both of these materials are found in various colors, including green and brown.) To use floral tape properly, apply it with tension, because that allows the waxed tape to adhere to itself as you wrap. Floral foam is the basis for several projects in the book, and it's always handy to have on hand if you plan to dry your own flowers. It works wonderfully as a foundation for the dried flowers while you are sealing or removing silica gel, for instance. I usually store dried flowers mounted in foam blocks.

Floral pins are used to secure natural materials to a base. Sealants, floral preservatives, and acrylic sprays, discussed on pages 92 and 93, are important supplies. A good pair of garden snips or floral shears will probably come in handy, and a pair of pruners will be helpful if you are working with thick-stemmed material or twigs, as for making the kitchen trellis on page 111. You'll need a pair of wire cutters, too.

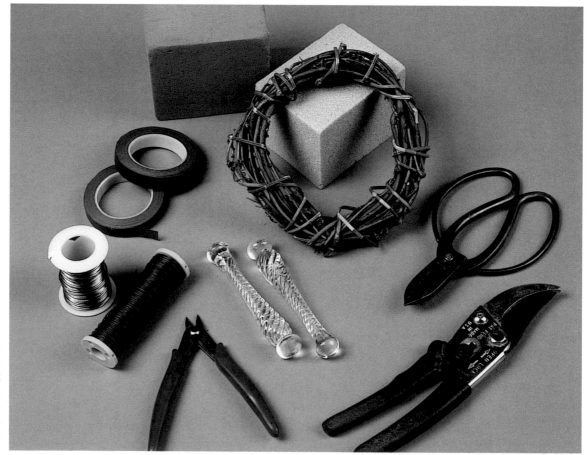

Here are some of the floral tools and supplies you will use, including foam, wreath forms, garden shears, pruners, pestles, wire cutters, wire, and floral tape.

CRAFTING TOOLS AND SUPPLIES

Most of the things that you need are very basic crafting supplies and need little explanation. A hot glue gun and glue sticks, decoupage medium, clear-drying craft glue, miscellaneous brushes, and scissors are essential to many of the projects. Basic sewing equipment, including a sewing machine, needles, and thread, etc., are used to make the sachet bag on page 124, as well as for several other projects. Beads, beading needles, and beading thread are used in a few of the projects, and ribbons embellish several of them. Paper, both utilitarian and decorative, is an important ingredient in many of the projects. You'll need some sort of measuring device, a tape measure or ruler, and a pencil, pen, or marker. Most likely, you'll want to protect your work surface, perhaps with newspaper, craft paper, or waxed paper.

There are some specialized tools used in the book, like the eyelet punch used for the boxes on page 127. This project might give you a chance to work with some new equipment. Of course, each set of instructions will detail the tools and supplies that you'll need to create that project.

Incorporate a new technique like simple embossing into your dried flower crafting.

Pictured are many of the general crafting tools and supplies you will use to create the projects in this book. You probably already have most of them, such as a glue gun, tape measure, sewing needles, beads, buttons, scissors, and paintbrushes.

CRAFTING TECHNIQUES, TIPS, AND CONSIDERATIONS

You can use dried or pressed flowers to embellish a craft project, like the perky little blossoms in the collection on page 120. Or you might add dried materials as an ingredient in a project, like the soap and body products in the guest baskets on page 136. You can also use dried flowers as the basis for a project, as with the table runner on page 139. The techniques you use in each project will probably be very familiar to you, but the preserved material itself may have special characteristics that you need to keep in mind while you work. Here is some advice.

Embellishing a Project with Flowers

Generally speaking, use only clear-drying craft glue or decoupage medium if your project calls for a finishing coat of adhesive on top of the flowers. Other kinds of glue may leave you with a dull, clouded flower, not the vibrant specimen that you want. But even these two types have their differences. While I was experimenting with the curtain on page 141, I found that I could use craft glue successfully on the pink pansies, for instance, with no negative effects. But when used on the yellow varieties, the glue dried quite unattractively on the surface, and I switched to decoupage medium. It

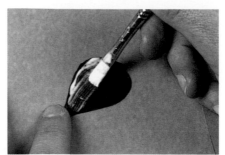

To apply glue or decoupage medium to the back of a pressed petal, make the brush strokes from the inside to the outer edge of the petal (or from the center of the flower outward, as the case may be).

bears repeating that you should experiment with just a few specimens, using all the techniques you have in mind, before you begin a final project. It may save you some disappointment.

When you are applying clear glue or decoupage medium on individual petals and don't plan to apply a top coat, try to use just the amount needed to coat the petal and no more. You may find that any excess will be impossible to remove from your base material, and it might spoil the appearance of your project. Use these supplies as sparingly as possible.

A flat paintbrush seems to work well when applying adhesives to the surfaces of pressed flowers. Work toward the outer edges of the flowers or petals, as shown in the photo above, making sure you don't paint decoupage over the blooms and onto your work surface—or you will have glued the flower to your table! The delicate nature of pressed flowers makes it difficult to remove them in these cases. I've lost many a nice blossom with a

careless application of glue. Be attentive as you work.

Your paintbrush is also an excellent tool for placing flowers on your project. Use just a bit of adhesive on the back of the flower, and then move it into place with the paintbrush, as shown in the photo below. While tweezers can also be used to transfer pressed flowers, the paintbrush method is virtually trouble-free.

Use a small paintbrush dipped in glue or decoupage medium to place the pressed flowers; dab the brush onto the back of the flower and move it into position.

Using Flowers as an Ingredient

Some interesting and unexpected things can happen to dried flowers when they are used in the crafting process. For instance, the purple disappears from pansies when they are placed into a soap medium. Oftentimes, commercially prepared dried flowers are dyed, and this color will then leach out when certain types of liquid ingredients are used. But the pansies that lost their color were pressed right from my garden, so dye was not the culprit. It's simply the nature of the plant itself. However, be advised that most store-bought materials will have been dyed and sealed, and these products may react with the ones you intend to use. A little test is probably in order before you begin.

This same phenomenon occurs with some types of sealants, too, such as water-based liquid products. These may cause certain colors to run, but they can also produce a rather intriguing antiqued look over the rest of the surface. You might find this to be a desirable quality in your final project, so experiment at will.

Making Flowers the Basis of a Project

Several of the projects that have the flowers themselves as the basic material also require floral foam. Though it is relatively easy to sink the stems into the foam, it may be helpful to make holes for the stems first; that way, you don't have to be overly concerned about possibly breaking a stem while you work. A variation of this technique is also used in the shadow box on page 117; it's demonstrated in the photo at right.

Of course, dried flowers are not as pliable as fresh flowers, and they won't have the graceful drape of a freshly cut blossom. But there are a few tricks that you can employ to make working with these items easier. Floral preservatives, discussed on page 92, are often used by professionals before and after they begin

If you're certain that the flowers you're incorporating into a project have been dyed, like these neon pink beauties, you may want to test them first to make sure that they are color-fast.

to work; the preservatives soften the dried materials, which makes it easier to manipulate them while you are creating an arrangement. If you are using purchased materials and want to reshape the stems a bit, you can steam them just slightly and hold them in position as they dry. (You can rejuvenate a crushed bloom with this method, too.)

Because air-dried materials tend to have very straight stalks, you may wish to add some gentle curves with the following method. While the flowers are still fresh, insert a wire near the top of the stem for about an inch (2.5 cm). Then, gently wrap the wire around the length of the stem. After the flower has wilted just a bit, bend the wire to create some curves, and then allow it to dry fully.

When making an arrangement, particularly one like the stook on page 134, remove all the materials from their packaging and arrange the items so you can easily pick them up. Though this seems like a very simple idea, it

Pierce holes into floral foam or foam core board with an awl and then place the flowers, as shown.

When you're dividing long material into shorter working pieces, be sure to break the stem at the proper point to prevent having any visible stems in your arrangement.

really makes your work much easier if everything is readily accessible. Further, try to determine the desired height of the specimens that you're using and trim the stems first, if necessary.

To divide long specimens into shorter lengths, as you'll do for the wreaths on page 146, be sure to break the stem at the proper point, because you don't want any visible stems in your project. The stem should be snapped just at the location of the right thumb, as shown in the photo above. Then, you'll have a stem at the bottom of the left piece, and no visible stem at the top of the right piece. Repeat for as many pieces as needed, and glue the stem ends into place.

In most instances, arrangements using dried flowers are best worked from the center out, to prevent possible damage to the stems; with this method, you're not working over the material you've just placed. This may be contrary to the methods

you use for fresh flowers, but try to plan your arrangements with this technique in mind, particularly if you're incorporating tall specimens.

Working Tips

Make sure that your material has been properly stored and kept fresh. If you add stale ingredients to a project such as the coasters on page 129, they won't release the lovely lavender scent as intended. This advice applies to all the projects, because they will certainly have more impact if the flowers you use are colorful and vivid, not faded and dusty.

Dried and pressed flowers are delicate. I've found that it's helpful to have a bit more material on hand than I really need, to account for breakage, bungled glue jobs, or other mishaps.

Keep an eye on the ventilation in your work space; pressed flowers can blow away with the slightest breeze, and you certainly don't want them to take flight into a container of decoupage medium! Consider the ambient humidity, too; if you are working with flowers that are not sealed, they could begin to absorb moisture quite rapidly.

Finally, each set of project instructions will give you some additional advice pertinent to that specific project, so look for some more tips in that section of the book.

DESIGN CONSIDERATIONS

Since you don't have to be concerned with containers that are waterproof when using dried flowers, you can

Though dried flowers are delicate, they're not as fragile as you may think. They can be easily manipulated and arranged with just a bit of care.

be very creative with the kinds of vessels you choose to use for arrangements. Basketry is an obvious example, but how about a bark container, paper or cardboard boxes, sections of bamboo or a pile of striking stones? Any kind of found object that can be used as a container is at your disposal: The possibilities are endless.

Texture can create some visual interest in your projects; take a look at the burlap ribbon and corrugated cardboard on page 108 to see how these materials help highlight the delicate beauty of the pressed flowers.

Professional floral designers now say that the old rules about the ratio of the height of the container to the flowers can be tossed out the window. Now it's far more important to size the arrangement in relation to its placement in your home, so consider where you plan to use it. If it's on your dinner table, you want your guests to be able to converse and see each other clearly, so don't use a tall arrangement as a centerpiece.

Don't be overwhelmed by the quality of professionally produced arrangements you may have seen in floral shops or in people's homes. Some professional floral designers actually deconstruct flowers petal by petal, dry them in silica crystals, and then reconstruct them to use in arrangements, adding stems created from other materials. And many of those breathtaking dried floral displays have probably been treated with colored floral sprays to enhance the hue of the blooms. The professionals are, after all, professionals, so please remember that the goal of this book is to enjoy crafting with dried flowers. If you are new to this medium, allow some time to become acquainted with the nuances of working with preserved materials.

PURCHASING TIPS

Since dried materials can be expensive, make sure that you are purchasing top-quality flowers. Since they are generally sold in cellophane packages, inspect them to make sure

You don't need professional training to create a beautiful arrangement with dried flowers.

Purchased materials can be very lovely, and you may find some unusual items in stores, such as the Protea shown at center bottom of the photo above.

the flowers are mostly intact; if you see lots of loose material in the package, keep on looking. Likewise, since many of the store-bought materials have been dyed, make sure their color hasn't faded.

Many florists also carry preserved materials. Though their prices are likely to be higher than at a craft store, their flowers may be locally grown, probably handled less, and perhaps in better condition. Lastly, try to determine the amount you need as best you can, to avoid unnecessary expense.

MAINTENANCE CONSIDERATIONS

Now that you have created a project with dried flowers, there are several things you can do to increase its longevity. Obviously, over the course of time, the materials will age. But some sources say that dried flowers can be kept for years if cared for properly.

First, keep your projects out of the bright sun to reduce fading. Try to avoid placing dried materials in rooms that can be damp or humid, like a bathroom or kitchen. (A few projects in this book are delightful exceptions to this rule, however.) If your project becomes dusty, you can use a hair dryer on a low, cool setting to disperse the particles. Try a paintbrush, too, for a quick touch-up.

Finally, for safety's sake, you should keep your projects away from

To keep your dried flowers looking this lovely, seal them well; keep them in a dry place; and don't display them in direct sunlight.

sparks and flames, as the materials are, of course, very dry. The sealant products are flammable as well.

GETTING STARTED

If you're interested in working with dried flowers, I think you'll find this book will satisfy your curiosity. The information presented lets you get involved at a level that suits you and your lifestyle, either starting with your own materials or with purchased ones. You may find that you can appreciate the subtleties of flowers a little bit more when you work with them as closely as you will in these projects. Now, turn the page and begin!

Flower Fun

There are many simple ways you can use dried flowers in crafting or decorating so fast and easy that they really don't need detailed instructions. Here are a few additional suggestions to incorporate preserved floral materials into your life:

⚘ Decoupage individual petals or whole pressed flowers onto paper and line your drawers. A bit more elegant than regular shelf paper, don't you think?

⚘ Similarly, take a few petals or small flowers and glue them to the inside of an envelope; it adds a nice touch for a special piece of correspondence.

⚘ There are several different ways you can adorn gifts with dried or pressed flowers. When you are tying a ribbon into a bow, place a few stems of your favorite dried flowers in the knot. Sprinkle a handful of petals over a wrapped package for a stunning presentation, or attach a large, dramatic flower like a peony with metallic wire, rather than ribbon.

⚘ For a twist on wrapping paper, use two layers of paper and place pressed flowers between the two; just make sure the material on top is transparent or translucent, so use cellophane or vellum, for example.

⚘ Armature wire, available from art and craft suppliers, can be used as a sleek, modern way to bind bunches of flowers into simple, stand-alone displays.

⚘ Create whimsical stems for dried flowers from wire. Use pliers to bend or wrap the wire into the design of your choice, remove most of the original stem, and use floral tape to attach the lengths of wire to the remaining stem. Don't worry about covering up the tape.

⚘ Fill a clear vase or bowl with flower heads instead of fruit; large showy species are perfect for this idea.

⚘ Use pressed flowers to create custom switch plates for your walls. At your local home improvement center, you can find clear plastic switch plates designed to be backed with wallpaper; instead, use a decorative paper and pressed flowers or foliage of your choice.

Drawer Pulls

DESIGNER: JOAN MORRIS

Aren't these wonderful? And so simple, too. The glass craft stones create the illusion that the flowers are embedded in the drawer pulls; they also produce a magnifying effect that brilliantly displays the blossoms. Retrofit any cabinet using this technique. The stones aren't perfectly circular, so expect these pulls to be delightfully imperfect.

YOU WILL NEED

Clear glass craft stones, 1¼ inches (3.1 cm) in diameter

Decoupage medium

Small paintbrushes

Statice, assorted colors

Pansies

White paint

Hot glue gun and glue sticks, or cyanoacrylate glue

Concave drawer pulls, 1⅜ inches (3.5 cm) in diameter, from a home improvement store

Screwdriver

VARIATION

The stones are available in pastel tones, too, and you may find these useful in coordinating a look for your home decorating. This method can be used to create ornamentation for curtain tiebacks (add a pin finding to the back of the stones) or to make elegant magnets (add a magnet or adhesive magnetic strip to the back).

1 On the flat side of a glass stone, paint on the decoupage medium. Then, place alternating colors of statice on the lower part of the glass piece, arranging them in a half-circle. Paint on a little more decoupage medium. As shown, place the pansy face down behind the statice layer, using individual petals if desired. Cover the rest of the glass piece. Paint a light layer of decoupage medium on the back of the pansy to flatten the petals. Let dry. Repeat for as many drawer pulls as needed.

3 Glue the flower-covered stones to the drawer pulls. Center the stones on the pulls and press in place. Be certain to use enough glue to securely fasten the stones, since the pulls may get a lot of use. Let dry.

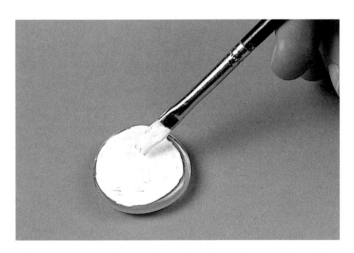

2 Paint over the back of the glass piece with white paint, completely covering the flowers. This application of paint makes the glass stones opaque and prevents the finish of the drawer pull from detracting from the design of the pressed flowers. Let the piece dry, and then repeat for the other drawer pulls.

4 Choose a location for the hardware, then install the drawer pulls, using the screws that are sold with the hardware. Rotate the pulls as needed for the correct orientation of the design on the stones.

TIP: Glass craft stones and drawer pulls are available in different sizes, but the smaller sizes will be a bit more difficult to use for this project.

Translucent Lamp

DESIGNER: CORINNE KURZMANN

You may have admired a similar design in a trendy boutique, and now you can create your own using pressed flowers and translucent handmade paper. When you illuminate it, the flowers glow from within, displaying their intricate silhouettes. It's a lovely, subtle lighting treatment.

YOU WILL NEED

Lamp form—from a craft store

Light bulb

Ruler

Pencil

Translucent handmade paper (with petals, if desired)

Scissors or decorative-edged scissors

Pressed flowers

Decoupage medium

Paintbrush

Hole punch or nail

Small bookbinding screws

Vellum or squares of handmade paper (optional)

TIP: Remember that the paper you choose should be somewhat translucent. You may wish to experiment with different weights of paper before you begin, by wrapping them around the form when it's illuminated. That way, you can be sure that you'll obtain the desired results when your lamp shade is finished.

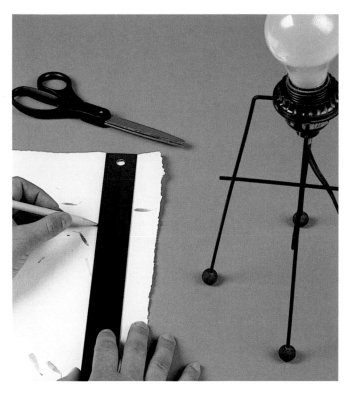

1   Measure, mark, and cut the paper to the desired size, based on your lamp form. Then cut a second sheet the same size, as you will need two layers of paper for the shade. Use decorative-edged scissors to cut the paper, if desired, or tear along the edges to create the same effect.

2   Lay one of the sheets of paper flat on a work surface and arrange the dried flowers. Then, use the decoupage medium to glue the flowers in place, being careful to use a minimal amount of decoupage so that it doesn't bleed through the paper.

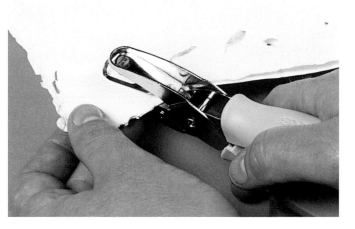

3   To align the holes for the shade, place one of the sheets of paper around the form and mark the locations of the holes that will fit on the frame. Next, place the paper back on your work surface and mark the spots to install the bookbinder's screws, spaced evenly along the edges of the paper. Then, align the two sheets and use the hole punch or nail to make the holes through both layers.

4   Put the two sheets together, with the pressed flower layer on the inside. Remove the caps on the lamp form, if necessary, to slip the paper onto the form; then replace the caps. Place the holes for the bookbinder's screws at the back post of the lamp form and insert the screws at the marked spots, as shown. Add layers of vellum underneath the screws or between the layers of paper if you feel that your lamp shade needs the extra support.

Floral Spheres

DESIGNER: TERRY TAYLOR

Your guests won't stop talking about this clever arrangement featuring helichrysum, better known by its common name, strawflower. It is very easy to grow, so you can plan this project in the spring, cultivate it through the summer, and enjoy it in the fall. Or, go ahead and purchase dried strawflowers now, if you just can't wait to make this centerpiece.

YOU WILL NEED

Polystyrene foam balls,
a variety of sizes

Pencil

Polystyrene foam square

Acrylic paint

Flat paintbrush

4 bunches of strawflowers

Hot glue gun and glue sticks

Small bowl or container

Vine-wrapped bamboo

Craft knife or small saw

Wire

Raffia

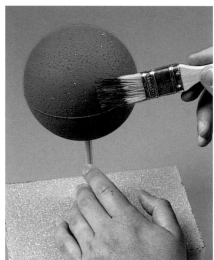

1 Use an old pencil to temporarily position one of the balls into the polystyrene foam. Paint the ball with a coat of acrylic paint that matches the color of your strawflowers, and let it dry completely. Don't skip this step, because it keeps the color of the ball from peeking through your glued plant material.

2 Remove the flower heads from the stems, leaving as little stem material as possible. Hot glue the strawflowers to the top of the ball, as shown, placing the flowers as close together as possible. After you have partially covered the ball, take it off its pencil stand and move it to a small container so you can rotate the ball as needed to finish gluing on the flowers. Repeat steps 1 and 2 to create the desired number of spheres.

3 Cut three equal lengths of bamboo to use for a tripod. Cross two sticks at an angle, as shown, and wrap them tightly with wire where they cross. Try to make this joint very secure, as this forms the base of the tripod.

4 Fiddle with the placement of the third leg of the tripod; this is art, not science! When you are satisfied with the way it looks and stands, use a bit of hot glue to hold the three sticks together. For extra security, wrap a length of wire around the tripod, as shown.

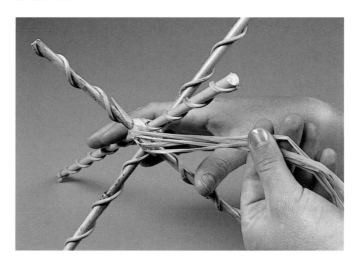

5 To cover the joint in the tripod, use raffia to disguise the wire and hot glue. You may need to use several lengths of raffia, using a bit of hot glue to secure the strands. Repeat steps 3, 4, and 5 to build as many tripods as needed.

VARIATIONS

Hot glue still-pliable autumn leaves to a ball, and then randomly wrap metallic thread around and around the ball to accent them. Cover the balls with dried seedpods of lunaria (money plant) for a sleek, wintertime look. Use this same technique on a smaller scale to create holiday ornaments.

Blooming Gift Bags

DESIGNER: VALERIE SHRADER

*Why use a bow when you can use a flower instead?
Here's a new way to adorn a gift without wrap or ribbon. Use dried petals
to create your own fanciful flowers, adding beads or metallic threads to enhance
your design. Collaborate with nature to make great cards, too.*

Waxed paper

Dried lisianthus and Gerbera daisies, individual petals

Decoupage medium

Flat paintbrush

Parchment paper—from a kitchen specialty shop

Heavy book

Scissors

Assorted beads

Beading needle

Beading thread

Corrugated gift bags, assorted sizes

Burlap ribbon

Silver metallic thread

Sewing needle

2 After the flower is dry, trim around the parchment paper to create the frame for the flower, as shown. Depending upon the type of beads you choose, either sew them carefully at the center of the flower or glue them in place with the decoupage medium. If you glued beads into the center, let the glue dry before you proceed to the next step.

1 To make the beaded flowers on the large bag, first cover your work surface with waxed paper. Create the flower shape on a piece of parchment paper by carefully painting decoupage medium onto the back of the petals, as shown, and gluing them into place, one at a time. Try not to let the decoupage spread onto the parchment paper. Smooth the petals into place gently with your fingertips. Place a layer of waxed paper over the top, and then let your flower dry thoroughly inside a heavy book.

3 Before you attach the flowers, first decide on their placement on the bag. Then, paint decoupage medium onto the back of the center of the flower and press it onto the bag. Place the bag on its back while the decoupage is drying.

4 To create the flowers on the burlap ribbon, first cut the ribbon to the length of your bag. Then place a small dab of decoupage medium on the back of the first petal and begin to build your flower at the desired location along the ribbon. Press into place, and add more petals as needed. Paint decoupage medium on the top of the petals also, working from the inside to the outer edge, to secure them in the design. Let dry, then embellish the center with silver beads. Use the silver metallic thread to attach the ribbon to the bag, taking just a few stitches at the center of the ribbon at the top and bottom of the bag.

TIP: Experiment with other wide-petal flowers to create this look. Some species of poppy dry to a beautiful, translucent finish, for example.

You can have a lot of fun using complete flowers with this process, too, as you can see in the photo below. Use pressed daisies, and decoupage them onto a piece of natural burlap; then make a pocket on the front of the bag by attaching the burlap with metallic thread. Or dry osteospermum blooms and glue them onto parchment paper, stitch the paper onto a piece of white burlap with decorative thread, and glue the entire piece onto the top of a corrugated box. Lastly, many dried flowers look beautiful when they are decoupaged onto mesh ribbon—they almost seem to melt into the fabric.

Kitchen Trellis

DESIGNER: SUSAN MCBRIDE

This beautiful arrangement of twigs, twine, and blossoms is decorative and functional, too, because you can use this trellis as a drying rack for herbs or flowers. Use found materials from your yard to create the twig framework, and embellish as desired with your favorites from the garden. Enlarge this design if you need more drying space.

YOU WILL NEED

Large-gauge sewing needle

Dark brown thread

Rubber gloves

Dried flowers and herbs—oregano, yarrow, chili peppers

Scissors

Hemp twine

9 thin hardwood twigs

2 thick hardwood twigs

Pruners or garden snips

TIP: Try to hang your trellis in a dry area in the kitchen, away from the humidity of boiling water.

VARIATION

Consider an Asian influence for this project, and use bamboo to create the trellis. Look for decorative twine if you want a more polished look.

1 Using the needle and the brown thread, carefully pierce the chili peppers and thread them onto a length of thread about 7 inches (17.8 cm) long. (Since the chili peppers contain capsaicin which burns the skin, you should wear rubber gloves. If you don't, you'd better not rub your eyes while you're working on this portion of the project!) Once you have about a dozen peppers on the thread, tie them together in a circle.

2 Cut the stems of the oregano to about 4½ inches (11.4 cm). Bind three to five stems together with a length of hemp twine about 18 inches (45.7 cm) long. Make three small bouquets, and then use the same technique to make two small yarrow bouquets; be certain to leave enough twine to tie the bouquets onto the twig trellis. Set aside.

3 Find twigs with about the same diameter, and use the pruners or garden snips to cut nine twigs to a length of about 12 inches (30.5 cm); these twigs will form the horizontal supports for the trellis. Find two thicker twigs and cut these to a length of about 18 inches (45.7 cm); these are the vertical supports. Take the thinner twigs and bind the edges into three bundles of three twigs each, as shown. Attach these bundles to the longer, thicker twigs by tying on with hemp twine. Since this is a rustic design, the binding doesn't have to be exact, but do trim the edges to keep it neat.

4 Attach the herb bouquets and the bunches of peppers to the twig trellis as desired. Take a length of the hemp twine and create a loop for hanging, being sure that you tie the knots securely so that the trellis doesn't fall.

Decorated Lampshade

DESIGNER: TERRY TAYLOR

A length of ribbon and a few dried flowers will dress up any lamp shade. This is a quick and easy project, readily adapted to your décor, and a good one for a beginner to get the feel of working with dried materials. Have a little fun with this decorating idea; it's the perfect excuse to experiment with color and texture.

YOU WILL NEED

Lampshade

Tape measure

Ribbon

Scissors

Sewing needle

Thread

Hot glue gun and glue sticks

Dried flowers

VARIATION

Create some simple holiday looks for your home with this technique. It's an easy and inexpensive way to add seasonal color; attach small pinecones or berries, perhaps, or small glass ornaments to accent the dried flowers you choose.

1 Determine the circumference of your lamp-shade, and then cut a length of ribbon two to three times that measurement. The longer the ribbon length, the fuller the ruffle you'll create. Consider the type of flowers you will use as you decide how full to make the ruffle.

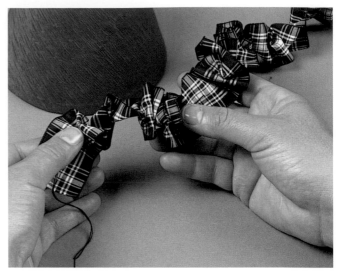

3 Gather the ribbon on the thread by pulling the basting stitches. Use your fingers to evenly distribute the gathers as desired. When you are satisfied with the appearance of the ribbon, knot the thread.

2 Thread your needle with a double strand of thread, in a color complementary to your ribbon. Knot the end. Sew a line of ¼-inch (6 mm) basting stitches down the center of the ribbon, but leave the thread in the needle.

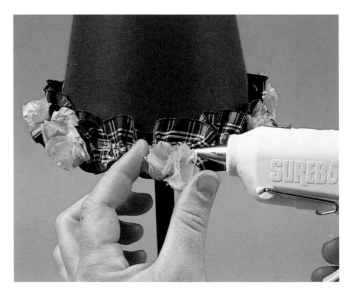

4 Hot glue the ribbon to the base of the shade, letting the ribbon extend approximately ½ inch (1.3 cm) below the base of the shade. Then, hot glue flowers to the ribbon; place them by sight or measure to ensure the flowers are evenly distributed along the ruffled border.

Tonal Arrangement

DESIGNER: VALERIE SHRADER

Take a minimalist approach when you create this arrangement of larkspur, using only similar shades of blue. Start with a distinctive organic container, and then plan your arrangement with only one type of flower for a lush, contemporary look. The effect is simple, yet dramatic.

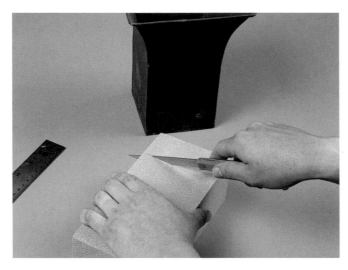

1   Fit the foam into the container. Use the kitchen knife to carve the foam into the proper shape to ensure a snug fit. Leave 1 or 2 inches (2.5 or 5.1 cm) of space between the top of the foam and the top of the container; this will allow you some working room to create the arrangement.

TIP: Your dried flower arrangements will last longer if they are not displayed in bright sunlight, so keep this idea in mind when you use this project to decorate your home.

VARIATION

In the right container, you can use a dense arrangement of stems that are all the same height to create a carpet of flowers.

2   Snap the stems of the larkspur to the desired length; use the snips for this step if your flowers have thick stalks. Then begin to build the arrangement in the middle of the foam, starting with the longest stalks of light blue larkspur. Angle the ends of the stems toward the center to create a spray of blossoms. Continue to add the light blue larkspur until you've used about two-thirds of the first bunch, slightly decreasing the height as you work.

3   Now, begin to intersperse a few stalks of the dark blue larkspur, gradually using less light blue larkspur and more dark blue stems. Continue to angle them toward the center and decrease the height of the larkspur, creating a full, luxurious arrangement. When you are content with your project, spray it with floral preservative, if desired.

Compass Shadow Box

DESIGNER: JOAN MORRIS

Does this design look familiar? It's based on a quilting pattern, and it offers infinite possibilities for variations in color and texture. Use all pressed flowers, for instance; for a more rustic feel, add some twigs or acorns. You'll find that it's simple to disassemble the shadow box to craft this project.

Foam core board, ½ inch (1.3 cm) thick

Ruler

Pencil

Utility knife

Shadow box, 8 x 8 inches (20.3 x 20.3 cm)

White paper (optional)

Scissors

Transfer paper

Assorted dried flowers

Hot glue gun and glue sticks

Awl

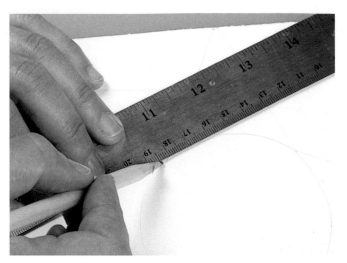

2 Trace or draw your chosen design onto the white paper. (To replicate this design, use the template on page 153.) Then take the transfer paper and trace the design onto the foam core board; however, if you're confident in your drawing skills, simply transfer the design directly to the foam core board.

1 Measure and mark the foam board to create a piece that is 7¾ × 7¾ inches (19.7 × 19.7 cm). Using the utility knife, cut the piece to these dimensions, as shown; after you've cut this piece, make sure it fits tightly inside the shadow box. Next, measure, mark, and cut the piece of paper to 7¾ × 7¾ inches (19.7 × 19.7 cm).

3 Decide which flowers to use in each element of the design, balancing the color and shape of the materials. Remove the flowers from their stalks; if possible, leave a short stem at the base of the flower to insert into the board. Start from the center of the design and use the glue gun to place the flowers; use the awl to make a hole for the materials with stems, place the flowers into the holes, and then glue into place. Flat materials, like eucalyptus, can be glued directly onto the board.

4 When you've completed the design, carefully place the frame over the foam core board, inserting it into the box. Hang or display as desired.

TIP: Since quilting books inspired the design in this project, you might look to these sources for other ideas.

VARIATION

The shadow box in this project was painted to complement the colors of its dried flowers. You may choose to retain the natural finish of your box, if it enhances your design; you could also make a box from salvaged materials, if you're handy with tools.

More Flower Fun

☙ Create your own botanical pictures with pressed flowers and foliage. Find a frame you like, and then add the dried materials. Use a layer of linen or decorative paper underneath the flowers for contrast, if desired.

☙ Find some salvaged items and use them to display dried flowers. Look for some pieces of old ceiling tin and glue on miniature roses; put two or three together for a grouping. Likewise, you might discover some old barn planks filled with fortuitous cracks; cut the planks into short pieces and insert some stems into the planks, and then hang for a rustic display.

Flower Power Collection

DESIGNERS: ALLISON SMITH & TERRY TAYLOR

Sock it to me! These projects have in common the use of some fun little pressed flowers in funky neon colors, reminiscent of the '60s. Add decoupage and a dash of imagination to create this groovy grouping of items.

YOU WILL NEED

(FOR THE VOTIVES)

Craft glue

Water

Small container

Small soft paintbrush

Lime green votive candles

Small pink pressed flowers

Paraffin

Double boiler

Plastic container

Wax paper

(FOR THE PILLARS)

Tape measure

Tall glass emergency candle

Orange high-fiber handmade paper

Scissors

Decoupage medium

Foam paintbrush

Small orange pressed flowers, coordinated with the paper color

(FOR THE FRAMES)

Patterned tissue paper

Scissors

Paper frame

Decoupage medium

Small container

Small paintbrush

Small pink pressed flowers

Craft glue

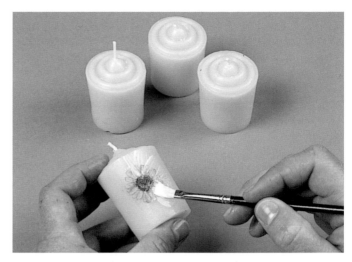

1 To craft the votives, begin by diluting the glue with water by one half. With the paintbrush, apply a small amount of glue onto the candle where the flower is to be placed. Press the flower onto the candle and gently paint over the candle to seal it, as shown. Be careful not to make bubbles in the glue by overworking it. Let the votive dry completely before the next step.

2 Use an old plastic container to melt the paraffin in a double boiler. Once you use a container to melt wax, it can't be used for any other purpose; on the other hand, the paraffin can be used again and again for other projects. When the paraffin is completely melted, hold the candle by the wick and quickly dip it only *one time* into the paraffin. Make one swift motion as you dip and remove. Don't allow the candle to sit in the paraffin bath, or it will cloud

the colors of the candle and flower. Repeat steps 1 and 2 for as many votives as desired; then, let them dry on wax paper.

each with a small dot of decoupage medium. Lastly, seal by painting over the entire candle with decoupage medium.

3 To decorate the pillar candle, first measure the candle and cut the paper to the dimensions of the candle, adding 1 inch (2.5 cm) to the height and ½ inch (1.3 cm) to the circumference of the candle. Cover the candle with decoupage medium; if the medium is too thick, thin it down with water. Place the paper on a flat surface, and then put the candle on top of the paper and roll the candle so the paper adheres to it, as shown. Smooth it with your hands.

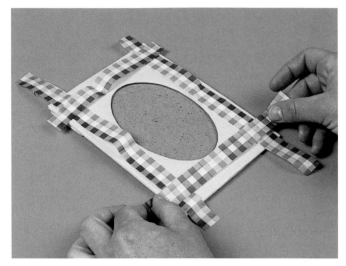

5 For the decorated frame, cut the tissue paper into strips proportionate to your frame. Arrange the strips as you would like to see them on the frame, as shown; you might try several arrangements until you find one that you like. Cut the strips slightly longer than the frame's dimensions; you will eventually fold the strips around the back of the frame. For now, set the strips to the side.

4 Turn the candle upside down and spread decoupage medium onto the bottom of the candle. Press the paper down and allow it to dry. Affix the flowers randomly to the candle, as shown,

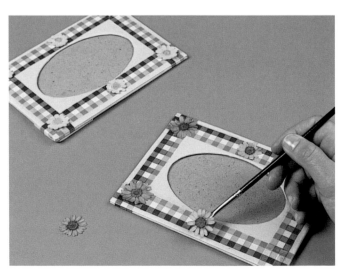

6 To decorate the frame, pour a small amount of decoupage medium into the container. Brush a coat of the medium onto the frame the width of one of your strips. Lay one of the strips of tissue onto the

medium, and use your fingers or the brush to smooth the tissue into place. Adhere all of the strips in this manner. Then brush the medium onto the back of the frame and fold over all of the tissue ends. Smooth them into place. Allow the strips to dry and then use white craft glue to adhere pressed flowers to the face of the frame, as shown.

TIP: Be sure you leave enough space to insert the photo after you've enhanced the picture frame.

VARIATIONS

Press colorful autumn leaves and use them instead of flowers in any of these projects. Rather than a paper frame, use a wooden frame; simply paint the frame before you apply the tissue and dried floral embellishments.

Ribbon Sachet Bag

DESIGNER: JOAN MORRIS

This delicate creation is the perfect complement to a fragrant blend of potpourri. If you want to make your own potpourri, choose your favorite materials and assemble the mixture. Then exercise a little patience, as it will take about six weeks to cure. In the meantime, find some glorious ribbons to make this bag, and dream about the scented result.

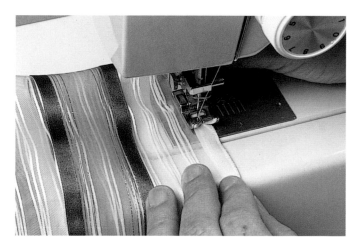

2 Find the center of the ribbon by folding it in half lengthwise, wrong sides together, so that the narrow ribbon is on the outside. Machine stitch the sides together close to the edges to form the bag, making sure the wired edges do not get caught in the seam.

3 To make a potpourri, choose fragrant dried materials and place them in a bowl; add 1 tablespoon (15 ml) of fixative for each cup of potpourri. (The potpourri for this project was chosen to coordinate with the color of the ribbon.) If desired, add just a few drops of essential oil for extra fragrance. Mix thoroughly and place in the paper bag; shake well, then roll the bag tightly to remove excess air. Store in a dark location and shake once a day for a week; then shake once a week for the next five weeks.

1 To make the bag, begin by placing the 2-inch-wide (5.1 cm) ribbon in the center of the 5-inch-wide (12.7 cm) ribbon. Hand stitch the narrow ribbon onto the wider ribbon along its length, using invisible thread. (A sewing machine may also be used for this step, if desired.) Turn under a ½-inch (1.3 cm) hem on both raw edges and stitch in place.

If you plan on placing your sachet bag deep within a drawer, you can omit the floral decoration in step 4 so it will lie flat.

4 To decorate your bag, glue three or four eucalyptus leaves together to form a base. Then add a layer of dried material, next a circle of statice, and finally a single dried flower in the center, gluing each layer on successively. Lastly, glue the arrangements onto the center of the ribbon.

5 When the potpourri is ready, fill the ribbon bag within 2½ inches (6.4 cm) of the top. Then, gather the bag about 2 inches (5.1 cm) from the top and secure with a rubber band. Wrap the ¼-inch-wide (6 mm) ribbon around the rubber band and make a bow. Of course, if you don't want to make your own potpourri, you can purchase it ready-made and add it to the bag.

Rose and Moss Boxes

DESIGNER: TERRY TAYLOR

This is a versatile project with as many variations as there are colors of paint and types of dried flowers. The plain boxes are like blank canvases, ready to be transformed to suit your mood and tastes. Use these embellished boxes to store treasured mementos, or to store nothing at all, for that matter—they don't have to be functional to be appreciated.

YOU WILL NEED

Paper boxes

Off-white acrylic paint

Paintbrushes

Masking tape

Metallic acrylic paint

Paper towels

Tape measure

Pencil

Hole punch

Eyelet punch and eyelets

Dried miniature rosebuds

Scissors

Reindeer moss (or similar dried moss)

Hot glue gun and glue sticks

1 yard (.9 m) of ribbon

VARIATIONS

Use bright paint colors and tiny strawflowers for a summery look. Or, for an autumnal accent, glue tiny acorns around the box lid. Dried poppy seed heads and a dash of wintry white glitter sprinkled all over the box would make an unusually festive holiday decoration.

1 Paint the lid and box with one coat of acrylic paint. Let them dry thoroughly, and then apply a second coat of paint. Let the box dry completely.

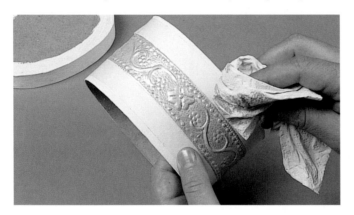

2 Place a length of masking tape above and below the embossed band around the box. Paint the band with metallic paint, then quickly wipe off the paint, as shown. Remove the tape when dry.

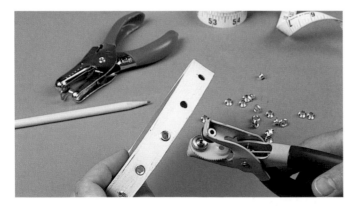

3 Measure and make an even number of marks around the rim of the box lid, spacing them at regular intervals. Use the hole punch to pierce a hole at each mark. Then, use the eyelet punch to set an eyelet in each hole, as shown.

4 Trim the stem from the bottom of each miniature rosebud. Hot glue a single row of closely spaced rosebuds around the edge of the box lid. Then fill in the center of the box lid with reindeer moss, attaching it with hot glue, as shown.

5 Cut the ribbon to the desired length. Then thread the ribbon through the eyelets. Wrap the ends of the ribbon with masking tape, if desired, to make it easier to thread. Lastly, tie a bow with the ribbon ends.

Aromatic Coasters

DESIGNER: ALLISON SMITH

These sweet little coasters are filled with a surprise—lavender, which releases its fragrance each time you set your hot mug atop them. Make a set of four to safeguard your furniture, and you'll be helping your state of mind at the same time with the soothing aroma of lavender, known for its relaxing properties. Choose an antiqued fabric for this mood-lifting project.

YOU WILL NEED
(FOR FOUR COASTERS)

Paper

Compass

Scissors

Pins

¼ yard (22.9 cm) of floral print fabric

Sewing machine

Thread

Wooden spoon

Iron and ironing board

Lavender flowers

Spoon

4 decorative buttons, each 1 inch (2.5 cm) in diameter

Sewing needle

Embroidery floss

1 Use the compass to make a paper pattern that is 5¼ inches (13.3 cm) in diameter; cut it out with the scissors. Then, pin the paper to the fabric and cut out the circles; to make four coasters, you'll need eight circles.

2 Place two of the circles with their right sides together. Then, sew them together using a ⅝-inch (1.6 cm) seam allowance. Leave a 2-inch (5.1 cm) gap in the seam so you have an opening to fill the coasters with lavender.

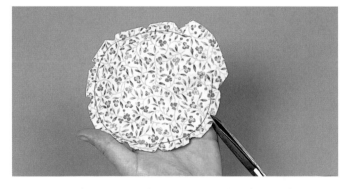

3 Trim the seams along the inside edges. Then snip along the inside edge close to the seam line, as shown, but avoid cutting the seam. Turn the coaster right side out and push out the edges with the end of a wooden spoon. Press flat.

4 Fill the coasters with lavender to a depth of approximately ¼ inch (6 mm), and distribute the lavender evenly inside the coaster. (Lavender is available in bulk, with the flowers already removed from the stalks. This form of lavender is ideal to use in this project.) Hand stitch the opening closed.

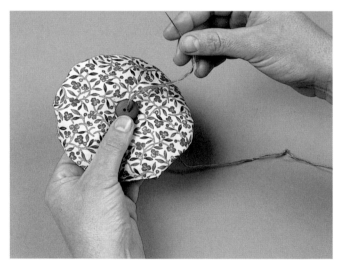

5 Sew the button onto the center of the coaster using the embroidery floss; choose a color of floss and button that complements your fabric. Tie a decorative knot on top and trim the ends. Repeat steps 2 though 5 to make the other three coasters.

VARIATIONS

Experiment with sachet or fine potpourri to fill these coasters, too; a translucent fabric would provide an elegant touch.

Wrapped Mirror

DESIGNER: TERRY TAYLOR

The elegant and exotic pitcher plant is showcased on this decorative accent mirror. The intricate wrapping of the raffia creates the perfect textured backdrop for the dried pitchers. Don't even think about making this project for a gift; you need to keep this mirror for yourself.

Polystyrene foam form, 1½ × 9 × 12 inches
(3.8 × 22.9 × 30.5 cm)

Ruler

Marker

Serrated kitchen knife

Raffia

Scissors

Hot glue gun and glue sticks

Mirror glass, 6 × 8 inches
(15.2 × 20.3 cm)

Dried pitcher plants

Decorative button or bead

Mirror hanger

2 Wrap the raffia around the width of the top and bottom of the frame. Hot glue the ends of the raffia to the back of the frame as you work. Don't skimp on the raffia! Too much is better than too little; otherwise, you'll have foam peeking out unexpectedly (and probably unpleasantly, too).

1 Measure and mark a 5 × 7-inch (12.7 × 17.8 cm) rectangle in the center of the foam form. Use the serrated kitchen knife to saw out the rectangle. Save the rectangle and recycle it into some other craft project.

3 Now wrap the raffia around the length of the sides of the frame, from top to bottom. Again, be generous with the raffia, and use an amount consistent with that on the top and bottom of the frame. Hot glue to the frame as you work, as in step 2.

Be certain to use only cultivated pitcher plants (members of the genus *Sarracenia*) in this or any other project, as most varieties are endangered in the wild.

VARIATIONS

Wrap several stems of dried wheat with raffia in place of the pitcher plants. Or, hot glue trimmed bamboo stalks to the edges of the wrapped frame.

4 Wrap the middle sections of the sides, top, and bottom of the frame with raffia, as shown, so that all of the foam is covered. As in the previous steps, hot glue the ends to the back of the frame.

More Flower Fun

✿ Add some romance to a strand of paper lanterns by decoupaging dried flowers or petals onto the globes.

✿ You can preserve edible flowers by sugaring or crystallizing them; paint the petals or flowers with a wash of egg white, then use a strainer to sprinkle on the sugar. Leave them to dry in a warm location, and use them within three days as decorations for desserts. One of the loveliest cakes I've ever seen was decorated with sugared native violets.

✿ For a simple but elegant display, place a row of single dried roses along the wall. It's the perfect decorating touch for a guest room.

5 Use the hot glue gun and affix the mirror to the back of the frame. Then glue the pitcher plants to the frame. If desired, accent the plant material with a decorative button or bead, as shown, and add the mirror hanger.

New Age Stook

DESIGNERS: VALERIE SHRADER & TERRY TAYLOR

Here is the evolution of the stook—the shocks of corn or wheat that farmers left to dry in the field. The wheat in this arrangement keeps it true to its origins, but the addition of the Protea sends this stook straight into the twenty-first century. This is also the same basic technique used to create posies—smaller arrangements usually made with fresh flowers.

YOU WILL NEED

6 stalks of Protea

3 packages of wheat

Floral tape or twine

Wire

Wire cutters

Mesh ribbon, wide and narrow

Scissors

Decorative paper

1 Place all the materials within reach, and spread them out so they are easy to grab; once you begin to assemble the stook, it's difficult to put it down without compromising its shape. Arrange the tape or twine so that you're working with the loose end of the spool or roll, but keep it in one continuous strand.

2 Take three or four pieces of wheat to begin the stook* and wrap tightly with the tape just under the heads of the wheat. Continue to add three or four stems at a time until you're happy with the size of the crown, wrapping at the same spot just under the heads after each addition.

3 Now, begin to decrease the height of the material in the stook. Take a handful of stems and add them at an angle, continuing to wrap tightly after each addition and still leaving tape connected to the roll. Add stems around all sides of the stook until you are satisfied with the shape, adding the Protea as desired.

*You may also see this referred to as a sheaf. Generally speaking, a stook is made from a single variety of flower, but artistic license was taken for this project.

4 Wrap lengths of wire around the tape; this stabilizes the stook so you can add the decorative elements. Next, cover the wire with a layer of mesh ribbon; then a layer of decorative paper; and finally a layer of narrow mesh ribbon. Use the hot glue gun to secure each layer as you add it, gluing each addition to the layer underneath it if necessary.

5 To make the stook stand upright, you will need to trim the ends. First, determine how tall you want the stook, and gradually cut the stems to that length. Then you may need to snip the ends of stems, as shown, so the stook is balanced; keep trimming it until you are satisfied.

TIP: Once you get the hang of this technique, you'll want to try it with everything. Any dried material with a fairly long stem can probably be used to make a stook.

Herbal Guest Baskets

DESIGNERS: CORINNE KURZMANN & TERRY TAYLOR

Your visitors will be delighted to find this collection of aromatic gifts awaiting them. Decorate the sleek basket with a medallion of herbs and fill it with bath products to make your guests' stay especially enjoyable. These items are surprisingly easy to make, and you can find a variety of recipes if you want to make custom products for your visitors.

(FOR THE SOAP)

Soap or candy molds

Cooking spray

Paper towels

Clear glycerin melt-and-pour soap

Kitchen knife

Microwave-safe container

Microwave oven

Lavender

Soap colorant (optional)

Decorative papers and ribbons

(FOR THE FOOT BATH)

¼ cup (59 ml) table or sea salt

Dried herbs—rosemary, peppermint, and kelp

Glass or ceramic container

Mortar and pestle (optional)

Essential oil (optional)

Decorative bag

(FOR THE HERBAL BATH TEA)

Dried flowers and herbs—lavender, comfrey leaf, rose petals, and passionflower

Tea bag or muslin bag

(FOR THE BASKET DECORATION)

Chrome basket

Aluminum tooling foil

Large craft punch

Stylus

Mouse pad

Hot glue gun and glue sticks

1 To make the lavender soap, first spray the molds with a light coating of cooking spray, then wipe the mold with your fingers or a paper towel, as shown. Cut the soap into chunks and place it in the microwave-safe container. Follow the manufacturer's instructions for melting the soap; you can also melt the soap in a double boiler if you prefer.

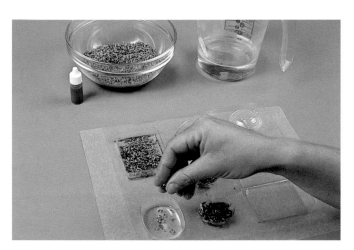

2 Pour a thin layer of melted soap in the molds. Sprinkle in lavender flowers as shown; add colorant if you wish. Then, fill the soap molds with melted soap and allow the soaps to harden. Invert the molds and release the soaps. Wrap each soap with decorative paper and ribbon to create a pleasing presentation.

3 To blend the foot bath, mix ¼ cup (59 ml) of salt and the desired amount of rosemary, peppermint, and kelp in a container. If you prefer a finer mix, use a mortar and pestle to grind the ingredients. You can add a few drops of essential oil for fragrance, if desired. Place the mixture in a decorative bag. To use, simply swirl into warm water.

5 To decorate the basket, punch out two medallions from the tooling foil. Use a stylus or other blunt object to emboss the front side of the medallion, as shown, working on a mouse pad to protect your surface. Place sprigs of lavender around the perimeter of the medallion and hot glue into place; then glue the two medallion pieces together. Affix the medallion to the basket with hot glue.

TIP: Contrary to common advice about dried flowers, encourage your visitors to leave this basket in the guest bathroom, as the humidity will release the aroma of the herbs in the medallion.

VARIATION

You can substitute most of your favorite herbs in these recipes.

4 For the herbal bath tea, add lavender, comfrey leaf, rose petals, and passionflower until you have about ¼ to ⅓ cup (59 to 79 ml) of herbal mixture. Seal in a tea bag or place in a muslin bag. To use, place the bag of herbs in 2 cups (473 ml) of boiling water, cover, and steep for 20 minutes. Then add the infusion to the bath.

Natural Table Runner

DESIGNER: BARBARA ZARETSKY

This exquisite tableau of twigs, flowers, and herb blossoms form a stunning natural table runner. Let spontaneity guide you when you create this decoration, and be willing to adapt your design as you proceed. Consider the surface of your table, your linens, and your glassware when you choose the floral materials. Here, yarrow and gold-rimmed glasses complement each other perfectly.

YOU WILL NEED

6 birch twigs

Scissors or floral snips

2 bunches of yarrow

2 bunches of Australian daisy

2 bunches of lavender

1 stalk of hydrangea

1 Set your table first, putting plates, silverware, glassware, and linens where you prefer. In this design, clear salad plates were placed atop the linens and dinner plates for a sleek, contemporary feel. Begin with the longest elements of the table runner— the birch twigs. Arrange as desired; clip to the appropriate length, if needed. Remember that you may want to adjust the size of your materials, as well as the arrangement, while you are working.

2 Add the yarrow, as in the photo above right, trying to array the materials naturally and casually. Next, add some bunches of Australian daisy, clipping the stems as desired and filling out the arrangement. Now, place the lavender under the flowers, perpendicular to the direction of the twigs.

3 To complete the table runner, add more yarrow as desired. Adjust the design as necessary, and then add some hydrangea for the centerpiece; use scissors, snips, or your fingers to remove pieces of hydrangea from the stalk as needed. Finally, cut or break off some small florets of hydrangea and distribute them around the table as desired.

Curtain with Pansy Streamers

DESIGNER: VALERIE SHRADER

This delicate curtain will remind you of spring all year round. The ribbon streamers can move with the breeze, so the flowers seem to float in the air. Though the construction of the curtain is simple, you could merely add the streamers to a ready-made sheer, if desired.

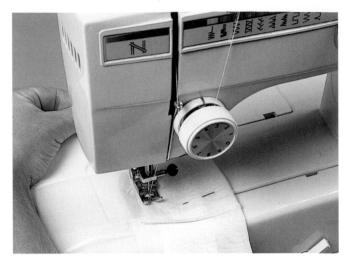

2 Cut out two pieces of sheer ribbon for the streamers, each the height of the curtain, plus ½ inch (1.3 cm). Pin the ribbon to the curtain, making sure that the streamers are straight. Baste into place, if desired. Then stitch the lengths of ribbon to the curtain while you make a 3-inch (7.6 cm) casing at the top of the curtain, as shown. (If you cut the fabric so the selvage is at the top edge of the curtain, you won't need to machine hem the casing first.)

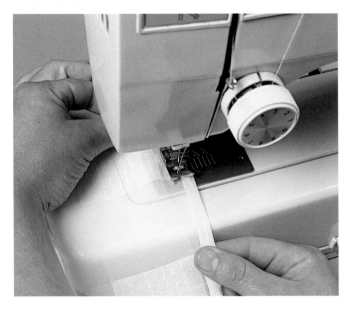

1 Measure the window where you plan to install the curtain. Then cut out a piece of fabric sized to the dimensions of your window, plus 2 extra inches (5.1 cm) in width and 4 extra inches (10.2 cm) in height. Make a narrow machine hem around the sides and bottom of the sheer, as shown. Sharp sewing machine needles can make a big difference when you are sewing with lightweight fabric.

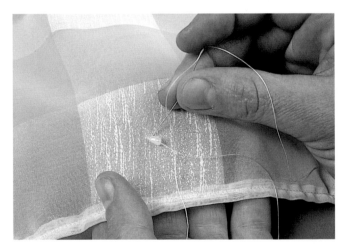

3 If desired, scatter seed pearls and attach with beading needle and thread. After you knot the thread to sew on each pearl, be sure to clip the tail completely, so it does not show through the curtain. If you want to embellish the curtain with pearls, be sure to do it at this stage, to avoid the possibility of damaging the flowers after they are added to the ribbon streamers.

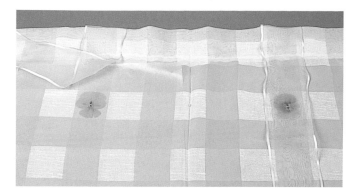

4 Place waxed paper between the curtain and the ribbon to protect the fabric. Plan to attach the pansies from the top down. Move the streamers out of the way while you decide where you want to place the pansies on the sheer, using the fabric underneath as a guide. The fabric used in this project made it easy to place the pansy in its proper place, with its distinct intersections of patterns; you may need to mark the spot where you plan to place the flowers, depending upon your fabric selection.

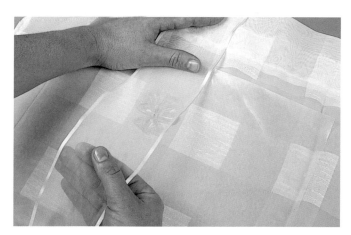

5 With a flat paintbrush, apply decoupage medium to the front of the flower, working from the middle out. Make sure that the entire surface of the pansy is covered with a thin coat of the medium. Place the pansy on the wax paper, face up, and use the wax paper to work the flower into the proper position, if necessary. Then gently place the ribbon on top of the pansy, as shown, and put a piece of wax paper on top of the streamer as you press the flower with your fingers, working from the inside out. Use wax paper to blot up any excess

decoupage. Continue in this manner and attach pansies as desired, alternating each streamer. Allow to dry completely on the waxed paper.

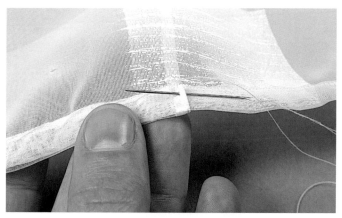

6 Use the fray retardant on the edge of the ribbon and allow to dry. Then turn the ribbon under and tack invisibly onto the hem of the curtain, catching only the back of the hem. Add the final pearl details if desired, one at the top of the ribbon and one at the bottom, to secure the streamer onto the curtain.

TIPS: You may need more fabric and ribbon than is listed here, depending upon the size of your window. Be sure to measure it before you purchase any material. When you are applying the decoupage medium to the pansies, try to coat the entire surface to achieve an even finish when the flowers dry. Don't use too much decoupage, however, or it may bleed through onto the curtain. Experiment with this technique before you begin your final project.

VARIATION

Make the ribbon streamers and attach them to an existing curtain. Delete the final seed pearls in step 6 if you prefer a free-flowing sheer.

Pavé Rose Basket

DESIGNER: ALLISON SMITH

In the language of flowers, white roses mean love, respect, and beauty, and this elegant project evokes them all. Use a pale and subtle approach like this one, or search for materials that are more dramatic if you want a bolder color scheme. Flowing silk ribbons add the perfect final touch.

YOU WILL NEED

Kitchen knife

Block of floral foam

Metal hanging basket

2 dozen white roses

Floral preservative (optional)

Metal primer

Paintbrushes

Small containers

Pale pink paint

Crackle medium

Off-white outdoor acrylic paint

1 yard (.9 m) of hand-dyed bias-cut silk ribbon, 2¾ inches (7.0 cm) wide

Scissors

Fray retardant

1 yard (.9 m) of hand-dyed bias-cut silk ribbon, ½ inch (1.3 cm) wide

Buttons

Hot glue gun and glue sticks

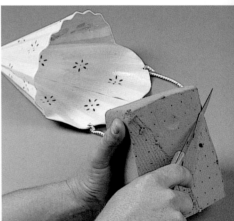

1 Using the kitchen knife, cut the floral foam to the shape of the basket. Make it just a little bit smaller than the container itself to allow room to arrange the roses within the basket. Remove the foam from the basket and set it aside. Spray the roses with preservative if desired.

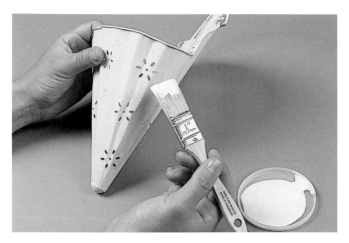

2 Prime the basket and allow it to dry. Paint with the pale pink paint and allow to dry; next, paint the basket with a thin coat of the crackle medium and allow it to dry for 20 to 30 minutes. Work quickly while you apply a thin coat of the off-white paint, as shown; apply it with smooth, even strokes, being careful not to paint over areas that have already been covered. Let the basket dry completely. The crackle finish will develop as this layer of paint dries.

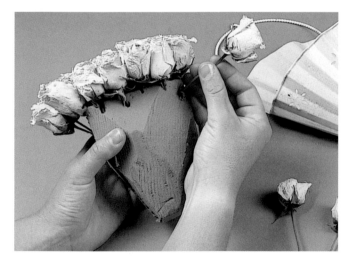

3 Snap the flower heads off the stems, leaving 3 to 4 inches (7.6 cm to 10.2 cm) of stem attached. Insert the flowers into the foam, packing them closely together. To create the pavé effect, make sure that the flowers are all approximately the same height. Set the foam aside while you decorate the handle.

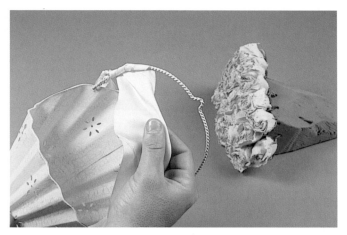

4 Attach the wide ribbon to one end of the handle by tying it in a knot, leaving about 8 inches (20.3 cm) extra hanging free on the side. Tightly wrap the ribbon around the handle. Tie the ribbon off on the other side, trim the ends, and treat with fray retardant.

5 Now, tightly wrap the narrow ribbon around the handle from end to end. Then, tie short lengths of the same ribbon to the handle. Hot glue the buttons onto the handle to disguise the knots.

TIP: The thickness of the coat of crackle medium will determine the size of the crackle on the finished product; a thin coat will produce a fine crackle, whereas a thick coat of crackle medium will produce a broader, coarser crackle.

Wreath Triptych

DESIGNER: JOSENA AIELLO-BADER

Find a special place to display this stunning group of wreaths—perhaps on a mantel or shelf. The differing hues of hydrangea unify the shades of the lavender and the larkspur, and the varied textures create visual interest. This basic idea can be translated into any color scheme that suits your mood or décor.

2 Gather up another cluster of lavender flowers, and then lay the second group of flower heads onto the wreath so they cover the hot glue from the first cluster. Continue in this same manner until the wreath form is covered. Remember to glue the flower clusters to the outside and inside of the wreath as well, not just to the front. Each cluster should be covering the hot glue from the previous one.

1 Since the lavender wreath is the most time-consuming and demands the most material, it will be demonstrated here. Gather in your fingers a cluster of five to eight lavender heads, putting most of the tips together. Cut the stems to a length of ¾-inch (1.9 cm) length. Cover the ends with hot glue and lay them down on the wreath form.

3 Once the wreath is covered with lavender and has a good shape, with even coverage and no gaps, hot glue the fern tips to the wreath. Again, make clusters of two to three tips, and be sure to hot glue them down into the flower heads—don't just place them on top. Do this evenly on the front of the wreath as well as on the inside and outside of the form.

4 Cut 1 yard (.9 m) of ribbon and pull it through the grapevine on the back of the wreath form. Tie a knot above the wreath where you want to make the bow—first a full knot and then a two-loop bow. Then trim off the extra ribbon.

FOR THE ADDITIONAL WREATHS

Though we use the same basic method to make all the wreaths, there are a few special considerations for the remaining two. To create the larkspur wreath at top right, you need to break the larkspur flower stems a few times to get clusters about the same size as the lavender. However, it is important that stems don't stick out of the clusters; they can be trimmed out once the clusters are hot glued onto the wreath form. Add the fern tips and ribbon as in steps 3 and 4.

The hydrangea wreath, at lower right, is a quickie. Simply break apart the large flower heads into smaller sizes that are still held together by a stem. Cover the bottom of the flower bunches with hot glue and stick them onto the wreath form; bunch the flowers right next to each other so that no grapevine shows. When you're happy with the shape of the wreath, add the fern tips and ribbon.

Sublime Stationery Set

DESIGNER: NICOLE TUGGLE

Make a special place for this portfolio on your desk. Like a flower, it's lovely yet delicate, so treat it gently; at the same time, it's very functional, keeping all of your letter writing materials together beautifully. Simply create more of the cards and the notepaper as needed, and enjoy this project for many seasons.

YOU WILL NEED

Thick decorative paper, 1 sheet cut to 10 × 17 inches (25.4 × 43.2 cm) and 1 sheet cut to 6 × 6 inches (15.2 × 15.2 cm)

Ruler

Pencil

Butter knife or bone folder

Clear-drying craft glue

Scissors

Small paintbrush

Foam brush

4 blank greeting cards, each 3½ × 5 inches (8.9 × 12.7 cm)

Gold decorative paper, 4 pieces cut to 2 × 3¾ inches (5.1 × 9.5 cm) and 1 piece cut to 2 × 5 inches (5.1 × 12.7 cm)

White decorative paper, 4 pieces cut to 1¾ × 3½ inches (4.4 × 8.9 cm) and 1 piece cut to 1½ × 4½ inches (3.8 × 11.4 cm)

8 pressed flowers

15 pieces of white paper, each 5 × 6½ inches (12.7 × 16.5 cm)

Awl

Large-gauge needle

Waxed linen or thick sewing thread

1 To make the stationery folder, take the large sheet of thick paper and lay it flat on the work surface. Measure and mark with a pencil ¼ inch (6 mm) from each edge. Fold each edge over and press down flat using a bone folder or the edge of a butter knife. Apply glue with the small paintbrush to glue each flap down, and let dry. With the paper lying long side toward you, mark the center point lightly with a pencil. Measure ½ inch (1.3 cm) out from that center point. Fold along these lines as shown to create the side spine of the folder.

2 To create the card pocket, put the smaller sheet of thick paper on the work surface. Measure, cut, and score the paper according to the template on page 154. Fold the top and bottom edges under ¼ inch (6 mm) and glue down; let dry. Fold the bottom flap and side flaps at the scored edges, and use the paintbrush to coat the surface with a thin layer of glue; then press together as shown, forming a pocket. Let dry.

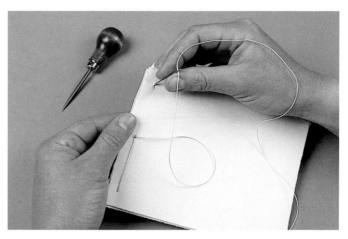

3 Use the foam brush to coat the back of the pocket with a layer of glue. Then, position it at the center point of the left inside cover of the folder and press down, working along the surface of the pocket's flaps with your fingers, or use the butter knife or bone folder as shown. Be careful not to crush the pocket. You want it to retain a rectangular shape, with the sides perpendicular.

5 To make the writing pad, line up the sheets of white paper in a small stack. Mark a series of holes that are ½ inch (1.3 cm) from the top of the paper. First, mark one at the center point, and then one at each side; the latter should be ½ inch (1.3 cm) from the side as well as ½ inch (1.3 cm) from the top. Use the awl and carefully perforate each point, making holes that go through the entire stack of paper. Thread the needle and knot the end, leaving about a 1-inch (2.5 cm) tail. Starting at the back of the stack, sew through the center hole. Sew through the left hole to the back of the paper. Sew back up through the center hole and back through the right hole, as shown above. Tie off at the center point with the tail of the thread, knot, and cut off any excess.

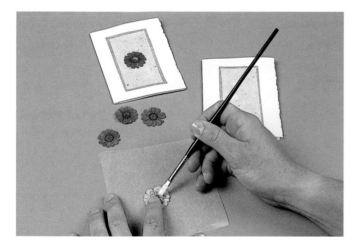

4 Embellish the cards by gluing a piece of the 2 × 3¾-inch (5.1 × 9.5 cm) gold paper at the center point of the card. Press the paper down with your fingers to eliminate any bubbles. Glue a piece of the 1¾ × 3½-inch (4.4 × 8.9 cm) white paper directly on top of the gold paper. Use the small paintbrush to coat the back of a single pressed flower with a thin layer of glue, taking care to cover each petal and the center point, as shown. Place the flower down on the center point of the white paper and press down very carefully. Repeat for the remaining cards.

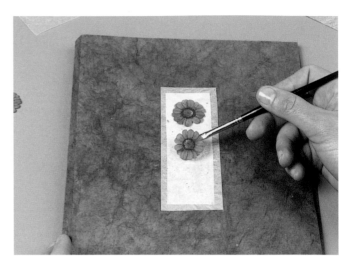

6 Hide the thread by covering the top edge of the writing pad with the decorative paper. Simply coat some paper with glue, wrap around the top edge, and cut off the excess from the sides. Let dry. Glue down a single pressed flower at the top center point. To attach to the folder, coat the back of the last page with a thin layer of glue. Center the pad over the right inside cover of the folder and press down, moving your fingers along the surface of that last sheet as shown, eliminating any bubbles and ensuring it is firmly attached. Let dry.

7 Embellish the cover of the folder by gluing down a piece of 2 × 5-inch (5.1 × 12.7 cm) gold decorative paper at the center point. Glue a piece of $1\frac{1}{2} \times 4\frac{1}{2}$-inch (3.8 × 11.4 cm) white decorative paper on top. Finally, glue three pressed flowers down along the center point. Let dry.

TIP: To remove the notepaper, use a ruler or other straight implement as a guide and rip each sheet off carefully as you use it. Remember that you can easily replenish your supply of cards and notepaper.

Quilting

KAROL KAVAYA & VICKI SKEMP

INTRODUCTION

DOES THE WORD "QUILTING" conjure up images of long-term projects, completed only after many arduous years? Do you picture grandmotherly types, whiling away the tedious hours of their golden years, bending over a vast expanse of patchwork to place tiny perfect stitches?

Well, as long-time quilters, we beg to differ. Quilting is perfectly adaptable to anyone, from kids to Gen X and beyond. While we happen to *like* those long-term projects that result in heirloom-quality king-size quilts, we also enjoy a quick project to scratch the quilting itch when there is little time for more. And these projects are a perfect introduction to those of you who want to try your hand at some of the various quilting techniques, without the commitment of time and money that a full-size quilt entails.

We will teach you traditional quilting techniques and patterns to create decorative and functional items for your home, as well as unique wearable items for yourself and for others. At the same time, though, we will also show you contemporary fabrics and modern color palettes that can be adapted to

your home and your personal sense of style.

In just a weekend you can create a striking wall hanging or an elegant evening bag. You can learn the technique of Hawaiian quilting, make a gift for a new baby, or a vest for yourself. If you have additional time to devote to a project, many can be embellished or quilted further. And somewhere along the way, you may discover that you have become a quilter.

What is special about quilting? It is an activity that incorporates design, creativity, and even math, that employs a relaxing, repetitive, meditative motion…usually, quilting can encompass as much or as little of the above qualities as you wish. The use of color and fabric speak to the senses of sight and touch. Then, there is the extra bonus of making something useful, as well as something beautiful and decorative. Furthermore, it is a living tradition that connects you with quilters of past times and faraway places. Over and over, we have found that people, even those who

do not quilt, respond to the craft on a very deep level. "My grandmother used to quilt," they may say, or "I have an old quilt my great-aunt made." There's something about quilting that warms the heart.

In quilting, as with most crafts, the creative process of is just as important as the result. Many people do not learn about technique anymore, because everything they use is purchased ready-made. Making something useful with your hands evokes satisfaction and happiness; we have witnessed this reaction firsthand as we participate in weeklong classes, one-day workshops, or as we help a friend with a project.

Most of us do not have to toil physically each day to provide for our wants; that is called progress. But many of us have found that *choosing* to make things with our hands, for ourselves or for others, is an activity that addresses deeper needs. In a creative endeavor, the combination of figuring out and carefully following instructions, focusing on a task, and attending to detail results in a real sense of accomplishment. Often, people are surprised at what they can create.

We hope you will be inspired by the designs, colors, and variety contained in these 19 projects. If you are new to quilting, this section contains the information to get you started and teaches you the skills to keep you going. We can just about promise that if you learn to quilt, you will continue to quilt—it is that rewarding. For those readers more advanced in this skill, we intend our projects to be challenging enough to keep you interested, and inspiring enough to be a springboard for your own ideas and variations.

To all of our readers—whether you make our projects for yourself, for your home, or for a gift—may you enjoy the process *and* the result.

A wise friend once said, "The most spiritual thing you can do is to make something beautiful, and to do it the best that you can."

QUILTING BASICS
GLOSSARY

BECAUSE QUILTING HAS SOME unique terminology, it will be helpful to check over this glossary before you read the introductory material and choose a project.

Appliqué. The attaching of a small piece of fabric to a larger piece of background fabric by hand or machine stitching.

Backstitch. In hand sewing, to loop back over the stitch you've just taken to provide additional strength. On the sewing machine, to reverse three or four stitches at the beginning and end of a seam to lock the stitches.

Baste. To join together the layers of a quilted piece with long hand stitches. Basting threads are removed after quilting. (Some quilters use safety pins instead of hand basting.)

Batting. The fluffy filler that is the middle layer of the quilt. Provides warmth and allows the quilting on the top layer to be more noticeable. Made of either cotton, cotton/polyester blend, polyester, wool, or silk.

Bias. The diagonal intersection of the lengthwise and crosswise threads of a piece of fabric, where the fabric has the most stretch. *True bias* is at a 45° angle to the straight grain.

Bias tape or binding. Strips of fabric, cut on the bias, used for binding edges. Purchase ready-made or make your own.

Blindstitch. An almost invisible hand stitch used for sewing hems, hanging sleeves, appliqués, and bias binding.

Block. Pieces of fabric sewn together to create a single unit; a traditional pieced quilt is made up of many blocks.

Ease in/ease to fit. To make two unequal lengths of fabric meet by gathering or pulling, in order to sew them together.

Echo quilting. To follow the pattern of quilting in a repetitive series of equally spaced rows of stitching.

Finger press. To use the fingertips instead of an iron to crease fabric or to press a seam.

Foundation piecing. Creating a quilting block using a muslin base; the fabric pieces are sewn to the base as they are sewn to each other.

Hanging sleeve. A strip of fabric sewn to the back of a quilt. A rod or dowel is inserted through the sleeve to facilitate hanging for display.

In-the-ditch quilting. Quilting done as closely as possible to a seam line or appliqué edge.

Machine hem. To hem using the sewing machine. Press the raw edge under ¼ inch (6 mm); fold the pressed edge to the desired depth of the hem, and stitch along the edge.

Completing a garment with echo quilting.

Mitered corner. A diagonal seam formed by two strips of fabric meeting at a 45° angle.

Outline quilting. Quilting that is done $\frac{1}{4}$ inch (6 mm) away from seams or appliqué pieces.

Patchwork. See **Piece.**

Piece. To sew together individual pieces of fabric to form a predetermined pattern; the fabric pieces are usually in geometric shapes.

Press. To use an iron in an up-and-down pressing motion, rather than a back-and-forth ironing motion.

Quilt backing. The bottom layer of the traditional three-layer "sandwich" that a quilt comprises (top, batting, backing).

Quilting. Small, even, running stitches through all the layers of a quilt; they hold the layers together and form a decorative pattern.

Quilting pattern. The design of the quilting stitches on the finished project.

Quilt top. The top layer of the quilt "sandwich," on which the quilting is executed.

Running stitch. The basic hand sewing stitch; the needle weaves in and out of the layers of fabric several times before it is pulled through.

Sandwich. To assemble the layers of a quilted project in preparation for basting and quilting.

Scant. As in "a scant $\frac{1}{4}$ inch (6 mm)," this means "absolutely no more than, possibly slightly less than" when you are sewing.

Seam allowance. The tiny, usually $\frac{1}{4}$-inch (6 mm) area of fabric beyond the seam line, between the sewn seam and the raw edge of the fabric.

Shadow quilting. Quilting that is done along the outline of a piece of batting that is placed between two layers of fabric, one or both of which is transparent; the top piece must be transparent to achieve the desired effect.

Staystitch. To stabilize a fabric piece by stitching $\frac{1}{8}$ inch (3 mm) from all raw edges; it prevents raveling. It also stabilizes foundation-pieced quilting projects.

Stencil. A pattern for a fancy quilting motif.

Strip piecing. Creating a quilting block using strips of fabric sewn to a muslin base.

Tack. To take a small hidden stitch in order to hold a piece of fabric in place.

Template. A pattern, usually made from plastic (for repeated use) or thin cardboard (for one-time use) that is used for tracing shapes onto fabric, which will then be cut out.

Topstitch. Machine stitching (sometimes hand stitching) done on the top or right side of fabric. A finishing stitch that is meant to be seen, topstitching can be sewn with matching or contrasting color thread.

Whipstitch. An overcasting hand stitch used to join edges.

Tools and Supplies

If you do any sewing, you probably already have many of the tools and supplies on hand. At its simplest level, quilting can be accomplished with only a needle, thread, and scissors, as well as old garments cut up for fabric and old blankets used for batting. Beautiful quilts have been made this way. But, we like to take advantage of some of the tools and supplies developed specifically for quilters.

Tools

Here are the tools you will need for virtually every project:

HOOPS

A 14-inch (35.6 cm) quilting hoop is helpful for the larger projects. If you do a project with embroidery, like the ones we have in this book, a small 4- or 5-inch (10.2 or 12.7 cm) embroidery hoop will be needed. Not every quilter uses a hoop all the time, especially on small pieces, but they are useful to keep the layers tight while you are working.

IRON AND IRONING BOARD

Pressing is essential at many steps of construction to produce crisp edges or creases. Many people who sew have an ironing board set up at the side of their sewing machines so that they are not tempted to skip this important step.

Note there is a difference between *ironing*, the back and forth smoothing used on yardage, and *pressing*, the lifting up and pressing down of the iron that is used to press seams and remove wrinkles without stretching the fabric or patchwork. You will iron your fabric before beginning a project; thereafter, you will press when required.

MARKING TOOLS

There are many options available for marking and transferring quilting patterns or motifs onto fabric, and there are advantages and disadvantages to each method. You will probably develop a preference for one tool over the course of time. You can choose from fabric-marking pencils in various colors; blue, water-soluble markers; purple vanishing markers; and even plain old mechanical pencils. However, *always* test markers on your fabric first to ensure that the marks can be completely removed. (Some sources say the blue markers damage fabric over

You are likely to have many of these supplies at home, including (left to right): an iron and ironing board, marking tools, measuring and cutting implements, and sewing machine and notions.

the course of time, and that the marks can even reappear months after they have seemingly been removed. Use with caution.)

Some projects lend themselves to marking before sandwiching and basting, some after. The tool you select will also be a factor; for example, disappearing pen marks *will* disappear, so you can't use it too far in advance of the actual quilting if you choose that type of marker.

MEASURING TOOLS

It is important to be precise when you are measuring and cutting fabric for the piecing we use in these projects. In patchwork and piecing, accuracy is important because a seemingly insignificant error repeated many times can lead to a big mess! You will need a measuring tape or stick, but you may find that another tool, such as a carpenter's square or right triangle, may also be useful. The gridded cutting mat for a rotary cutter is also an excellent measuring tool.

NEEDLES

Betweens, or quilting needles, are made short in order to produce the tiny stitches used in quilting. There is a range of betweens; the higher the number, the shorter the needle. Thus, a number 12 would be challenging for a beginner, so you may find it easier to start with a needle in the 5 to 10 range. Then, as your skill grows, switch to smaller needles.

Sharps are all-purpose needles, used in general sewing and for appliqué. We use sharps in many of our projects, so have some on hand.

Embroidery needles have large eyes to accommodate several strands of embroidery floss at once. You will need these for several of our projects.

SCISSORS

Have a pair of shears for cutting fabric, but use another pair of scissors for cutting paper and/or cardboard. (You will dull the edges of your fabric scissors if you use them on paper.) You may want to use small scissors or snips for cutting thread.

SEWING MACHINE

You do not need a Fancy Multi-Stitch Wonder to construct our projects. The simplest machine is all that is required, as we are doing only basic construction. In fact, any of the projects could be sewn entirely by hand, if so desired, but in our instructions we will assume that you are using a sewing machine.

STRAIGHT PINS AND PINCUSHION

We do not always pin when we are working, but when we do, we like the ones with brightly colored, round heads, as they are easier to see (and find if you drop them). You also need a pincushion, of course—the magnetic ones are terrific!

THIMBLES

Most quilters use a thimble on the middle or index finger of their quilting hand. There are various kinds of thimbles (metal, leather, and plastic, for example) and you should experiment to find what is comfortable for you.

ADDITIONAL TOOLS

We use the following tools in some of our projects:

Craft knife—for cutting card stock

Drafting compass—for making accurate circle patterns

Potter's rib—a nifty, sharp-edged wooden tool that we use for making creases on paper

Quilter's template plastic—semitranslucent material used to make templates; useful when you want to cut the same pattern a number of times

Quilting stencils—for marking quilt designs onto fabric

Rotary cutter, gridded cutting mat, and specially marked plastic ruler—not necessary, but once you learn how to use them, you will be amazed at how fast cutting goes

Ruler—for drafting patterns and marking fabric

Safety pins—1-inch-long (2.5 cm) brass safety pins can be used as a substitute for hand basting

Supplies

You should be able to find these supplies at your local craft, fabric, or quilting shop:

BATTING

In all our projects, we use batting that is 80 percent cotton and 20 percent polyester. There are many different types of batting, but we prefer this blend for its ease of use; it is very easy to quilt and can be used without a backing, as in our pillow project on page 184.

We purchase prepackaged batting that is available in the following sizes: craft, 36 × 45 inches (.9 × 1.1 m); crib, 45 × 60 inches (1.1 × 1.6 m); twin, 72 × 90 inches (1.8 × 2.2 m); full, 81 × 96 inches (2 × 2.4 m); queen, 90 × 108 inches (2.2 × 2.7 m); and king, 120 × 120 inches (3 × 3 m). The craft or crib size should be sufficient to create any one project in this book, but if you plan on purchasing batting for more than one project, you may wish to get a larger size. The batting may require prewashing, according to the instructions on the package.

Whichever batting you choose, it should be low loft; a fluffy batting would not suit the small scale of most of these projects. Some battings require closer quilting than others do; again, check your package for these requirements.

BIAS TAPE

Prepackaged bias tape comes in a variety of widths, folds, and colors, and we use it to bind the edges of some of our projects. See the individual project instructions for specific information regarding bias tape.

EMBROIDERY FLOSS

We have adorned some of our projects with embroidery, for which you will need embroidery floss. Again, see the individual project instructions for specific information regarding embroidery floss; though floss is purchased in six-strand skeins, our projects call for using only two strands of floss.

FABRIC

Most traditional quilters choose to use all-cotton fabric, because it feels soft and ages gracefully. If your project is one that will need to be laundered, use 100 percent mid-weight cotton, which you should prewash in warm or hot water, dry, and iron before cutting. (Be careful with imported fabrics, because the colors may bleed. Reds and blues seem especially prone to this.) If you are creating a piece that you will not wash, like the wall hanging on page 214, you will not need to be as concerned with the fabric's colorfast properties. We will talk more about choosing fabric on page 162.

MASKING TAPE

We use masking tape for marking straight lines on our projects. Some of our projects call for ¼-inch (6 mm) quilter's tape, which is available from your quilting supplier. You may also use standard masking tape, either ¾ inch (1.9 cm) or 1 inch (2.5 cm), depending on the project. Try to avoid using old tape, because it can leave a sticky residue on your fabric.

PAPER

When you are tracing pattern templates, you will need some sort of paper; freezer paper works quite well for this application. You may also use quilter's graph paper for measuring and cutting.

QUILTING THREAD

This is specifically designed for hand quilting and comes in a wide variety of colors. You can match the fabric on which you are quilting, or go for a contrast. Metallic quilting thread produces a striking effect, but should not be used in a project that will be laundered often.

SEWING THREAD

Use high-quality, general-purpose thread for machine piecing; select colors to match your fabrics. When sewing multicolored projects, light gray thread is a good choice. (If one of your fabrics is very light in color, a darker thread will show through the finished piece.) If only dark colors are being used in a multicolored project, dark gray thread works well.

UNBLEACHED MUSLIN

This economical, 100 percent cotton fabric is used (prewashed, of course) as the foundation for strip-pieced and crazy-quilt-style projects. We will discuss these special techniques in more detail on page 167.

Quilting tools and supplies—including batting, stencils, tape, marking tools, needles, and thread—surround these hoops.

PREPARATION FOR QUILTING

We will cover some quilting basics in this section and the following one, Quilting Techniques (page 166). Though each of the 19 projects has its own specific instructions, this information will provide useful background, and we suggest that you read through this material before beginning a project.

Choosing Fabric

When you have selected a project to make, you will next have to choose your fabrics. Will you try to match our color choices or will you go with something different—

something to match *your* décor and *your* personality? Color ideas may come from magazines, catalogs, quilting books, or nature—color is everywhere; just look.

You can also refer to the color wheel to help guide your choices. Anyone can achieve a pleasing effect by using analogous colors (colors next to each other on the color wheel, such as violet and blue, red and orange, etc.). A bold look will result from the use of complementary colors (colors opposite each other on the color wheel, such as violet and yellow, or reddish orange and bluish green, etc.). We used solid colors in most of our projects so the quilting stitches would be eye-catching; a busy print will hide quilting stitches almost entirely.

We have used fabrics that are 45 inches (1.1 m) wide. Our projects assume that you will be using yardage that

You will choose from a wide variety of fabrics and supplies for your quilting projects.

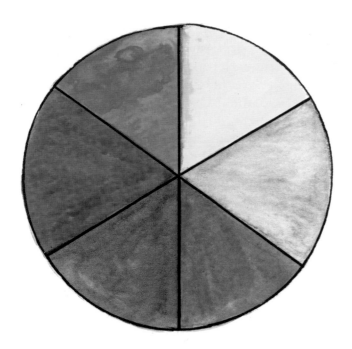

Measuring and Cutting

Because accuracy is very important in quilting, make sure you are measuring and then cutting a precise square, rectangle, or strip. You can choose several ways to measure and cut exact shapes: ruler and right triangle, quilter's graph paper, carpenter's square, or rotary cutting mat and ruler (even if you don't use the rotary cutter). Then, use shears or the rotary cutter (see below) to carefully cut your pieces.

When you are trying to cut batting to match a particular fabric shape, cut the fabric first and use that piece as a template. Then place the fabric shape onto the batting, pin in place, and cut out along the edge of the fabric.

To use the rotary cutter, begin by folding your fabric in half lengthwise to match the selvages. Place the fabric on the mat, and align the selvages with the bottom horizontal grid. Trim the right raw edge of the fabric at a right angle to the selvage. Place the ruler close to the raw edge, using the vertical grid to align and ensure a straight cut. Hold the ruler down firmly with your left hand, and cut

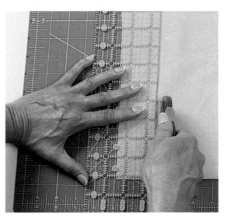

After just a bit of practice, the rotary cutter can be a very efficient way to cut fabric for quilts.

along the right edge of the ruler. Roll the cutter away from you while keeping steady pressure on the ruler. When you have a straight edge, you can proceed to cut strips in needed widths, as your project requires. Use the grid on the mat and/or the grid on the ruler to measure your widths.

Piecing

Many of our projects involve simple *piecing*: stitching square to square, triangle to triangle, etc., to create the designs in our book. (This construction is also called *patchwork*.) In all pieced projects, accuracy is extremely important—accuracy in marking, cutting, and sewing. Seams or corners will not match with a variation of as little as $1/8$ inch (3 mm). This is especially important when working on a small project where you may immediately notice any mistake. And remember, when sewing

is marked 45 inches (1.1 m) wide, but we are aware that some fabric so marked may actually be narrower. Our specifications allow for this discrepancy.

To reiterate, we prefer 100 percent cotton. Depending on the project, however, you may choose to use silk, satin, velvet, chiffon, etc. (The traditional crazy quilt uses an assortment of different fabrics, and we use an adaptation of this method in several of our projects.)

This is your most important supply, so choose it wisely and have fun while you are doing it.

PREPARING FABRIC

If you are using cotton fabric, remember to wash, dry, and iron it before cutting. This will take care of any shrinkage and also allow you to be sure that the dye in your fabrics won't run later.

Yardage Conversion

$1/8$ yard (.1 m) = $4\frac{1}{2}$ inches (11.4 cm)

$1/4$ yard (.23 m) = 9 inches (22.9 cm)

$1/3$ yard (.3 m) = 12 inches (30.5 cm)

$1/2$ yard (.5 m) = 18 inches (45.7 cm)

$3/4$ yard (.7 m) = 27 inches (68.5 cm)

1 yard (.9 m) = 36 inches (91.4 cm)

---

two pieces of fabric, the right sides should be together when you stitch.

Piecing and pressing go together. In most of our projects, when you have sewn one fabric to another, you will press the seam between them to one side, toward the darker fabric if possible. (Make it a habit.) Garment construction, like the vest on page 192, requires that some seams be pressed open. Follow the instructions given with the individual projects.

Finger pressing is sometimes an alternative to pressing with an iron. The small fabric pieces in the greeting card, potholder, baby bib, and evening bag projects were pressed with the fingertips, as were many steps in other projects. Finger pressing works beautifully and quickly.

One last (very important) note on piecing: If your sewing experience has been confined to standard garment making and you are accustomed to using ⅝-inch (1.6 cm) seams, please be aware that quilt piecing routinely uses ¼-inch (6 mm) seams. Unless you are directed otherwise in the individual project instructions, you should use a ¼-inch (6 mm) seam.

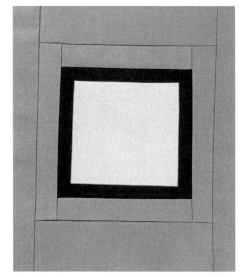

Simple piecing.

Sandwiching

After you have constructed the top of your quilting project, you will *sandwich* it to put together the top, batting, and backing layers. (A few of our projects don't involve sandwiching, but the majority of them do.) We use two different methods of sandwiching, depending on whether we plan to bind the edge.

THE BOUND EDGE

With this method, the backing fabric and the batting will be larger than the top piece by up to 3 inches (7.6 cm) on each side. Place the layers atop one another on your work surface with the backing fabric right side down; then the batting; and finally the top fabric, right side up, as shown in figure 1. Smooth the wrinkles out by hand.

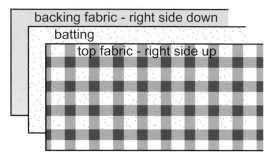

FIGURE 1. Sandwiching method for a bound edge.

THE CLEAN EDGE

Match all the edges of the fabric; the batting may be slightly larger. Smooth all the layers, making sure there are no lumps in the batting or wrinkles in the backing. Put the batting down first; then add the backing fabric, right side up; and lastly the top fabric, right side down, as shown in figure 2. Pin well around the edges. Stitch with a ¼-inch (6 mm) seam allowance, leaving a gap at one end for turning the piece right side out. Trim the batting almost to the seam line, being careful not to cut your fabric. Trim the corners, being careful not to cut the stitches. Turn the piece right side out, and blindstitch the gap closed.

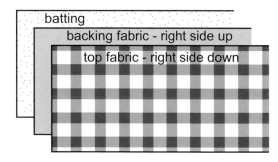

FIGURE 2. Sandwiching method for a clean edge.

Hand Basting

Once your piece is sandwiched, you are just about ready to quilt! But first, you will *baste* it to keep the layers in place while you work.

Figure 3 shows the standard basting pattern, taking long stitches through the piece.

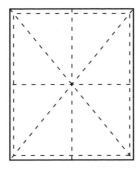

FIGURE 3. Standard basting pattern.

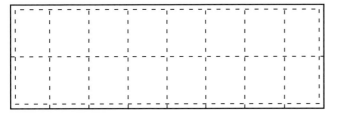

FIGURE 4. Rectangular basting pattern.

An alternative is the basting pattern used for long rectangular projects, shown in figure 4.

Marking and Transferring Quilting Patterns

If you are experienced with garment construction, the word *pattern* may have a different connotation than we use in quilting. A *quilting pattern* is the design of the quilting stitches on your project, as opposed to the piece of paper onto which your garment pattern is printed. (We may use the word *motif* to describe a quilting pattern as well.) A *template* is the term we will use to describe a pattern that will be used to cut out shapes; it will usually be made of paper or plastic.

Masking tape is great for marking straight lines in our projects. It is applied to one area at a time as you work; in general, you will not mark the entire project all at once. Often, you will mark a small section, quilt, and then move the tape for each successive section.

Curved lines require another kind of marking, preferably before the piece is basted. Place the fabric on a hard surface and draw the lines freehand, or mark using a plastic stencil and the marking tool of your choice (see page 159). Stencils come in a wide array of beautiful patterns—hearts, feathers, cables, flowers—we suggest you visit your quilting supplier to see what is available. Before

you go, however, be sure to measure the piece you will be quilting, so that you buy the right size of stencil.

In general, designs with curved lines take longer to quilt than those with straight lines. The complexity of the quilting in your design will partly determine how long your project will take to complete.

While we have included most of our quilting patterns in this book, you may find that it is simpler to purchase a stencil in a similar design and mark from that. Or, you can freehand the design onto the fabric, using our motif for inspiration. We encourage you to use whichever method works best for you.

Lastly, to use the templates for garment construction, you can simply trace some of the templates onto paper and use them as you would standard garment patterns. Some will need to be photocopied and enlarged. Seam allowances are included in all our templates.

This piece was marked with masking tape for the straight lines of quilting, and with a marking pen and stencil for the cable-patterned quilting.

QUILTING TECHNIQUES

Finally, it is time to quilt. A few of our projects work best when you place the piece into a quilting hoop. (Some of our projects, because of their size or fabric content, were quilted without a hoop.) When working with a small piece of quilting, appliqué, or embroidery—too small to use a hoop—you can sit at a table to support your work. Or, for maximum comfort, stretch out on the sofa with a firm pillow in your lap and spread the piece you are working on out on the pillow. Just be sure not to sew your project to the pillow!

Quilter's Knot

First, thread your quilting needle, using a length of quilting thread that measures slightly longer than the distance from your fingertips to your elbow. Grasp the end of the thread to the needle, and wrap the end of the thread around the tip end of the needle three or four times, as shown in figure 1 below. Then press the wrapped thread to the needle while you pull the needle all the way through the wrapped thread. You should have a tiny knot at the end; trim any tail.

FIGURE 1. Making the quilter's knot.

Setting Your Knot

Now that you have made the knot, push the needle into the quilt top approximately ¼ inch (6 mm) from where your quilting is to begin. Go into the batting, but not through the backing. Bring the needle back up to where the line of quilting is to begin. Pull gently until the knot rests on the surface. Take one or more sharp tugs to pop the knot through the top and hide it in the batting. Alternatively, many quilters begin by pushing their needle up from the backing, through the batting, and out through the top, then giving a tug to pull the knot through the backing and into the batting.

The Quilting Stitch

For quilting, you will use a simple running stitch with a single strand of thread. After you have set your knot, begin by inserting your needle straight down. Use the index or middle finger of the hand on top of the piece to push the needle through all layers. (You will want your thimble now, if you use one.) Use the index or middle finger of the hand underneath the piece to feel whether the needle has penetrated all the layers and to turn it back upward. You will be using a rocking motion, making one or two stitches at a time, working up to three or four at a time. Aim for consistency in the size of the stitches and the spaces between them. Small stitches are nice, but it is the evenness of the stitching that matters most.

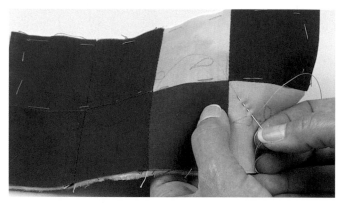

The quilting stitch; try to make the stitches consistent in size and spacing.

Ending Your Quilting

When you have come to the end of a line of quilting or when your thread becomes too short, secure your thread without making a knot. Make a double *backstitch* and hide the remaining thread in the batting.

Finishing Details

PACKAGED BIAS TAPE

When using bias tape, you will need to allow an extra inch (2.5 cm) of tape for the overlap. First, open out the tape completely. You will want the narrower side to be on the top of your project. Fold the raw end of the tape over ½ inch (1.3 cm) and pin in place, with the right sides of the tape and fabric together. Sew the tape on, continuing your stitching until the raw end of the tape overlaps your starting point by 1 inch (2.5 cm). Remove the pins. Neatly fold the tape over to the back of your work, covering the seam. Finally, blindstitch the tape to the back. (For more information on applying bias tape, see the instructions on the package.)

CUSTOM BIAS BINDING

We usually use packaged bias tape, but occasionally, when a perfect fabric match is desirable, we cut our own. To finish the edges of your project with a matching bias binding, take a square of fabric and fold it on the true bias at a 45° angle to the straight grain. Next, cut strips of the desired width parallel to the fold. You will then stitch the strips together, if necessary, to reach the right length for your project. Apply this binding as you would packaged bias tape.

HANGING SLEEVE

Our hanging projects require a sleeve to hold a rod or dowel. To make a hanging sleeve, you will need to cut a strip of fabric (preferably the same used for the backing piece of the project). The sleeve's length will be the same as the width of the piece to be hung, and its width will be determined by the size of the rod or dowel to be used. (See the individual projects for specific measurements.)

On the two long edges of the strip, turn the edges under approximately ½ inch (1.3 cm), and press or machine hem. Now turn the shorter edges of the strip under so no raw edges show, and hem. Pin the sleeve to the upper edge of the quilted piece. Hand stitch the sleeve to the back of the quilted piece along both long edges, and don't let the stitches show on the front. A dowel, stick, curtain rod, or branch can be inserted in the sleeve for hanging.

TOPSTITCHING

Topstitching, done by hand or machine, is a finishing stitch. In most of our projects that use this technique, we stitch ⅛ inch (3 mm) from an edge to create a crisp, tailored look. In the pillow cover project on page 184, topstitching is used to define the border.

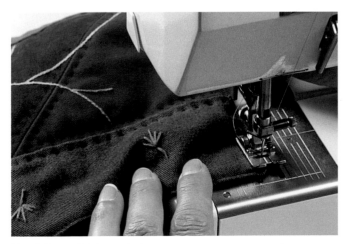

Topstitching to finish a project.

Special Techniques

FOUNDATION PIECING

Several of our projects use *foundation* piecing instead of patchwork piecing. (In foundation piecing, the fabric pieces are sewn to a muslin base as well as sewn to one another, whereas patchwork pieces are sewn only to one another.) There are many variations of foundation piecing, and they go by different names: stitch and flip, string piecing, strip piecing, etc. Our foundation-pieced projects are of three types: crazy-quilt-style piecing, as in the baby bib and the evening bag (pages 196 and 216); Log Cabin strip piecing, as in the potholders (page 202); and marked foundation piecing, as in the cards (page 205).

Crazy-quilt-style piecing uses randomly shaped scraps; all of ours happen to have straight edges, but you can use this method with curved pieces, although it is harder. You begin by placing the first scrap right side up at one edge of your muslin foundation. You then place a second scrap right side down on top of the first, aligning the two edges that you want to stitch together. Sew along that edge with a ¼-inch (6 mm) seam, then open the pieces right sides out and press. Add the third scrap, right side down onto the right side of the previously stitched scraps, aligning one edge as before. Stitch and press. Your object is to cover the entire muslin foundation, and it's okay if your scraps extend beyond

Placing the first two pieces in a crazy-quilt construction.

the edges of the foundation muslin. When the foundation is covered, you will trim the scraps along the edge and *staystitch* all around the piece for stability.

Trimming the edges after completing a crazy quilt project.

Log Cabin strip piecing is similar to the method above, but you begin with a square placed in the interior of your foundation piece and sew strips around that square. You sew a strip to one side of the square and continue adding strips around the square. Press after each piece is added.

An adaptation of Log Cabin piecing; this project is also marked for quilting.

Marked foundation piecing differs from the first two methods in that your foundation muslin is marked with a pattern of lines along which you sew to create a specific image. The marked foundation also has numbers that tell you the order of stitching. You sew with the marked side of the muslin facing you, with the fabric placed against the unmarked side. This is unlike the previous two examples, where the fabric is on the top while you are sewing. Open and press the fabric scraps after sewing each seam.

In all foundation piecing, the fabric scraps applied to the muslin will be unsecured around the outer edges. The project will be easier to work with in subsequent steps

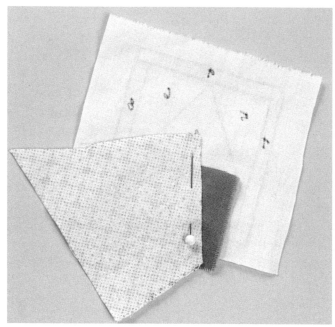

This sequence of photos illustrates the steps in marked foundation piecing: above, pinning the first two pieces prior to sewing; below, stitching the pieces together with the marked foundation on top.

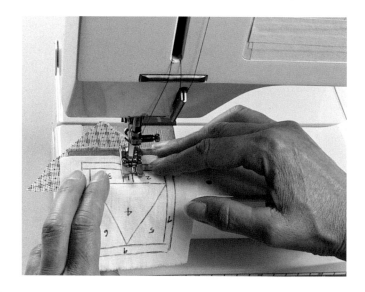

if you staystitch the edges; machine stitch ⅛ inch (3 mm) from the raw edge to stabilize the edges.

The individual projects that use these methods will provide specific instructions on the application of these techniques.

APPLIQUÉ

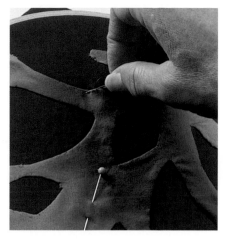

Stitching an appliqué.

To appliqué a piece of fabric onto a background fabric, as in the Hawaiian appliqué project on page 194, begin by pinning or basting the appliqué piece to the background fabric. There are many appliqué techniques, but the one we like best involves the blindstitch and no prepressing. You simply turn under the raw edges of the piece as you appliqué. You could mark a fine pencil line to turn on, but we generally just eyeball a ⅛- to ¼-inch (3 to 6 mm) margin and turn under.

To appliqué, thread your needle and make a small knot in one end of the thread. Bring your needle up through the folded edge of the piece you are appliquéing so the knot is hidden in the fold. Insert your needle into the background fabric, just under the fold of the appliqué, next to where the needle came out of the piece. Pull the needle up through the background fabric and catch the edge of the fold about ⅛ inch (3 mm) away. Continue around the whole piece using a blindstitch. Hide your finishing knot on the back.

EMBROIDERY

Embroidery is a beautiful embellishment for many quilted items. In fact, it is crucial for traditional crazy quilts, which actually have only embroidery and no real quilting. On a couple of our projects, we have incorporated crazy-quilt techniques with traditional quilting, and added a bit of embroidery, too. We use only two strands of floss, separated out from the six that are in a standard skein of embroidery floss. See page 228 for illustrations of the stitches that we used.

Essentials Kit

You are likely to need all of the following items on each project that you create, so we will not list them on every page of instructions. Here are the tools and supplies that you should have on hand for each project:

- **Iron**
- **Ironing board**
- **Quilting needles**
- **Quilting thread**
- **Pins**
- **Pincushion**
- **Scissors**
- **Sewing machine**
- **Sewing thread**
- **Tape measure**

Last advice....

Remember those ¼-inch (6 mm) seams—and happy quilting.

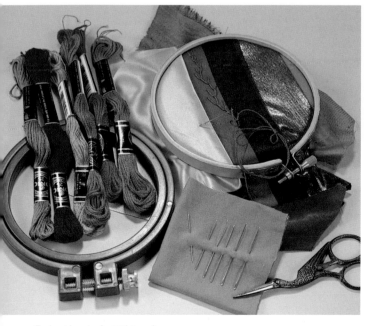

Embroidery tools and supplies.

Celestial Potpourri Bags

These delightful little confections feature shadow quilting; be sure to select a sheer fabric to appreciate the beauty of this technique. Use these bags to scent your drawers, or as quick-and-easy party favors.

YOU WILL NEED (PER BAG)

Essentials kit	Paper
¼ yard (.23 m) of chiffon or similar transparent material	Pencil
	Gold metallic quilting thread
Templates (page 222)	Potpourri mix
Batting scrap	⅓ yard (.3 m) of narrow gold ribbon

MEASURE AND CUT

Chiffon: 1 rectangle, 7 × 22 inches (17.8 × 55.9 cm)

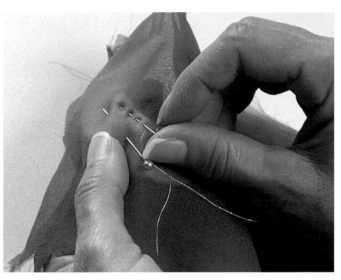

1 Fold the chiffon in half vertically so that it is now 7 × 11 inches (17.8 × 27.9 cm). Stitch along the short raw edge and one long raw edge. Turn right side out and press.

3 Quilt around the batting shape with the gold thread, first working along the edges of the design to hold the batting in place. Then fill up the image with echo quilting as desired. Leave the trailing ends of the threads, if you want.

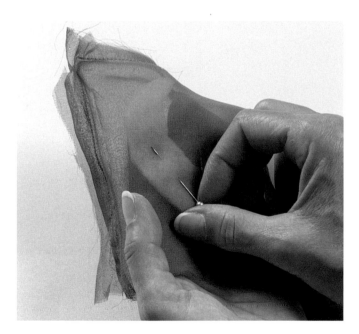

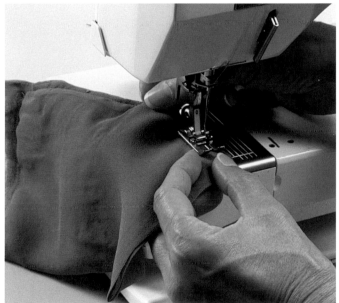

2 Trace the desired template and cut it out; then pin the pattern to the batting scrap, and cut out the shape. Center the batting shape on one half of the rectangle, between the layers of chiffon. Pin in place.

4 Fold the rectangle horizontally, right sides together, and stitch the side and bottom. Turn the bag right side out. Fill it with a potpourri mix of your choice, and tie the bag closed with the gold ribbon.

USE ¼-INCH (6 MM) SEAMS THROUGHOUT

Delicates Travel Pouch

Here is an elegant way to pack and safeguard fine hosiery, silk scarves, jewelry, etc. This bag can be packed flat or rolled up to fit in a corner of a suitcase. You will learn to mark both straight and curved lines for quilting when you create this project.

YOU WILL NEED

Essentials kit

⅓ yard (.3 m) of pale green fabric

⅓ yard (.3 m) of cream or white satin

1 package of craft-size batting

Purchased cable stencil or quilting pattern (page 219)

Fabric marking pen or pencil

Paper

Black permanent marker

¾-inch (1.9 cm) masking tape

Pale green quilting thread

2 yards (1.8 m) of lavender ribbon

MEASURE AND CUT

Pale green fabric: 1 rectangle, 10 × 26 inches (25.4 × 66 cm)

Cream fabric: 1 rectangle, 10 × 26 inches (25.4 × 66 cm)

Batting: 1 rectangle, 10 × 26 inches (25.4 × 66 cm)

USE ¼-INCH (6 MM) SEAMS THROUGHOUT

1 Transfer the cable pattern onto the perimeter of the pale green fabric, as shown in the photo. If you prefer to use the pattern on page 219, trace it onto a piece of paper with the permanent marker, and then place the paper under the fabric. Now, trace the design onto the fabric with a marking pen or pencil. Pin or baste together the green rectangle and batting. Quilt the cable motif.

2 Use the masking tape to create the lattice pattern shown, and quilt along both sides of the tape. Remove the tape and basting when your quilting is completed. If there are any markings remaining from step 1, remove them as directed.

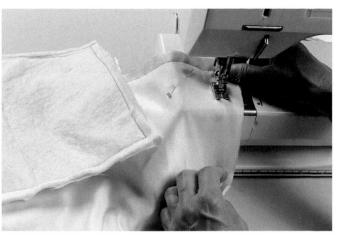

3 Pin the satin rectangle to the quilted layers, right sides together. Stitch around the edges, leaving a 4- or 5-inch (10.2 or 12.7 cm) opening in the middle of one end. Turn right side out and slipstitch the opening closed.

4 With the right side of the bag facing you, fold to create a pocket with a depth of 9½ inches (24.1 cm). The right sides will be together, so now is the time to stitch the sides of the pocket.

5 Turn the bag right side out. Cut four 18-inch (45.7 cm) ribbon ties, and tack them onto the bag.

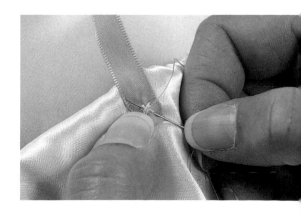

Silk Pillbox Hat

This stylish headgear stands out because it is made of silk. When determining your hat size, be sure to measure and calculate carefully so you get a good fit.

YOU WILL NEED

Essentials kit

Drafting compass

¼ yard (.23 m) of teal fabric

¼ yard (.23 m) of teal print fabric

⅓ yard (.3 m) of pink fabric

1 package of craft-size batting

Gold metallic quilting thread

Quilting pattern (page 221) or purchased stencil

Fabric marking pencil

TO DETERMINE YOUR HAT SIZE

Measure your head at the point where you will wear the hat. This measurement—plus ½-inch (1.3 cm) seam allowance—will be the length of your band. The band's width will be 4 inches (10.2 cm). To draft a circle of a suitable size, refer to the chart below. If your head measurement differs from those given, choose the next size up for your circle's diameter. You can then ease it in to fit the band that is your correct size.

For Head Circumference	Make Circle Diameter
22" (55.9 cm)	7" (17.8 cm)
22⅜" (56.8 cm)	7⅛" (18.1 cm)
22¾" (57.8 cm)	7¼" (18.4 cm)
23⅛" (58.7 cm)	7⅜" (18.7 cm)
23½" (59.7 cm)	7½" (19 cm)

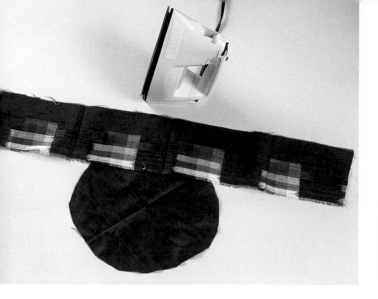

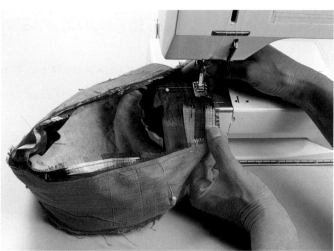

1 Measure and cut a circle of the appropriate size from the solid teal fabric and a circle from the pink lining fabric. Referring to your head measurement, cut a 4-inch-wide (10.2 cm) band from the teal print fabric and the pink lining fabric, being sure to add the ½-inch (1.3 cm) seam allowance to your head measurement. Staystitch all edges to prevent the silk from fraying. Cut a circle from the batting. Fold the two fabric circles into quarters, and press lightly to make four equidistant marks.

3 Carefully trim the batting to the seam line. Turn the outer shell right side out. Repeat step 2 with the lining fabric, but omit the batting and quilting. Pin the outer shell (turned right side out) inside the inner shell (turned inside out), matching seams and equidistant points. Pin along the edge and stitch as shown, leaving a gap of about 2 inches (5 cm) on either side of the seam.

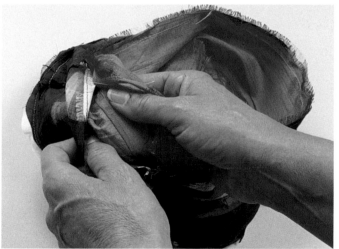

2 Place the ends of the outer band right sides together and stitch. Press the seam to one side. Fold and press to find four equidistant points, with the seam being one point. Transfer the quilting pattern onto the right side of the teal fabric circle; draw a freehand design based on our pattern, or use a purchased stencil. Pin the batting to the teal circle, and quilt. Now, pin the quilted top to the teal outer band as shown, right sides together, matching the four equidistant points. Stitch all the way around, easing in any fullness.

4 Turn the hat right side out, pulling carefully through the 4-inch (10.2 cm) gap. Press. Blindstitch the gap closed.

Variation: Add batting to the band, and quilt it in addition to the top. Use a star or spiral for the quilting pattern on top.

USE ¼-INCH (6 MM) SEAMS THROUGHOUT

Silk Pillbox Hat **175**

Brightly Colored Bunting

Don't worry about the cold on a winter outing when baby is tucked into this bunting. It is simple to construct and quilt, and the quilting pattern will give you a good opportunity to perfect your stitch. It will make an excellent present for a newborn.

USE ¼-INCH (6 MM) SEAMS THROUGHOUT

Essentials kit

1 yard (.9 m) of lime green print fabric

1 yard (.9 m) of royal blue fabric

1 package of craft-size batting

¾-inch (1.9 cm) masking tape

Fabric marking pencil

Royal blue and lime green quilting thread

Quilting hoop

Silver snaps, sizes 1/0 and 2/0

MEASURE AND CUT

Lime green print fabric: 1 rectangle, 24½ × 33½ inches
(62.2 × 85.1 cm)

Royal blue fabric: 1 rectangle, 24½ × 33½ inches
(62.2 × 85.1 cm)

Batting: 1 rectangle, 26 × 35 inches
(66 × 88.9 cm)

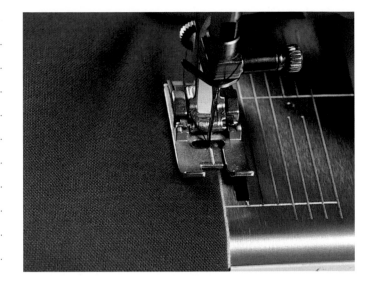

2 Trim the batting almost to the seam line, being careful not to cut the fabric. Trim the corners. Turn the bunting right side out; turn the unfinished seams under, and blindstitch the gap closed. Measure 7 inches (17.8 cm) from the bottom edge, and mark each side with masking tape. Then topstitch around the top and sides as shown, ⅛ inch (3 mm) from the edge, starting and stopping at the marked spots. Remove the tape.

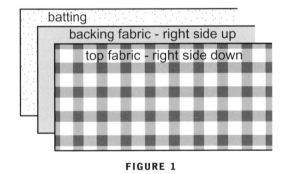

FIGURE 1

1 Sandwich the layers as in figure 1: Place the lime green and blue fabrics with their right sides together and edges aligned. Then, place these fabrics onto the piece of batting. (The batting will be slightly bigger all the way around.) Pin the three layers together along the edge, pinning well to keep all the layers in place when stitching. Sew around the edge, but leave a gap on one short edge for turning right side out.

3 Mark the bunting for quilting with a wavy freehand design that runs both horizontally and vertically. Baste. Place the bunting into the hoop and quilt, using royal blue thread for the vertical lines and lime green for the horizontal lines. Remove the marks and basting.

Now, pin the bottom of the bunting with the wrong sides together, and sew ¼ inch (6 mm) from the edge, backstitching at the beginning and end. Run another line of stitching near the first one for added strength.

4 Fold the sides of the bunting toward the center, overlapping the front by ¾ inch (1.9 cm), as shown in the photo. Pin along the overlap, and place a piece of masking tape 6¼ inches (15.9 cm) from the bottom of the bunting.

6 Mark places to sew five size 1/0 snaps on the front of the bunting, to be hidden by the overlap; sew on the snaps. Fold the front corners down about 7½ inches (19 cm) to form the collar of the bunting. Mark a spot for a size 2/0 snap underneath each point of the collar; sew on the snaps.

5 With the bunting face up, stitch the front closed about ⅜ inch (9.5 mm) from the edge of the overlap, starting at the bottom of the bunting and sewing to your mark. Sew the top row of stitching several times to reinforce, as shown. Remove the tape.

Wine Bottle Carrier

Plan to arrive in fashion with this carrier in hand, color coordinated for either Bordeaux or Chablis. The sturdy construction ensures that your wine will have a safe journey to its destination.

Essentials kit

½ yard (.5 m) of red fabric

¼ yard (.23 m) of black fabric

⅛ yard (.1 m) of white fabric

1 package of craft-size batting

Quilting patterns (page 219) or purchased stencils

Fabric marking pencil

Red quilting thread

Black fabric: 2 rectangles, each 4½ × 14½ inches
(11.4 × 36.8 cm)
1 square, 4½ × 4½ inches (11.4 × 11.4 cm)

Red fabric: 6 rectangles, each 4 × 4½ inches (10.2 × 11.4 cm)
4 rectangles, each 4 × 14½ inches (11.4 × 36.8 cm)
1 square, 4½ × 4½ inches (11.4 × 11.4 cm)
2 strips, each 3½ × 10½ inches (8.9 × 26.7 cm)

White fabric: 2 rectangles, each 4 × 4½ inches
(10.2 × 11.4 cm)

Batting: 4 rectangles, each 4½ × 14¼ inches (11.4 × 36.2 cm)
1 square, 4½ × 4½ inches (11.4 × 11.4 cm)
2 strips, each 2¼ × 10½ inches (5.7 × 26.7 cm)

1 Piece the two bicolored panels together, using three pieces of 4 × 4½-inch (10.2 × 11.4 cm) red fabric and one piece of 4 × 4½-inch (10.2 × 11.4 cm) white fabric per panel. Baste the large pieces of batting to the wrong side of each panel, making sure the batting is ¼ inch (6 mm) below the fabric at the top. Also, baste the appropriate size of batting to the black panels and the square of black fabric. Now, draw a freehand design for quilting on one panel, using the vine and grapes motif (see page 219). Mark the remaining three panels with the woven diamond pattern (see page 219) or with your own stencil. Do not mark within ½ inch (1.3 cm) of any edge. Quilt all four panels; the diamond motif is shown in the photo. Remove the basting on the sides. Remove the quilting marks.

2 Placing the right sides together, sew one black panel, top up, to the black 4½ × 4½-inch (11.4 × 11.4 cm) bottom, starting and stopping ¼ inch (6 mm) from the ends. Double-stitch this seam for strength. Repeat on the opposite side with the other black panel, and then sew a red-and-white panel onto one of the remaining sides of the bottom, as shown in the photo.

USE ¼-INCH (6 MM) SEAMS THROUGHOUT

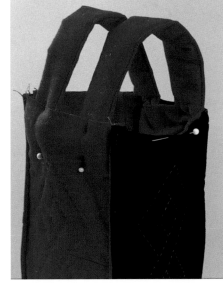

3 Pin and sew the long edges of two adjacent panels, right sides together, as shown. Start your stitching at the bottom edge of the fabric and sew to the top, reinforcing with backstitching at both ends. Pin and sew the other side, bottom to top, backstitching as before. Now, sew the remaining red-and-white panel onto the bottom, as in step 2, then sew to each black panel as above. Turn the carrier right side out. Topstitch all four lengthwise seams, 1 inch (2.5 cm) from the bottom to 1 inch (2.5 cm) from the top. Remove the basting on the bottom.

5 Construct the red liner with the four long red rectangles, sewing the side panels to the red square bottom as in steps 2 and 3, and turn it right side out. Turn the carrier inside out, and place it inside the liner. (The wrong sides will be together.) Match the bottom corners of the carrier and the lining, and tack both of the bottoms together in several places. Now turn the carrier right side out; place a bottle inside for weight, pull the liner to its full height, and straighten. Pin the handles in place as shown, inserting 2 inches (5.1 cm) of each raw end between the layers of the carrier. Pin the top together, turning the raw edges inward and matching up the four seams.

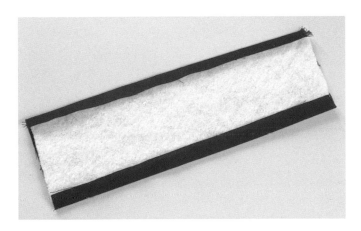

4 To make the handles, press the two long red strips under about ¹⁄₂ inch (1.3 cm) on each long edge. Center the remaining strips of batting on top of the wrong side of the fabric, as shown. Fold the fabric and batting in half, with the right side out. Stitch the handle closed along its length, ¹⁄₈ inch (3 mm) from the edge.

6 Remove the bottle and stitch around the top, about ¹⁄₈ inch (3 mm) from the edge. Triple-stitch for added strength.

Variation: You can machine quilt this project with satisfactory results; use red thread and your sewing machine's largest straight stitch. You can also quilt the bottom of the carrier, if desired.

Batik Tablecloth

Liven up your dining area with this exotic table covering. The quilted patterns in the border complement the design of the batik print; you could quilt the border simply at first and add more stitching at your leisure.

YOU WILL NEED

Essentials kit

1¼ yards (1.1 m) of batik fabric

¼ yard (.23 m) of turquoise fabric

2 yards (1.8 m) of khaki fabric

1 package of crib-size batting

¾-inch (1.9 cm) masking tape

Light yellow quilting thread

MEASURE AND CUT

Batik fabric: 1 square, 42 × 42 inches (106.7 × 106.7 cm)

Turquoise fabric: 2 strips, each 1½ × 42 inches (3.8 × 106.7 cm)
2 strips, each 1½ × 44 inches (3.8 × 111.8 cm)

Khaki fabric: 2 strips, each 13 × 44 inches (33 × 111.8 cm)
2 strips, each 13 × 55 inches (33 × 139.7 cm)

Batting: 2 pieces, each 5 × 54 inches (12.7 × 137.2 cm)
2 pieces, each 5 × 44 inches (12.7 × 111.8 cm)

USE ¼-INCH (6 MM) SEAMS THROUGHOUT

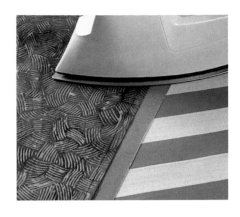

1 Stitch one of the 42-inch (106.7 cm) narrow turquoise strips to one side of the batik square, right sides together. Repeat on the opposite side of the square with the other 42-inch strip. Sew the 44-inch (111.8 cm) turquoise strips to the remaining sides of the square. Press the seam allowances outward, as shown.

2 Pin the 13 × 44-inch (33 × 111.8 cm) khaki strips to the narrow turquoise strips on two opposing sides, right sides together. Stitch and press the seam allowance toward the outer edge. Press the outer edge under ¼ inch (6 mm). Next, fold and press the wide khaki

strip so the exposed seam on the back of the tablecloth will be covered by the pressed edge of the strip. Unfold the strip and place the 5 × 44-inch (12.7 × 111.8 cm) batting strip along the crease; pin if desired, and then baste as shown, below left. Remove the pins.

3 Fold the khaki strip back over to cover the seam once again, and blindstitch as shown above. Repeat steps 2 and 3 with the opposite side.

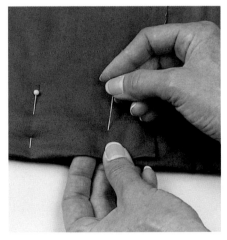

4 Now, using the 13 × 55-inch (33 × 139.7 cm) khaki strips, repeat steps 2 and 3 on the remaining two sides. These strips will extend ½ inch (1.3 cm) on either end. Fold in the unfinished ends, pin in place as shown, and whipstitch the ends closed.

5 Use the masking tape to create a weave pattern in the border. Quilt along one side of the tape for your basic line, and then along the other side of the tape for your second line. Now pull up the tape and lay it along the second line; quilt along the other side to create a third line. Repeat this procedure as necessary, and remove all tape and basting when you have completed the quilting. The photo above illustrates the possibilities of simple and/or more complex quilting in the border.

Tip: Make a set of matching napkins for this piece. You will need an additional yard of fabric; we chose the turquoise cloth. Cut four 16½-inch (41.9 cm) squares, and machine hem the unfinished edges. You don't have to use this project for dining, necessarily; it will also adorn (or hide) any nondescript table.

Lazy Day Pillow

The soft colors and simple lines of this pillow evoke a summertime feeling, and illustrate the possibilities of easy four-patch block construction. It would be wonderful in a hammock, wouldn't it?

Cream fabric: 1 square, 10½ × 10½ inches (26.7 × 26.7 cm)

Yellow fabric: 1 square, 10½ × 10½ inches (26.7 × 26.7 cm)

Green fabric: 1 square, 10½ × 10½ inches (26.7 × 26.7 cm)
2 strips, 2½ × 28 inches (6.4 × 71.1 cm)

Blue fabric: 1 square, 10½ × 10½ inches (26.7 × 26.7 cm)
2 strips, 2½ × 28 inches (6.4 × 71.1 cm)
2 rectangles, 20 × 24½ inches (50.8 × 62.2 cm)

Batting: 1 square, 25 × 25 inches (63.5 × 63.5 cm)

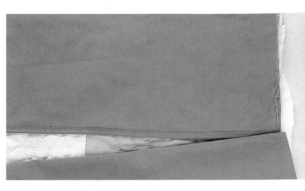

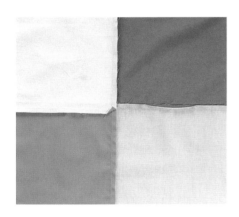

1 Stitch the fabric squares together as in the photo, and then press the seams to the darker side. Find and mark the horizontal center of one of the blue strips, which you will use for the border. Match this center mark to the center seam of the pillow front, and pin the blue strip to the pillow front, right sides together. Stitch, starting and stopping ¼ inch (6 mm) from each end. Sew the other blue strip onto an adjacent side, and then sew the green strips onto the remaining sides of the pillow front, being sure to stop stitching ¼ inch (6 mm) from each end.

2 To miter the corners (see page 158), fold the pillow front horizontally. Place a ruler along the fold at one corner, extending over the border strips. Mark the border as in the photo, and sew along the marked line. Trim the mitered seam to ¼ inch (6 mm), and press to one side. Press the border seams outward. Repeat for each of the remaining corners.

3 Mark the center of each side of each square with a straight pin. Follow the design in the photograph to place the masking tape for marking the basic diamond shape. Pin or baste the pillow front to the square of batting. (A backing is not necessary.) Quilt the diamond shapes, and then quilt the rest of the square as shown, moving the tape to mark successive outlines on the pillow front. Remove all tape when finished.

4 After the front of the pillow cover is quilted, add the pillow back. Begin by machine hemming one long edge of each blue rectangle. Then, pin the long raw edge of one rectangle to the top of the quilted front, placing right sides together. Pin the second rectangle to the bottom of the pillow front, right sides together. The second piece will overlap the first. (The photo above shows the first rectangle as it is being covered by the second rectangle.) Stitch around all four sides of the pillow cover.

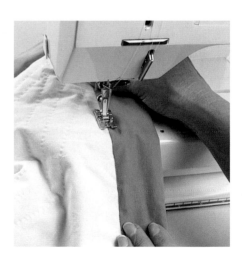

5 Turn the pillow cover right side out. Press. Topstitch as closely as possible along the border seam—not *in* the border. Lastly, insert the pillow form.

Baby Hat

*This cozy hat will keep the snow and wind off baby's ears. Choose a playful
print for this adorable project; though there are many construction
steps for this hat, none are difficult.*

YOU WILL NEED

Essentials kit

Templates (page 223)

Paper

⅓ yard (.3 m) of blue print fabric

⅓ yard (.3 m) of muslin

1 package of craft-size batting

¾-inch (1.9 cm) masking tape

Blue quilting thread

MEASURE AND CUT

Trace the hat template and ear flap templates onto paper and cut them out. To cut out the hat pieces, fold the print fabric and place the template on the fold. Cut out two pieces of blue fabric; then repeat for the muslin and batting, placing each on the fold and cutting two pieces. For the ear flaps, place the templates on the straight grain of the fabric, and cut out two pieces of blue fabric, two pieces of muslin, and two pieces of batting. Measure and cut two pieces of blue fabric for hat ties, each 1½ × 18 inches (3.8 × 45.7 cm).

2 Turn the hat piece right side out. Turn the unfinished edges in and blindstitch the gap closed. Baste the hat piece as shown to stabilize the layers. Quilt along a simple horizontal and vertical grid marked with the masking tape. Repeat steps 1 and 2 with the other hat piece, and then remove the tape.

1 Take one outer hat piece, one muslin piece, and one batting piece, and sandwich; place the fabrics right side together and place onto a piece of batting. Pin well and sew together, leaving a gap open at the bottom, as shown. Trim the batting almost to the seam line.

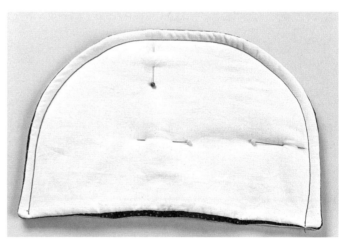

3 Place the two hat pieces with the right sides together. Pin and stitch around the curved top only; backstitch at each end of the seam.

USE ¼-INCH (6 MM) SEAMS THROUGHOUT

the curves. Turn the flap right side out and press. Turn in the unfinished edges ¼ inch (6 mm), and stitch the straight end closed. Repeat for the other flap.

4 To make the hat ties, finger press a ¼-inch (6 mm) fold along both long edges. Now, fold the tie in half lengthwise, right sides out, and finger press. Topstitch the tie closed ⅛ inch (3 mm) from the edge, stitching along the length and across one end. Repeat for the other tie.

5 Pin a tie to the right side of a blue ear flap piece, keeping raw edges even. Stitch across the curved edge of the flap. Repeat for the other flap.

6 Place a muslin flap on top of a blue flap, right sides together. Place a batting piece on top. Sew together with a ⅜-inch (9.5 mm) seam, leaving the straight edge open as shown. Trim the batting, and clip

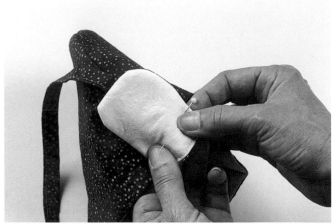

7 Pin a flap to one side of the hat, right sides together, centering it on the seam line with the edges even. Sew the flap to the hat, stitching ¾ inch (1.9 cm) from the straight edge. Repeat for the other flap.

8 Press up a ¾-inch (1.9 cm) hem on the lower edge of the hat, pressing the flaps out. Sew two rows of topstitching at the bottom edge of the hat, the first row ¼ inch (6 mm) from the edge, and again ¼ inch (6 mm) from the first row of stitching.

Tangy Table Runner

This piece will spice up any meal—not to mention the table. Add one part good food, one part good company, mix well, and savor. Measure, cut, and piece with precision, for there are lots of seams in this project.

YOU WILL NEED

Essentials kit

$1\frac{3}{4}$ yards (1.6 m) of lime green fabric

$\frac{1}{4}$ yard (.23 m) of yellow fabric

$\frac{1}{8}$ yard (.1 m) of teal fabric

$1\frac{3}{4}$ yards (1.6 m) of orange fabric

$1\frac{3}{4}$ yards (1.6 m) of print fabric

1 package of crib-size batting

Quilting pattern (page 220) or purchased stencil

Fabric marking pencil

$\frac{3}{4}$-inch (1.9 cm) masking tape

Quilting hoop

Lime green quilting thread

MEASURE AND CUT

(see figure 1)

Lime green fabric: 2 strips, each $5\frac{1}{2} \times 56\frac{1}{2}$ inches
(14 × 143.5 cm)
2 strips, each $3\frac{1}{2} \times 6\frac{1}{2}$ inches
(8.9 × 16.5 cm)
4 strips, each $5\frac{1}{2} \times 6\frac{1}{2}$ inches
(14 × 16.5 cm)

Yellow fabric: 3 squares, each 4 × 4 inches
(10.2 × 10.2 cm)
2 squares, each 3 × 3 inches
(7.6 × 7.6 cm)

Teal fabric: 6 strips, each 1 × 4 inches
(2.5 × 10.2 cm)
6 strips, each 1 × 5 inches
(2.5 × 12.7 cm)
4 strips, each $1\frac{1}{2} \times 3$ inches
(3.8 × 7.6 cm)
4 strips, each $1\frac{1}{2} \times 5$ inches
(3.8 × 12.7 cm)

Orange fabric: 2 strips, each $2\frac{1}{4} \times 56\frac{1}{2}$ inches
(5.7 × 143.5 cm)
2 strips, each $2\frac{1}{4} \times 20\frac{1}{2}$ inches
(5.7 × 52.1 cm)

Print fabric: 1 rectangle, $17\frac{1}{2} \times 57\frac{1}{2}$ inches
(44.5 × 146.1 cm)

Batting: 1 rectangle, $17\frac{1}{2} \times 57\frac{1}{2}$ inches
(44.5 × 146.1 cm)

USE $\frac{1}{4}$-INCH (6 MM) SEAMS THROUGHOUT

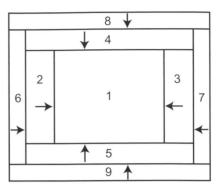

FIGURE 1: Block piecing sequence.

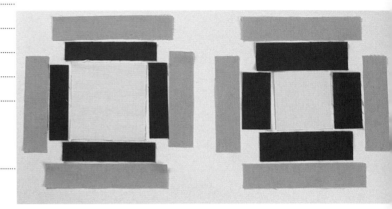

1 You will begin by assembling the pieced blocks from the small strips of lime green, yellow, and teal fabrics, as shown in the photo. Lay out a total of five blocks, three with the larger yellow blocks at the center and two with the smaller yellow blocks at the center.

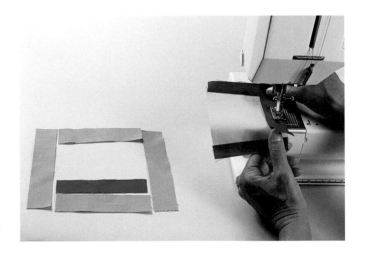

2 Assemble each block, starting with the center and sewing in the sequence indicated in figure 1, with the right sides of the fabric together. (Note that the sewing sequence will be correct for each style of block, despite a difference in the size of the pieces.)

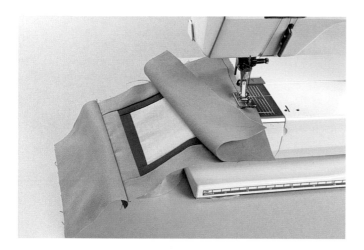

3 Sew the blocks together into a row as shown, alternating the lime rectangles with the pieced blocks. After you have sewn the row of blocks together, stitch the $3\frac{1}{2} \times 6\frac{1}{2}$-inch (8.9 × 16.5 cm) lime green strips to either short end of the row, right sides together. Then, sew the longer lime green strips to each long edge of the row, right sides together. Lastly, with right sides together, sew on the orange borders, first the long edges, then the short ends. Center the short borders so you will have an equal amount of fabric to turn over at each end.

5 Carefully pin along all four edges of the table runner, making sure to catch all three layers. Baste. Quilt, following the motif in the long lime borders and the center. Then quilt in-the-ditch along the seams of the pieced blocks and lime borders, along the long borders, and along a straight line formed by the teal edges of the pieced blocks. Remove the basting stitches and the tape.

4 Mark the top for quilting, drawing a freehand design using the motif on page 220 as a model; use masking tape for the straight lines. Next, sandwich the layers: first the top, right side down; then the batting, centered; and finally the print backing, right side up. Make sure the orange border extends equally on all four sides, as shown, as you will use the excess to create the border.

6 Fold the front borders over to the back, turn the raw edges under $\frac{1}{4}$ inch (6 mm), and blindstitch. Stitch the two short ends first, then the two longer sides, to form square corners.

Quilted Vest

Transform a simple garment into a one-of-a-kind fashion statement. You will appreciate the versatility of this reversible design, though the project does involve a fair amount of both sewing and quilting.

YOU WILL NEED

Essentials kit

An easy vest pattern

Red fabric

Print fabric

1 package of crib-size batting

Custom bias binding (page 167) to fit pattern, 1½ inches (3.8 cm) wide, or packaged bias tape

¾-inch (1.9 cm) masking tape

Red quilting thread

Button(s), thin silk cord for fastening loop (optional)

MEASURE AND CUT

Two fronts and one back in red fabric, print fabric, and batting, per pattern requirements

Note: Buy a pattern that is one size larger than your usual size, as the quilting will draw up the fabric. Ignore the sewing instructions and extraneous pieces in the pattern; you just need the pieces for the front and the back. Take the yardage requirements from the pattern, and when you are selecting fabrics, choose a solid fabric for the outside to highlight the quilting.

USE THE STANDARD ⅝-INCH (1.6 CM) GARMENT SEAM, EXCEPT WHEN APPLYING BIAS BINDING

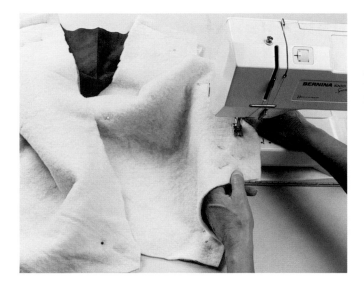

1 Beginning with the print fabric, place the vest fronts and the back right sides together, and stitch at the shoulders and sides. Press the seams open. Next, pin the batting pieces to the wrong side of the red fabric. As shown, stitch the red fabric together at the shoulders and sides, right sides together, as with the print fabric. Trim the batting close to the seams; press open. Place the print and red vests right sides together, and stitch the neck and the outer edges. Do not stitch the armholes.

3 To bind the armholes, measure and cut bias strips (see page 167) according to the circumference of the armholes, adding 1 inch (2.5 cm) for overlap. Fold the raw end of the bias binding over ½ inch (1.3 cm) and pin in place, with the right side of the binding against the outer side of the armhole. Sew the binding on with a ¼-inch (6 mm) seam; continue stitching until the raw end of the binding overlaps your starting point. Fold the binding over, turn the raw edge under, and blindstitch to the inside, as shown. Repeat for the other armhole. (You may also use packaged bias tape in this step, if you prefer.)

2 Clip the curves at the neck. Turn the garment right side out through one armhole. Press, concentrating on the edges so they look crisp.

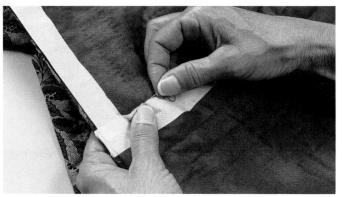

4 Using the masking tape, establish a quilting line along the edge and side seams of the vest, as shown. Quilt, filling up the body of the vest with echo quilting. Remove the tape when you are done. Add fasteners or ties, if desired.

Tips: Use metallic quilting thread—or a contrasting color—for more drama. Instead of a solid color for the outer fabric, choose a bold stripe or distinctive print, and use it as your quilting guide.

Hawaiian Quilting Appliqué

This heritage quilting technique from the islands makes a unique adornment for a shoulder bag. This method can also be used to create other decorative items for your home—a throw pillow or a wall hanging, perhaps.

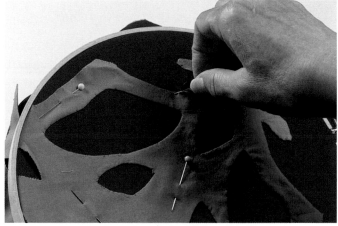

template or the one you made in step 1, and place it against the fold of the fabric; then trace around it. Cut it out, open, and press.

1 Trace the template for the appliqué onto a piece of paper, and cut it out. If you prefer, you can create your own template: Cut a paper square about 1 inch (2.5 cm) smaller than the finished size of the background square. Fold the paper in half, top to bottom. Fold in half again side to side. Finally, fold in half diagonally. (Yes, this is like those snowflakes you cut out as a child!) Experiment by cutting along the edges until you have a pleasing pattern when you unfold the paper. Keep it fairly simple and make your cuts rounded, as sharp angles are harder to appliqué properly.

3 Center the fabric appliqué on the background fabric, and pin in place. Place into the quilting hoop and appliqué with a blindstitch, turning under the edges of the appliqué as you go. (See page 169.)

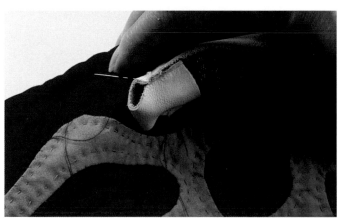

4 Pin or baste the appliquéd fabric to the batting. Echo quilt as desired. Turn the raw edges under and press. Pin the square to the bag and blindstitch in place.

2 Fold the turquoise fabric as described above (fold in half top to bottom, fold again in half side to side, and then in half diagonally). Use our paper

USE ¼-INCH (6 MM) SEAMS THROUGHOUT

Cats and Frogs Bib

This is a quick and easy project to welcome a little newcomer. It will also brighten a weary mother's day with its vivid colors and whimsical prints. This project will introduce you to crazy-quilt-style piecing— using scraps to create a design on a muslin foundation.

Essentials kit

Template, page 227

Paper

Pen

¼ yard (.23 m) of backing fabric

¼ yard (.23 m) of muslin

1 package of craft-size batting

Assorted fabric scraps for the front of the bib

Green quilting thread

1 package of green wide, single-fold bias tape

2 Trim the raw edges even with the muslin pattern, and staystitch around the perimeter of the bib. Pin or baste the batting to the back of the pieced top. Quilt as desired.

1 Trace the bib template onto paper with the pen, enlarge 200 percent, and cut it out. Place the paper template on the fold of the fabric, and cut; repeat for the muslin and batting. Begin covering the muslin in crazy-quilt style (see page 167) by placing a scrap right side up along one edge. Then place another scrap, right side down on top of the first scrap, matching the edges you want to join. Stitch along these matching edges as shown, sewing through the fabrics and the muslin. Open the pieces right side out and press. Repeat, this time aligning a third piece over your second scrap. Continue until the entire muslin piece is covered.

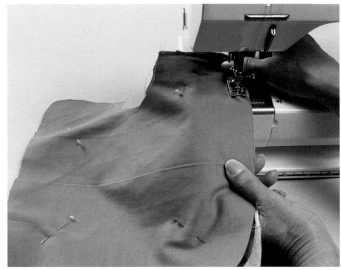

3 Pin the quilted top to the backing, right sides together. Stitch around the edges, leaving the neck area open. Turn right side out and press.

USE ¼-INCH (6 MM) SEAMS THROUGHOUT

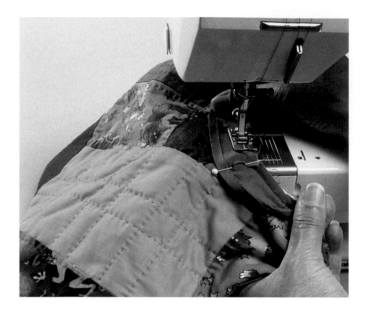

4   Measure and cut 50 inches (127 cm) of bias tape. Find the center of the bias tape, open it flat, and pin it to the center of the neck opening, right sides together. Pin all along the neck edge, and stitch through all layers. Backstitch.

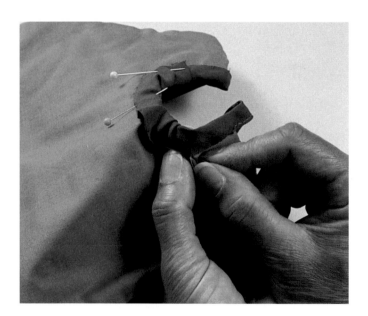

5   Fold the tape to the back, and pin the tape over the seam. Hand stitch, easing to fit. To make the ties, keep the remainder of the tape folded and topstitch it closed to the ends. Tie a knot in each end.

Variation: Use this method to cover muslin squares rather than the bib template. You can sew the squares together to make a pillow cover; if you feel ambitious, make a quilt for baby!

Lap Quilt

This Amish-inspired project is a soft and cuddly throw for a winter's day. Snuggle under its flannel backing and watch the snow fall, but don't forget the hot chocolate. If you want to learn to use a rotary cutter, this quilt provides a good opportunity to practice that skill.

YOU WILL NEED

Essentials kit

½ yard (.5 m) of royal blue fabric

½ yard (.5 m) of squash fabric

½ yard (.5 m) of red fabric

½ yard (.5 m) of black fabric

½ yard (.5 m) of purple fabric

1 yard (.9 m) of olive fabric

1½ yards (1.4 m) of mauve fabric

1½ yards (1.4 m) of navy blue fabric

3 yards (2.7 m) of gray flannel fabric

1 package of crib-size batting

Rotary cutter (optional)

Rotary mat and ruler (optional)

Paper or cardboard

White fabric marking pencil

¾-inch (1.9 cm) masking tape

Quilt hoop

Royal blue, squash, red, black, purple, and olive quilting thread

2 packages of black extra-wide double-fold bias tape

MEASURE AND CUT

Royal blue fabric: 3 squares, each 11½ × 11½ inches (29.2 × 29.2 cm)

Squash fabric: 2 squares, each 11½ × 11½ inches (29.2 × 29.2 cm)

Red fabric: 2 squares, each 11½ × 11½ inches (29.2 × 29.2 cm)

Black fabric: 2 squares, each 11½ × 11½ inches (29.2 × 29.2 cm)

Purple fabric: 1 square, 11½ × 11½ inches (29.2 × 29.2 cm)

Olive fabric: 2 squares, each 11½ × 11½ inches (29.2 × 29.2 cm)
2 strips, each 3½ × 39¼ inches (8.9 × 99.7 cm)

Mauve fabric: 2 strips, each 1½ × 35½ inches (3.8 × 90.2 cm)
2 strips, each 1½ × 44¾ inches (3.8 × 113.7 cm)

Navy fabric: 2 strips, each 2 × 46¾ inches (5.1 × 118.7 cm)

Flannel: 2 pieces, cut selvage to selvage at the midpoint of the entire yardage

Batting: 1 piece, 45 × 58 inches (114.3 × 147.3 cm)

USE ¼-INCH (6 MM) SEAMS THROUGHOUT

1 Sew the squares into rows, right sides together, according to the design shown in the photo. Press the seams to the darker side. Then sew the rows to one another, right sides together. Next, sew on the borders, all with right sides together, in this order: the longer mauve strips on the sides; the remaining mauve strips on the top and bottom; the navy strips on the sides; and finally the olive borders on the top and bottom. Press the completed top. Sew the two pieces of flannel together along their longer edges, right sides together. Press the seam open. Now sandwich the layers: flannel on the bottom, right side down, and then center the batting on the flannel. Now add the top, right side up, also

centered. Smooth the wrinkles and baste. You will have more flannel than you need; for ease of handling, trim it so that you have an excess of only 3 inches (7.6 cm) all the way around—*after* basting.

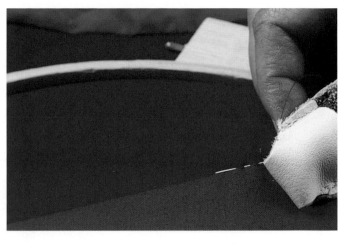

2 Measure and cut a 7⅜-inch (18.7 cm) square paper or cardboard template. Center the paper template on a middle quilt square. Carefully place masking tape around the perimeter of the template, as shown. Remove the template, and quilt along the inside of the square of tape.

4 Quilt-in-the-ditch around each block. Continue until you have quilted the entire top. Mark straight lines on the borders with masking tape, and quilt. Remove the basting thread and tape when you finish. Trim along all four sides of the quilt to align the three layers. To apply bias tape, first sew the two lengths of tape together in a ¼-inch (6 mm) seam. Then, fold over the raw end of the bias tape ½ inch (1.3 cm) and pin to the quilt, right sides together. Stitch, overlapping at the end. Fold the tape over to the back of the quilt, and blindstitch down by hand; be careful not to catch the quilt top with your stitches.

3 Use the roll of masking tape as the other template. Place it in the center of the quilted square, and trace along the inside with a fabric marking pencil. Quilt along these markings. Continue in this manner to finish quilting inside the squares.

Mrs. Mondrian's Potholder

Let modern art assume a traditional use in your kitchen. This project uses a different application of strip piecing, based on the time-honored Log Cabin square; the preparation is super fast and simple with a rotary cutter.

USE ¹/₄-INCH (6 MM) SEAMS THROUGHOUT

YOU WILL NEED

(for three potholders)

Essentials kit

½ yard (.5 m) of print fabric

1 package of craft-size batting

½ yard (.5 m) of denim

½ yard (.5 m) of unbleached muslin

¼ yard (.23 m) of each: pink, red, brown, dark green, medium green, and yellow print fabric

¼ yard (.23 m) of yellow fabric

Rotary cutter

Rotary mat and ruler

¼-inch (6 mm) quilter's masking tape

Red quilting thread

1 package of yellow wide, single-fold bias tape

1 metal D-ring

MEASURE AND CUT FOR THE POTHOLDER

Print fabric: 1 square, 10 × 10 inches (25.4 × 25.4 cm)

Batting: 1 square, 9½ × 9½ inches (24.1 × 24.1 cm)

Denim: 2 squares, each 9½ × 9½ inches (24.1 × 24.1 cm)

Muslin: 1 square, 12 × 12 inches (30.5 × 30.5 cm)

MEASURE AND CUT FOR THE PIECED TOP

(see figure 1)

Pink fabric (no. 1): 1 square, 1 × 1 inch (2.5 × 2.5 cm)

Red fabric (nos. 2 and 3): 1 strip, 1 × 4 inches (2.5 × 10.2 cm)

Brown fabric (nos. 4 and 5): 1 strip, 1 × 5 inches (2.5 × 12.7 cm)

Dark green fabric (nos. 6 and 7): 1 strip, 1 × 6 inches (2.5 × 15.2 cm)

Medium green fabric (nos. 8 and 9): 1 strip, 1 × 8 inches (2.5 × 20.3 cm)

Yellow print fabric (nos. 10 and 11): 1 strip, 2 × 10 inches (5.1 × 25.4 cm)

Yellow fabric (nos. 12 and 13): 1 strip, 3½ × 15 inches (8.9 × 38.1 cm)

Yellow fabric (nos. 14, 15, 16, and 17): 4 strips, each 1 × 10 inches (2.5 × 25.4 cm)

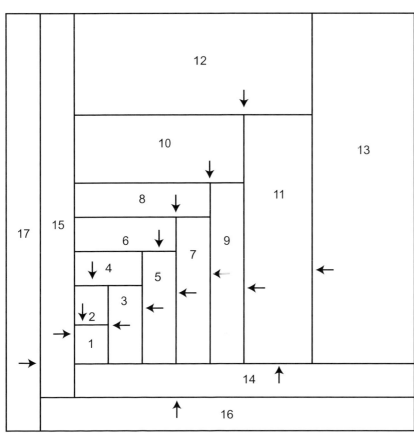

FIGURE 1. Potholder Piecing Sequence.

1 Align the pink square about 3 inches (7.6 cm) from the lower left-hand corner of the muslin square, right side up. Place the dark red strip on the pink square, right sides together, aligning the top, bottom, and left sides. (You will have excess fabric on the right side.) Stitch along the top.

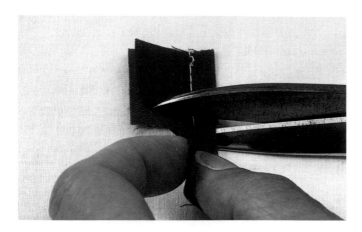

2 Trim off the excess fabric even with the pink square, as shown in the photo above. Open and press. Now lay the remaining red strip over pieces 1 and 2, align the right edges, and stitch along the right side. Open and press. Continue sewing in this fashion, following the order shown in figure 1; the arrows will indicate which edge to stitch first. (Note that each strip will be cut and the remainder used for the second strip in that color, as in steps 1 and 2, *except* for strips 14 through 17.) When you finish, measure to be sure that your piece is square. If it isn't, trim to a square.

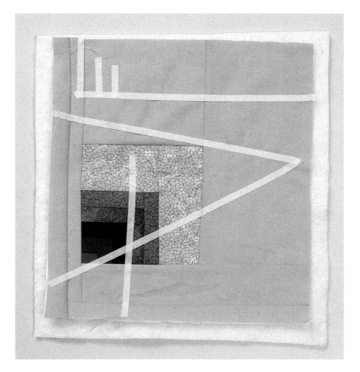

3 Use the masking tape to make random geometric shapes, as shown. Pin or baste the batting square to the back of the strip-pieced square. Quilt along both sides of the tape, removing it when you are finished.

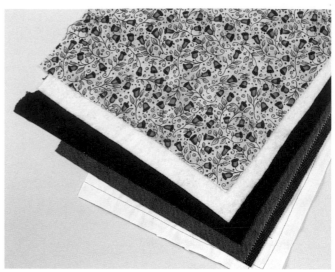

4 Pin together the quilted square (right side down), two denim squares, and backing print square (right side up). (If you prefer extra insulation, add another square of batting, as shown.) Open the bias tape, fold over the raw end ½ inch (1.3 cm), and pin to all four sides, placing the right side of the bias tape against the right side of the front. Stitch the bias tape to the potholder, overlapping the ends. Fold the tape over and blindstitch in place on the back, mitering at the corners. Attach the D-ring with needle and thread.

Variation: Once you have perfected this technique, you can vary it to create your own designs. For example, alter this piecing design to create a companion potholder to this project. You can also increase the dimensions of the potholder and make a complementary hot pad; because of the small amounts of fabric needed for this project, you will have enough left over to create both of these accompanying pieces.

Greeting Cards

Delight your friends with these charming cards, and make use of your fabric scraps, too.
You can use this foundation piecing method to create cards for any occasion.

YOU WILL NEED

(for one card)

Essentials kit	Craft knife
1 sheet of blank card stock, 11 × 17 inches (27.9 × 43.2 cm) from print shop or office supply store	Pattern (figure 1)
Large paper cutter—at the print shop	¼ yard (.23 m) of muslin
Metal-edged ruler	Black extra-fine-point permanent marking pen
Pencil	Scraps of fabric
Wooden pottery rib (or similar tool)	¾-inch (1.9 cm) masking tape
White plastic or vinyl eraser	Glue
Cardboard	Envelope

Card stock: 1 piece, 6 × 14 inches (15.2 × 35.6 cm); use the large paper cutter where you purchase the card stock

Scraps of fabric: Approximately 3 × 3 inches (7.6 × 7.6 cm)

Muslin: 1 square, 3½ × 3½ inches (8.9 × 8.9 cm)

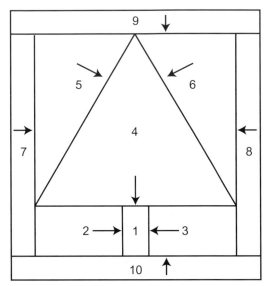

FIGURE 1. Card Piecing Pattern.

2 Open the paper, making sure the short section is at your left. Measure and mark the center of the middle section on the inside of the card. Now, measure and mark a 2½ × 2½-inch (6.4 × 6.4 cm) window, placing it 1 inch (2.5 cm) below the top of the paper and centered with the previous mark. Place the cardboard underneath the paper to protect your work surface, and cut along the lines with the craft knife, using the ruler as a guide.

1 Measure and lightly mark with pencil the length of the paper at 4½ inches (11.4 cm) and 9¼ inches (23.5 cm). Fold at each mark and crease with the rib. Erase the marks.

USE ¼-INCH (6 MM) SEAMS THROUGHOUT

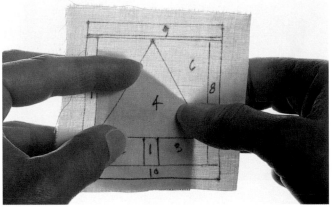

3 Trace the pattern from figure 1 onto the muslin, using the permanent marker. Press the fabric scraps before you begin sewing (and then finger press as you go). Now you are ready to do the foundation piecing (see page 168). Place the wrong side of your fabric against the unmarked side of the muslin; the marked side of the muslin will be at the back of the finished block. Hold the foundation and fabric up to a light source to help you see the marked lines, as shown. Make sure your fabric covers the shape with at least a ¼-inch (6 mm) seam allowance extending all the way around. Pin piece 1 in place.

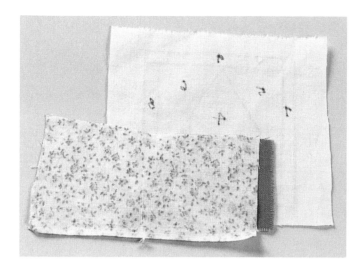

4 Place piece 2 on piece 1, right sides together. Working from the marked back (holding the muslin so that the black lines and numbers are facing you), stitch along the marked line between numbers 1 and 2, sewing through both layers of fabric and the muslin foundation. Begin and end your sewing a few stitches beyond the end of the line.

5 Trim the seam allowance to approximately ¼ inch (6 mm) as you go, being careful not to cut the foundation fabric; you will need to fold the pieces out of the way as you trim, as shown. Open piece 2 right side out and finger press. Add the remaining pieces in numerical order according to the pattern, right sides facing, finger pressing and trimming seams as you go.

Tip: Turn the sewing machine wheel by hand to carefully stitch the quilted picture to the card.

6 To "quilt" the finished picture, use contrasting color thread and a large stitch on your sewing machine. Stitch around the design. Finally, stabilize your piece by stitching all around the block, ⅛ to ¼ inch (3 to 6 mm) away from its border. Place the fabric picture face down, and put a piece of masking tape on the top and bottom.

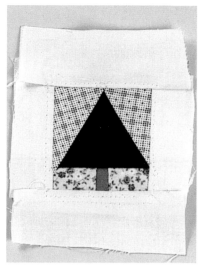

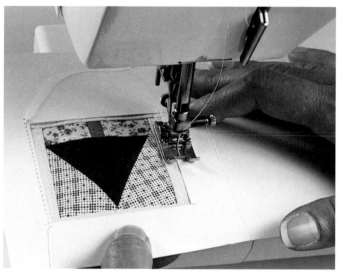

7 Turn the pieced picture face up. Place the card stock, right side up, over the picture, centering it in the window. Press down on the card to affix the tape. Place it under the sewing machine foot, right side up, being careful that the machine foot doesn't mar the card stock. Use the window as a guide, and slowly stitch along the sides of the window with a large stitch, as shown. Remove the masking tape before you stitch along the top and bottom of the window. Glue the flap shut; insert the card into an envelope when needed.

Variation: Add another decorative touch by stitching the front flap closed instead of gluing it down. You could use a fabric with a preprinted image for your picture, like a frog, sun, moon, etc.

Embroidered Window Valance

Add an elegant touch to your window with this valance, constructed of brushed denim in rich colors. You will enjoy the lush texture of this fabric; it is the perfect backdrop for quilting and embroidery.

YOU WILL NEED

Essentials kit

¼ yard (.23 m) of maroon brushed denim fabric

¼ yard (.23 m) of dark green brushed denim fabric

¼ yard (.23 m) of medium green brushed denim fabric

⅔ yard (.6 m) of black fabric

Fabric marking pencil

1 skein each of cream, blue, light brown, moss green, gold, and silver-gray embroidery floss

Embroidery needle*

Embroidery hoop (optional)

1 package of crib-size batting

Black quilting thread

Quilting hoop (optional)

Wooden dowel (to fit valance)

*See embroidery stitches on page 228.

MEASURE AND CUT

Maroon fabric: 4 squares, each 5⅞ × 5⅞ inches (14.9 × 14.9 cm)

Dark green fabric: 4 squares, each 5⅞ × 5⅞ inches (14.9 × 14.9 cm)

Medium green fabric: 2 strips, each 3 × 40½ inches (7.6 × 102.9 cm)

Black fabric: 1 piece, 10½ × 40½ inches (26.7 × 102.9 cm)
1 strip, 3 × 40 inches (7.6 × 101.6 cm)

Batting: 1 rectangle, 12 × 43 inches (30.5 × 109.2 cm)

USE ¼-INCH (6 MM) SEAMS THROUGHOUT

1 Cut the maroon and dark green squares on the diagonal, yielding eight triangles of each color. Match each maroon triangle with a green triangle, being sure to place the softer, brushed right sides together. Sew the pairs of triangles together along the diagonal to make eight two-color squares. Press the squares open, with the seams to the darker side. Sew the squares together to form a row. Placing the right sides together, sew a medium green strip to each long edge of the row. Press the seams outward; press the top.

2 Using the fabric marking pencil, draw a freehand design onto the top; embroider along your design, using only two strands of floss. (You can use an embroidery hoop if desired, but the denim has so much body that you may not need one.) Remove the marks when finished. Note the gradation of colors used in the embroidery, as shown in the photo.

Tips: This valance measures 38½ inches (97.8 cm) from end to end. For a different size, add borders to lengthen or remove some squares to shorten. (If you haven't embroidered for a while, you may want to practice on scrap fabric before working on the finished valance.)

Variation: For a more rustic look, use a branch from the woods to hang this valance.

3 To sandwich the valance: Place the batting on a work surface and smooth; then place the black piece of backing on top, centered, with its right side up. Place the pieced top on the backing, right side down, aligning the edges of both fabrics. Pin well around the edges. Stitch with the fabric side up, being sure to catch all three layers. Leave a 6-inch (15.2 cm) gap at one short end for turning the valance right side out. Carefully trim the batting, as shown above.

4 Trim the corners. Turn the valance right side out. Fold the edges of the gap inward, and blindstitch closed. Quilt around the inside of each triangle and along the edge of each long border. (Use a quilting hoop if desired.) With your machine, topstitch around the valance, ⅛ inch (3 mm) from the edge, as shown. Make a hanging sleeve (see page 167) from the black fabric strip, and attach using a blindstitch. Insert a wooden dowel through the sleeve to hang.

Evening Star Place Mat

Elongated pieces are a slight challenge, but the effect is worth the effort. To achieve the best results, follow the instructions closely. Use an assortment of off-white fabrics to create this simple ornamentation for your table; it's beautiful, functional, and patterned after the traditional evening star motif.

YOU WILL NEED
(for four place mats)

Essentials kit	Fine-point pen or pencil
¼ yard (.23 m) of off-white gingham fabric	1 sheet of quilter's template plastic
⅓ yard (.3 m) of green fabric	¾-inch (1.9 cm) masking tape
¾ yard (.7 m) of off-white print fabric	Quilting hoop
1 yard (.9 m) of off-white print fabric (for the back)	Off-white quilting thread
1 package of craft-size batting	Quilting pattern (page 221)
Templates (page 226)	

Gingham fabric: 1 rectangle, 4 × 5½ inches (10.2 × 14 cm)

Green fabric: 4 triangles from template A
4 triangles from template B

Off-white print fabric: 4 triangles from template A
4 triangles from template B
4 rectangles, each 4 × 5½ inches (10.2 × 14 cm)
2 strips, each 2 × 11 inches (5.1 × 27.9 cm)
2 strips, each 2 × 18½ inches (5.1 × 47 cm)

Off-white print fabric (for the back): 1 rectangle, 14 × 18½ inches (35.6 × 47 cm)

Batting: 1 rectangle, 14 × 18½ inches (35.6 × 47 cm)

2 Placing the right sides together, pin all the green A pieces to the off-white B pieces, and pin all the off-white A pieces to all of the green B pieces. *Note that the A and B pieces will be offset and should not meet exactly; when pinning, make sure that the B piece extends ¼ inch (6 mm), as in the photo.* This offset creates the seam allowance that will allow the four triangles to meet to form a rectangle. Stitch all the pieces together and press the seam allowances to the darker side.

1 Trace template patterns A and B onto the quilter's template plastic and cut out on the line. Next, place these templates onto the fabric, align the arrow on the template with the straight grain of the fabric, and cut according to the list above. Trace the templates onto the fabric carefully, and then cut on the marked lines *precisely.*

3 Next, you will make rectangles by sewing together the bicolored triangles. To make sure you will have the proper seam to allow the triangles to form a rectangle, place the bicolored triangles together (right sides facing each other), and hold them up to a light source. At the point where the two diagonal seams meet, there should be a ¼-inch (6 mm) seam allowance, as shown in the photo. Stitch all the triangles together to form four rectangles.

USE ¼-INCH (6 MM) SEAMS THROUGHOUT

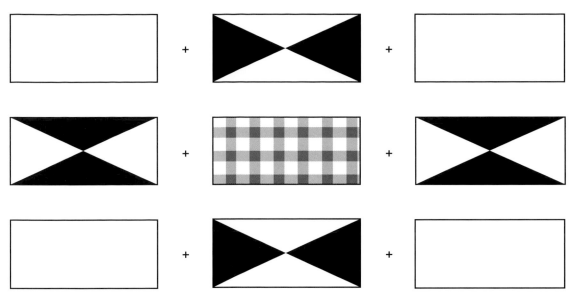

FIGURE 1

4 Piece the rows as illustrated in figure 1, adding the off-white print rectangles. Now, line up the seams and sew the rows to one another; press. Sew the shorter off-white strips on the sides for borders, and press. Then stitch the remaining strips onto the top and the bottom, backstitching at the beginning and end of each border. Press the top of the place mat.

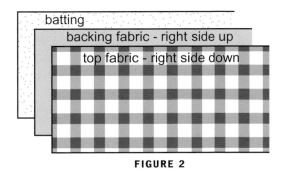

FIGURE 2

5 Sandwich the layers and pin together: batting at the bottom, then the back, right side up; and last the top, right side down. (See figure 2.) Sew together, leaving a gap at one end. Trim the corners and trim the batting close to the seam line. Turn right side out and gently push the corners out to a point. Turn the unfinished raw edges inward and blindstitch the gap closed.

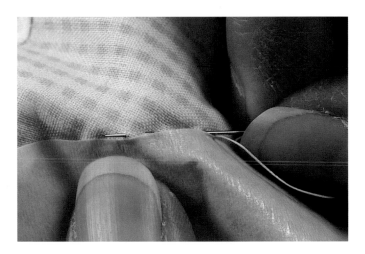

6 Baste. Then mark the top for quilting with the masking tape, finding the midpoint on each side of the center rectangle; form a central diamond here. (See the quilting pattern on page 221 for reference.) Extend the lines through the border, but do not quilt through the green fabric. Put your place mat into a hoop and quilt, working from the center out. Outline quilt around every green piece, extending into the border. Now, quilt around the entire place mat, 1/4 inch (6 mm) from the outer edge. Remove the tape and basting.

Tip: Remember—you have enough fabric left for three more place mats!

African Women Wall Hanging

Your quilting skills and your imagination can enhance a piece of unique fabric. Here, a design featuring African women carrying gourd vessels is enhanced with quilting and beads. There are many pictorial fabrics available; choose one that captures your fancy and embellish it as your heart desires.

Print fabric: 1 rectangle, $10\frac{3}{4} \times 18$ inches (27.3×45.7 cm)
1 rectangle, $9\frac{1}{2} \times 18$ inches (24.1×45.7 cm)

Maroon fabric: 1 rectangle, $6\frac{3}{4} \times 18$ inches (17.1×45.7 cm)
1 strip, $2\frac{5}{8} \times 18$ inches (6.7×45.7 cm)

Green fabric: 1 rectangle, $7\frac{1}{2} \times 18$ inches (19×45.7 cm)
1 strip, 2×18 inches (5.1×45.7 cm)
1 strip, 3×38 inches (7.6×96.5 cm)

Black fabric: 1 rectangle, 19 inches $\times$ 37 inches (48.3×94 cm)

Batting: 1 rectangle, approximately 21×40 inches
(53.3×101.6 cm)

2 With the marking pen or pencil, draw a freehand quilting design on all the solid-colored fabric. Sew the wooden beads on to complement these designs. Now sandwich the layers: black fabric on the bottom, right side down; batting in the center; then the multicolored panel on top, right side up. Baste. Place the hanging into the quilting hoop (careful of your beads!). Quilt along the design of the print fabric in several places on each panel to secure the batting; quilt the solid panels.

1 Sew the 18-inch-wide (45.7 cm) fabric pieces together in the following order, from left to right: wide maroon, wide print, narrow green, narrow maroon, narrow print, and wide green. Press the seams to one side. (Be sure to do it now, because you can't press after the beads have been sewn on.) With quilting thread and needle, add the colored beads to the print fabric, making all the knots on the back of the fabric.

3 Remove all marks and basting thread. Trim the batting and backing fabrics to the size of the top, if necessary. Sew the bias tape around the raw edges of the front of the wall hanging, right sides together; fold over and blindstitch on the back. Make a hanging sleeve (see page 167) from the remaining strip of green fabric and attach, as shown. Insert the dowel or rod through the sleeve.

Crazy-Quilt Evening Bag

This bag is a jewel of an accessory for a simple cocktail dress, combining sumptuous fabrics with romantic embroidery. It may use crazy-quilt construction, but the effect is dazzling—definitely not crazy....

YOU WILL NEED

Essentials kit

Templates (page 225)

⅛ yard (.1 m) of unbleached muslin

Permanent marker

Scraps of silk, satin, and velvet fabrics

Skeins of embroidery floss in various colors

Embroidery hoop

Embroidery needle*

¼ yard (.23 m) of pink silk

¼ yard (.23 m) of black velvet

1 package of craft-size batting

1 yard (.9 m) of black medium cord

6 inches (15.2 cm) of black thin cord

Decorative button

*See embroidery stitches on page 228.

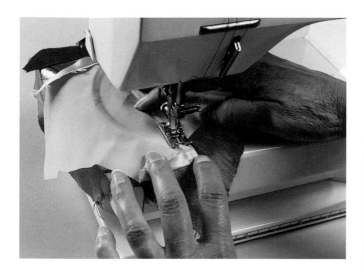

1 Transfer the templates onto paper, enlarge 200 percent, and cut them out. Use the pocket template to cut one piece from the muslin. Sew the silk, satin, and velvet scraps to the muslin in random fashion, using crazy-quilt piecing (see page 167). Begin with one scrap right side up. Then add the second scrap, right side down on the first scrap, and stitch along one edge through all layers. Open and press. Continue in this fashion, as shown above, until the entire piece of muslin is covered. Trim the sewn scraps even with the muslin edge. Staystitch around the pocket a scant $\frac{1}{8}$ inch (3 mm) from the edge.

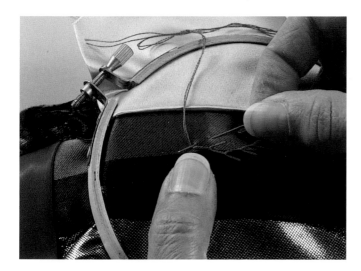

2 Embellish the pocket with embroidery, but use only two strands of the embroidery floss to fit the small scale of this project. (See page 228 for embroidery stitches.)

USE $\frac{1}{4}$-INCH (6 MM) SEAMS THROUGHOUT

3 Next, cut one pocket from the pink fabric. Pin the pink lining to the completed crazy-quilt pocket, right sides together. Stitch across the top only. Turn the pocket right side out and press. As before, staystitch the raw edges together with a scant $\frac{1}{8}$-inch (3 mm) seam.

4 Using the templates, cut one front and one back from the black velvet. Repeat for the batting. Baste the batting pieces to the back of each velvet piece. Lay the velvet/batting back piece on your work surface, velvet side up. Now place the embroidered pocket on the back piece, embroidered side down, aligning the straight bottom edges. Place the velvet/batting front piece on top, velvet side down. Align the bottom edges. (Note that the curved top of the bag is pictured at the bottom of this photo.)

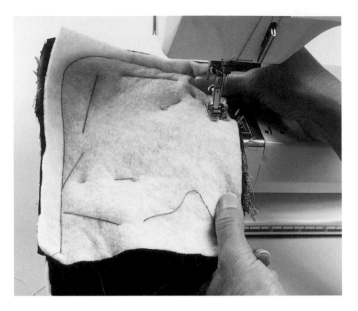

5 Pin; stitch the sides and the bottom, through all layers. Turn right side out.

7 Cut the medium black cord to the desired length for a shoulder bag. Tack each end between the lining and the velvet bag at the side seams, as shown. Turn the raw edges of the black velvet flap and the lining flap under about ⅛ inch (3 mm). Pin together and hand stitch to finish the top. Cut the thin black cord to the desired length, and make a loop by sewing the two ends together in the center of the underside of the flap. Sew the decorative button onto the center of the front pocket.

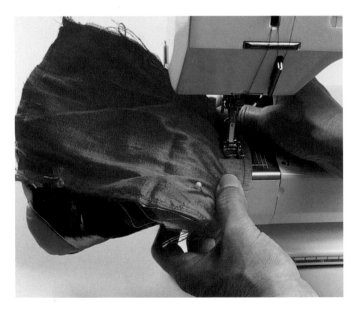

6 Using the templates, cut the front and back pieces from lining fabric. Placing right sides together, pin and sew. Leave the lining wrong side out, and stitch the front top edge of the lining to the front top edge of the velvet bag, right sides together. Push the lining into the velvet bag.

WINE BOTTLE CARRIER (WOVEN DIAMONDS), PAGE 179

DELICATES TRAVEL POUCH, PAGE 172

WINE BOTTLE CARRIER (VINE AND GRAPES), PAGE 179

TANGY TABLE RUNNER, PAGE 189

EVENING STAR PLACE MAT, PAGE 211

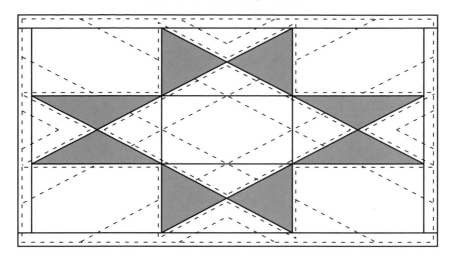

SILK PILLBOX HAT, PAGE 174

TEMPLATES

CELESTIAL POTPOURRI BAGS, PAGE 170

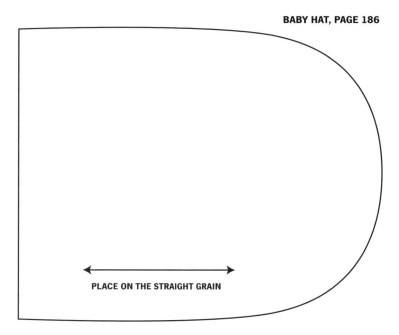

PLACE ON THE STRAIGHT GRAIN

EAR FLAPS

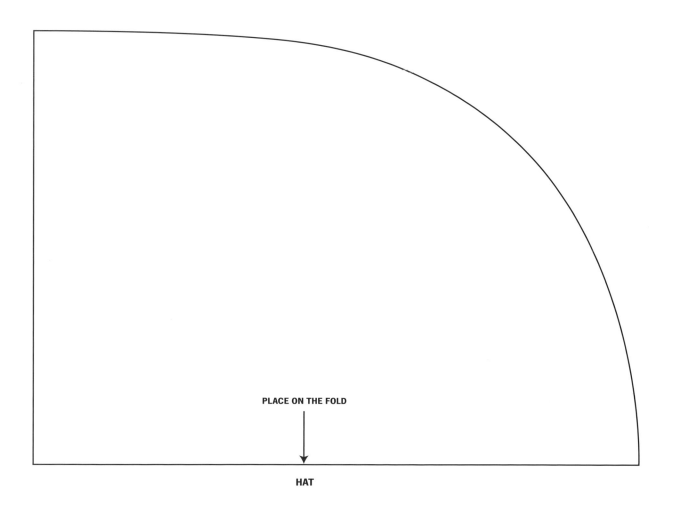

PLACE ON THE FOLD

HAT

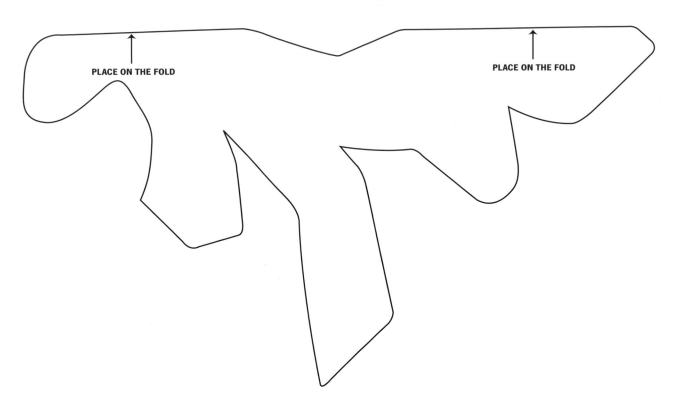

PLACE ON THE FOLD

PLACE ON THE FOLD

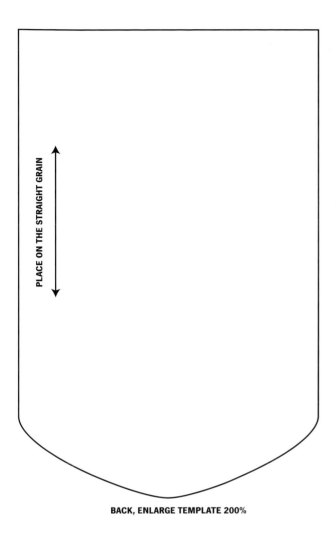

PLACE ON THE STRAIGHT GRAIN

BACK, ENLARGE TEMPLATE 200%

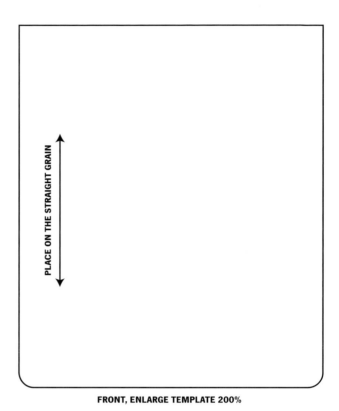

PLACE ON THE STRAIGHT GRAIN

FRONT, ENLARGE TEMPLATE 200%

PLACE ON THE STRAIGHT GRAIN

POCKET, ENLARGE TEMPLATE 200%

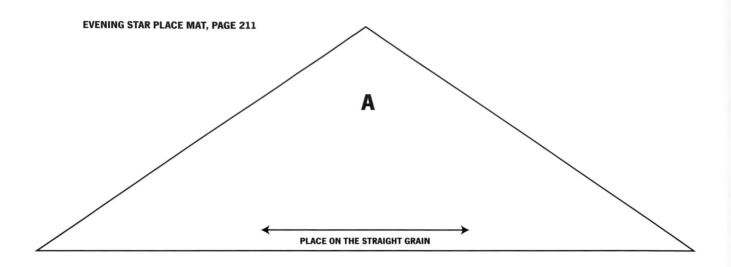

A

PLACE ON THE STRAIGHT GRAIN

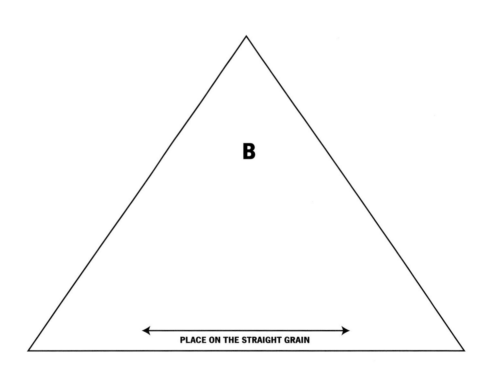

B

PLACE ON THE STRAIGHT GRAIN

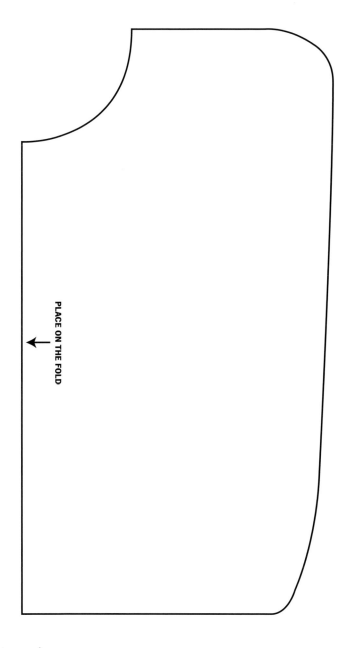

PLACE ON THE FOLD

Embroidery Stitches

SHEAVES

FEATHER STITCH

CHAIN STITCH

SPLIT STITCH

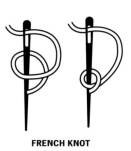

FRENCH KNOT

**DETACHED CHAIN STITCH
(LAZY DAISY)**

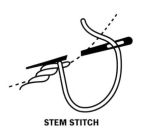

STEM STITCH

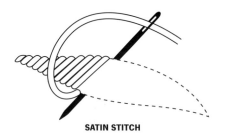

SATIN STITCH

Macrame

JIM GENTRY

INTRODUCTION

Macrame: Lace-like webbing made by knotting cord, yarn, or other materials. Why knot? Well, we always have. We teach our children to tie their shoes, we anchor our tents on overnight camping trips, we tie our dinghies to the dock, and we lovingly tie fanciful ribbon bows on gift packages. We use knots every day, though today we're more likely to use a wire core twist-tie or an elastic bungee cord instead of knotted cord. The act of knotting—whether practical or artistic—has an appeal that, once discovered, can become a lifelong pleasure.

Knotting as a practical skill is likely as old as man. Vines, stripped bark, grasses, and animal sinew were used in a variety of ways in early cultures. Using knotted adornments defined early cultures, and reflected the development of intelligence, skill, and the early structures of the civilization.

Historic artifacts illustrate man's creative effort through the ages. Elaborately knotted military regalia in both European and Asian cultures, reflected an interest in creating beauty and symbolizing power through texture, pattern, and color. We find major examples of the creative use of knotting (as a popular form of women's needlework) in the Victorian era, due to the increased varieties of ready-made materials and the rise of leisure time. Seafaring men on nineteenth century sailing ships used the materials at hand (and the idle hours of life at sea) to knot complex works for loved ones at home.

As a young boy growing up on a farm I remember large hanks of golden-colored sisal string hanging in the barn. The string had a practical use: it held together harvested bales of hay. When the strings were removed from the bales to feed the livestock, the sisal was saved for future use. It was secured in an orderly fashion to a wooden beam with a lark's head knot (though I didn't know what the knot was called at the time). I used this abundant supply of sisal to pull toys, secure firewood to a small red wagon, and create a precarious barn loft swing secured with simple overhand knots. It was a fiber that I became intimately familiar with in all its uses. In graduate school, I had the good fortune to study with professors who allowed me to explore the uses of fiber other than in the weaving studio. The art of macrame was undergoing a revival in the twentieth century. It was everywhere: in craft books, art exhibitions, and in items from everyday popular culture. I was roped in by knotting, so to speak.

During a leave of absence from teaching art in the public school system, a visual arts residency provided me with the opportunity to pursue the craft of knotting on a full-time basis. I designed and sold knotted projects, both simple and complex—belts, bands, neckpieces, bags, and sculptural forms—created using the inherent qualities of fiber and how it may be shaped through knotting.

Why knot, you ask? Because knotting materials appeal to the senses—the textures delight our touch and the colors seduce the eye. The art of knotting is portable and requires few tools, if any, aside from the human hand. In a world of mass-produced goods, the act of creating objects with simple materials—for practical use or artistic pleasure—has not lost its appeal. That's why knot.

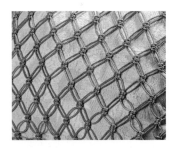

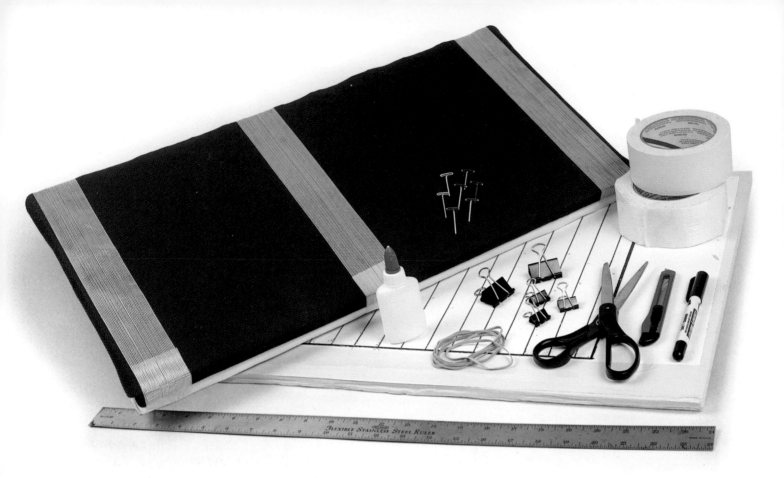

MACRAME BASICS

Knotting materials, a cutting tool, a knotting board, and your hands are basically all you need to create a project with macrame. Any additional tools you might need for specific projects are inexpensive and easy to acquire. In fact, you probably have many of them on hand already: scissors, a ruler or tape measure, masking or duct tape, sewing needles, a box cutter or craft knife, T-pins, paper clamps, and clear-drying waterproof glue.

CREATING A KNOTTING BOARD

A covered fiber board is an essential working surface for most macrame projects. It's a portable and flat surface that's easy to work on. In addition, you can easily pin cords to its porous surface. A single-layer board covered with fabric will work for many projects. If you anticipate several macrame projects in your future, you may want to create a more versatile two-panel board, covered with contrasting fabrics (black and white are good choices). The double thickness of the board makes it sturdier, and you can work on the side that provides the best contrast for the cords in your project.

YOU WILL NEED
Fiberboard ceiling panel (a panel for modular ceilings), measuring 24 × 48 inches (61 × 122 cm)*
2 lengths of fabric in contrasting colors, each measuring approximately 16 × 24 inches (40.6 × 60.9 cm)
Ruler
Craft knife or box cutter
Stapler and staples
Sturdy tape (fiber-reinforced strapping tape, duct tape, or masking tape), at least 2 inches (5 cm) wide
* You'll find this panel at most home improvement stores in the ceiling tile section.

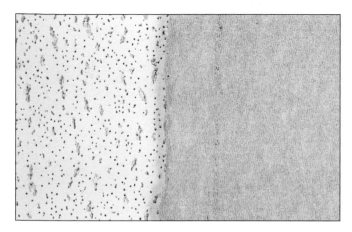

1 Examine your panel. You'll see that it has two different-looking sides. This is important. You'll want to work on the less porous side when you knot: it's smoother and will hold pins better than the rough-textured side.

2 Measure and mark your panel to create two rectangles. Each rectangle should measure 12 × 18 inches (30.5 × 45.7 cm). Cut the panel with a craft knife or box cutter.

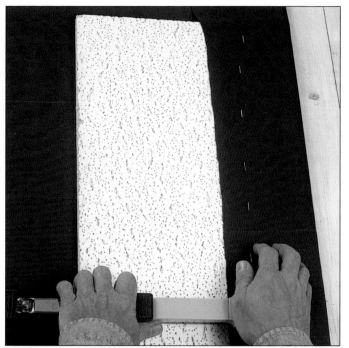

3 Spread one length of fabric on a flat, smooth work surface. Center a panel—smooth side down—on one color of fabric. Fold one long fabric edge onto the back of the fiber board. Staple the edge of the fabric to the board. Cover the raw edge of the fabric with a long strip of duct or masking tape. Pull on the opposite edge of fabric to tighten the fabric on the front. Staple the fabric to the board. Tape the edge if you wish. Repeat this process with the fabric edges at each end. Create a second panel in the same way using the second color of fabric.

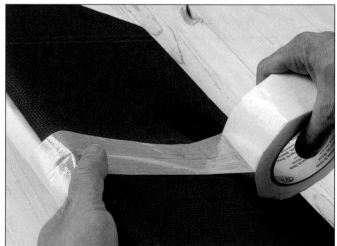

4 Hold the two fabric-covered panels back to back. Wrap a strip of tape around the center of both boards. Then wrap tape at each end around the boards.

KNOTTING MATERIALS

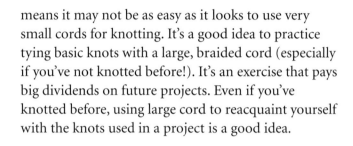

There's a vast array of knotting materials of all colors and sizes available in craft stores, needlework shops, discount stores, and even home improvement centers. A choice between synthetic versus natural materials is a personal choice or may be dictated by the specific project.

Rayon, nylon, polypropylene, and even plastic, are favored synthetic fibers, to name just a few. Cotton, wool, silk, linen, sisal, and blends are readily available in a wide range of colors and textures. But don't limit yourself to what you would normally define as fiber. Soft, pliable, and brightly-colored wire can be found in craft stores. Precious metal wires in silver and gold are available for the truly adventurous knotter.

When you choose threads or cords for a project, keep in mind how the piece is going to be used. Soft fibers like wool and silk may lose knotting definition, and may not be very strong. The lovely and soft turquoise-colored wool you covet may not be the most practical choice for a sturdy shopping bag. Instead, look for a brightly colored sisal or nylon. A beaded, silk pet leash might appeal to Fifi's sense of style, but a more durable, waterproof nylon cord is a better choice. But why make a hatband with rugged leather lacing if you have your heart set on silk? A silk hatband won't receive much wear and tear, so choose what your heart desires.

In short: choose a sturdy fiber if you expect lots of wear and tear; choose what you will if you foresee a gentle life for the item.

It's essential to note that the smaller the cord, the greater the challenge of the project. That doesn't mean it can't be done; it just means it may not be as easy as it looks to use very small cords for knotting. It's a good idea to practice tying basic knots with a large, braided cord (especially if you've not knotted before!). It's an exercise that pays big dividends on future projects. Even if you've knotted before, using large cord to reacquaint yourself with the knots used in a project is a good idea.

EMBELLISHMENTS AND HARDWARE

Beads are an integral part of many designs. They're readily available in a bewildering array of sizes, shapes, and materials. It's always a good idea to purchase the knotting material for your project before you choose beads and findings. Though you can enlarge the holes in beads to some extent, it's easier to select beads that already fit the threads you're using in a project. Read through the knotting directions to determine how many strands need to fit through a bead, then take a sample of your strands to the bead store. Following this simple hint will make your project a pleasure, rather than a trial, to work on.

O-rings and swivel snap-hooks are useful for anchoring cords for projects such as the water bottle tote (page 282) and the pet leash (page 250). Wooden or bamboo rings, twigs or dowels also may be used for anchor bars. But don't limit yourself! It's great fun to use found objects or unexpected anchors in your knotting designs.

KNOTTING TERMS AND DEFINITIONS

Macrame, like knitting, crochet, tatting, and weaving, is a system of creating a fiber structure. Unlike other methods, which depend upon looping or threads running over and under each other, macrame creates a structure with secured knots—that is, tying knots with selected cords, regrouping cords as needed, and tying more knots.

A thread is a cord is a strand is a...

Threads, cords, strands, ropes. They all mean the same in macrame instructions: a length of fiber. Writers like to use different terms to pep up their prose. In one project instruction, you may be told to regroup the strands and tie double half hitches with the cords. Knot with what you have!

Abbreviations

You'll find abbreviations in every set of instructions for crochet, knitting, and other fiber projects. These abbreviations make reading the instructions easier and less repetitive and save time and valuable space. In the instructions for the projects in this book you may read "tie a row of reverse double half hitches (RDHHs)." The next time this knot is used in the instructions you will read "tie a row of RDHHs."

Active and Inactive Threads

Active threads are being worked, *inactive* threads are those not being used to tie knots. In macrame, threads are continually changing their function; inactive threads may become active threads (and vice versa) in the very next step of a design. If directions tell you to "make these threads inactive," it means to not use the threads in that step.

Alternating and Regrouping

For most projects, cords will be separated into and worked in groups. A group of four is most commonly used, but groups of two, three, or any other number may be used. Most, but not all, designs are created using a total number of cords divisible by four.

Regrouping cords is simply a process of joining a specified number of cords from two adjacent groups. Each project will describe how cords are to be regrouped in each step as needed.

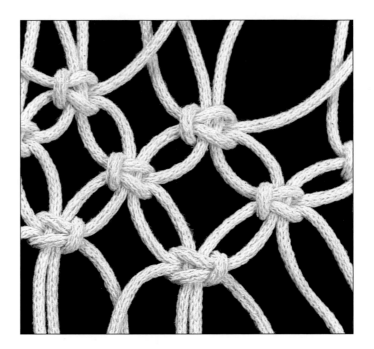

The word *alternating* is frequently used in macrame design language. For example: "Tie five rows of alternating square knots, using 16 total strands." This means that the first row will have four single square knots. You will regroup the cords and tie a second row of three square knots. The cords at each end of the row will be inactive. Regroup again and tie a row of square knots.

The place mat (page 248) and market bag (page 286) projects use such alternating structures as an integral part of their designs.

Anchoring Cords

To tie cords, they must be taut or offer some resistance to the act of tying. This is achieved by attaching or anchoring the cords in some fashion, which also helps to keep the threads in order. Each project will specify how the cords should be mounted.

A *slip-loop knot* (page 239) is used when threads are small and may be hard to identify as separate strands. This knot is easy to remove: you simply pull one end of the loop and the knot is removed. The slip-loop knot is a variation of the overhand knot.

The *overhand knot* (page 238) is used when cords are heavy and individual strands are easy to see. If you're working from one end, the knot may remain for the duration of the work or may be removed at any point after the work is underway (if its not an integral part of the design). In projects worked from the midpoint, the knot must be removed before completing the design in the opposite direction.

A *lark's head knot* (page 238) is used when there is a fixed anchor for the knotting cords. An O-ring, buckle, snap-hook, or separate length of cord are all fixed anchors. These fixed anchors are usually an integral part of the project design.

Cord Length

Generally if cords are no longer than 3 yards (2.7 m), they will be fairly easy to work with, and time will be saved by leaving them loose. The key to working with long cords is to have an uncluttered and clear, open work area. In addition, when each knot is begun, keep the loop open for the cord you are pulling through to form the knot.

Some knotters wind long cords into bundles which are often referred to as "butterflies." The bundles may be secured with rubber bands, tied with a short cord, or held with paper clamps. But other knotters find this method cumbersome. As you work, you will discover which you prefer—using bundles, or leaving the cords free.

Dimensions of Finished Projects

Remember that all dimensions for finished projects are approximate. The dimensions are based on the specific materials used and how tightly (or loosely) the project is knotted. No two knotters knot with the same tension. But don't worry, the cord lengths in each project are sized generously to compensate for this effect.

Knotting and Knot-Bearing Strands

Cords have two primary functions in macrame: *knotting* and *knot-bearing*. A knot-bearing strand is usually held taut, and the knotting strand is moved around the taut strand. It should be noted that cords change functions. A knot-bearing strand in one step may become a knotting strand in the next step.

Level of Difficulty

Four different elements determine the level of difficulty for a specific project. These elements are: the size of thread used, the number of knots used, the number of design changes in the project, and the scale of the project.

The projects in this section are divided into three levels of difficulty: easy, somewhat difficult, and moderately difficult. Start with an easy project if macrame is a new craft for you. The projects found on pages 244 through 262 are designed for beginners.

If you're an old hand at macrame or have knotted some of the easy projects in this book, look for more challenging projects on pages 265 through 286. The last three projects in the book are moderately difficult.

Sinnet

A *sinnet* of square knots results from two or more knots being tied with the same four cords. If the instructions are to tie a sinnet of 17 square knots, don't panic. Tie 17 square knots.

Working Methods

Different projects require different working methods. The working method to use is determined by the design of the project itself. There are three working methods used to create the projects in this book.

Knotting in the round is creating a continuous structure with no edges. It results when the knotting cords are anchored continuously around an object or holding form. The eyeglass case (page 271), key ring pouch (page 275), and shopping bag are examples of knotting in the round. All are worked from the top down, then closed (tied off) at the bottom of the design.

Knotting from one end is simply working from one end to the opposite end. It's used when the strands needed to complete the project are relatively short or when the project must be anchored at one end. The watchband (page 278) and the water bottle tote (page 282) are good examples of this working method.

Knotting from the midpoint is working from the center or midpoint of a design. It's useful when working with very long cords. The working length of the cords is divided in half (usually with an overhand knot). You work the design as directed, turn the knotting board, and work the design again. The place mat (page 248) and the hatband (page 260) are both examples of this method of working.

BASIC KNOTS

You've read about knots and how to use them. Now, let's look at a knot as if you've never seen one before. Knots are known by different (and sometimes colorful) names. In this section you'll find a photograph and an illustration for each knot you'll use for projects in this book. More importantly, you'll learn how each one is tied! Refer to this section often if you're a novice knotter.

Square Knot (SQKT)

The square knot is a secure, non-slipping knot made over

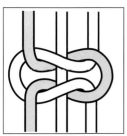

a central core or knot-bearing strand of one or more threads. The knot-bearing strand should be kept taut when you make this knot. Practice this knot. Practice it again and again. You'll soon develop a personal method for holding the core cords taut.

Pass the right-hand cord over the core cords and under the left-hand cord, leaving a little loop on the right. Then pass the left-hand cord under the core cords and up through the loop. Pull the cords to tighten the first half of the knot.

Then pass the left-hand cord over the core cords and under the right-hand cord, leaving a little loop on the left. Now, pass the right-hand cord under the core cords and up through the loop. Pull the cords to tighten the finished knot.

Half Knot (HK)

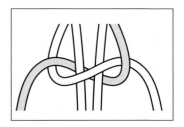

This is simply one half of the square knot. When tied repeatedly, it results in a spiral sinnet of half knots. The spiral may twist clockwise or counter-clockwise depending on which cord—the left or the right—is placed over the core threads.

Half Hitch (HH)

This knot is made of a single loop over one or more knot-bearing threads. Hold the knot-bearing thread taut, loop a knotting strand around the knot-bearing strand, then pull it into place.

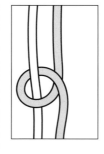

Alternating Half Hitch (AHH)

Not really a single knot, but a knot pattern, is created by alternating the thread used as the knot-bearing strand. Tie a half hitch, then switch: the knot-bearing cord now becomes the knotting cord. Then tie another half hitch. When two strands of different colors are used, a predictable and decorative pattern results.

Lark's Head Knot (LHK)

This is the knot most commonly used to anchor doubled cords. Find the midpoint of your cord and fold it in half forming a loop. Bring the looped end of the cord under the anchoring cord (ring, buckle, or dowel) from the top. The free ends are placed through the loop and the loop is pulled tight.

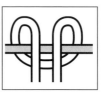 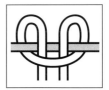 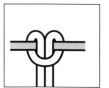

Overhand Knot (OK)

You use this basic knot almost daily without thinking about it. Try tying your shoes without it. It's used to anchor cords at the beginning of projects and as a finishing knot. Make a loop. Bring the end of the cord behind the loop and out through the loop. Pull it tight.

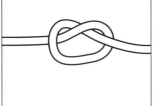

Slip-Loop Knot (SLK)

This a variation of the overhand knot. Begin by creating a loop around two fingers. Then reach through the loop and pull the free strand or strands through the loop forming a second loop. Pull it snugly, but keep an open loop as you create a knot below.

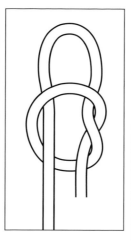

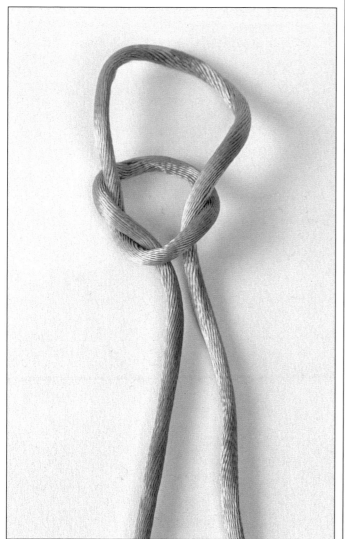

Double Half Hitch (DHH)

Double half hitches and square knots are the most frequently used knots in macrame. When a series of knotting strands are used to tie double half hitches on the same knot-bearing strand, a ridged row or line results.

Tie a half hitch around a taut knot-bearing cord. Tie another half hitch with the same knotting strand around the cord. Pick up the next free knotting strand and repeat. It's really that simple.

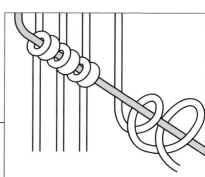

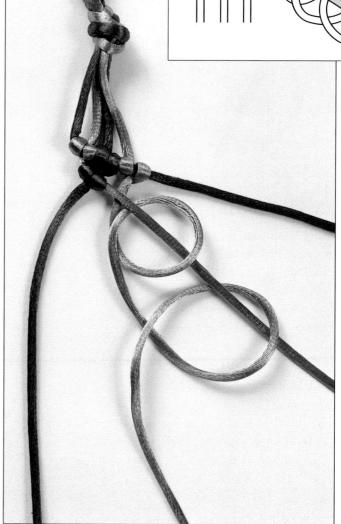

Reverse Double Half Hitch (RDHH)

This is a versatile knot that has the look of the lark's head knot turned to the side. The first step of the reverse double half hitch is a simple half hitch. The second step is slightly different: Pass the knotting strand under and around the knot-bearing strand and down through the loop created. It sounds simple, but here's the hitch (so to speak):

When you knot on the right side of a design, the knot-bearing strand should be held with the left hand, and the knotting strand held with the right hand.

When working on the left side of the design, you should hold the knot-bearing strand with the right hand and the knotting strand with the left.

It will feel awkward at first, but with practice it becomes comfortable and ensures a consistent knot pattern.

Coil Knot (CK)

This is similar to an overhand knot. It adds a decorative accent to the loose ends of strands, and it keeps strands from unraveling.

Make a large overhand knot. Before you close that knot, take one cord end and wrap it four times (or more) around the looped strand, then pull the knot firmly into place.

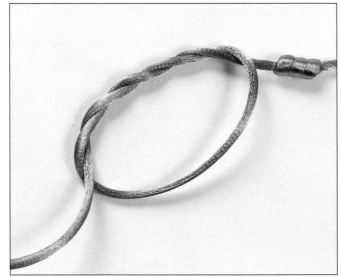

Gathering Double Half Hitch (GDHH)

Use this knot when you need to bring together a number of cords spread across a design.

Tie double half hitches in the usual way. However, instead of placing knotting strands aside after they are used, combine them with the knot-bearing cord just used. This process continues across the design until all strands are gathered in a bundle at the end of the knotted row.

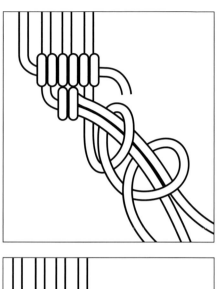

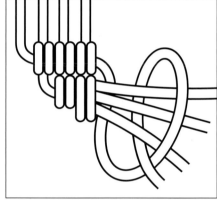

Three-Ply Braid

This simplest of braids is created using three strands or three groups of multiple threads. A braid works well in many knotted designs as a transition from one pattern to the next. And it works up quickly!

You have strands on the left, center, and right. Pick up the left strand and place it over the center strand. Then pick up the right strand and place it over the center strand. The sequence does not vary: left over center, right over center. If the sequence is interrupted, you'll see your mistake at once.

Four-Ply Braid

Yes, it's slightly more complicated than the three-ply braid. It creates a rounded rather than a flat braid. When you use more than one color, lovely patterns appear in the braid. Practice this braid and then practice it again.

Maintain constant tension on all the strands as you braid. Pick up the left strand. Bring it behind the next two strands and back in between them. Pick up the right strand. Bring it behind the adjacent two strands and, again, back in between. Repeat this sequence until you have the desired length.

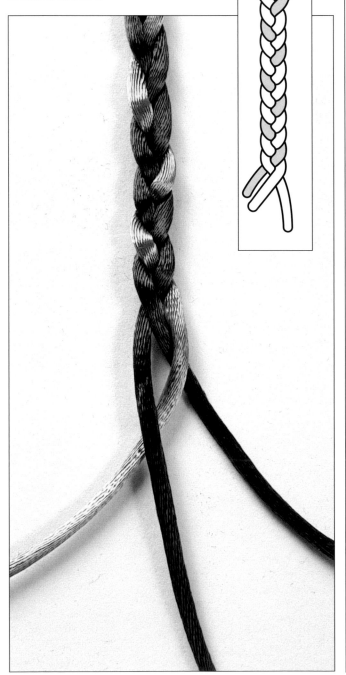

QUICK KNOT REFERENCE

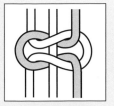

**SQUARE KNOT
(SQKT)**

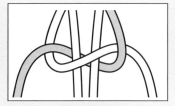

**HALF KNOT
(HK)**

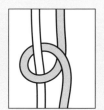

**HALF HITCH
(HH)**

**ALTERNATING
HALF HITCH (AHH)**

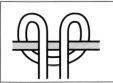 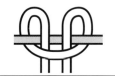 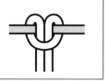

LARK'S HEAD KNOT (LHK)

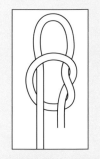

**SLIP-LOOP KNOT
(SLK)**

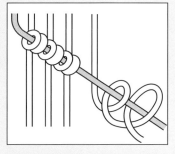

DOUBLE HALF HITCH (DHH)

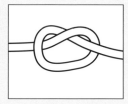

**OVERHAND KNOT
(OK)**

**REVERSE DOUBLE
HALF HITCH (RDHH)**

**COIL KNOT
(CK)**

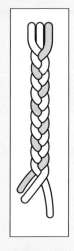

**THREE-PLY
BRAID**

FOUR-PLY BRAID

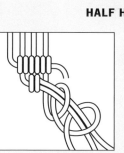 

GATHERING DOUBLE HALF HITCH (GDHH)

Snug-as-a-Bug Mug Rugs

Tie up these thirsty coasters to protect your table. They're extremely easy to knot. Make a set of them to match the place mats on page 248 and several more sets to use as gifts.

DIMENSIONS OF FINISHED PIECE

3 × 5 inches (7.6 × 12.7 cm)

KNOTS AND WORKING METHOD

Overhand knot (OK), square knot (SQKT)

Knotting from one end

Preparing the Materials

For each coaster, cut 20 pieces of cord, each one measuring 26 inches (66 cm) long.

1 Tie a set of four cords with an OK about 3 inches (7.6 cm) from the end. Make five sets in all.

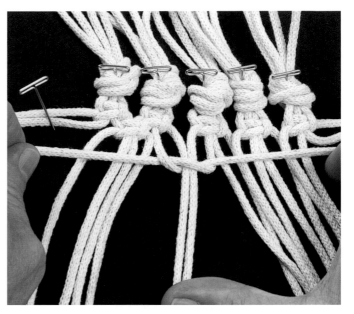

3 Start at the left. Place two cords to the side; they are now inactive. Make a SQKT using the next four threads. Make a row of SQKTs, leaving two inactive at the end of the row. Knot a total of 13 rows of alternating SQKTs. Pull the ends of the last row of knots securely. Trim the cord ends with scissors as desired.

2 Anchor the five sets of cords to the knotting board side-by-side, with a T-pin through each OK. Tie one SQKT in each group of four threads. Make sure the knots line up side-by-side.

4 Remove the T-pins and untie the OKs. Pull the ends tightly and trim the cord ends.

Soft Suede Belt

Oh, so retro...but chic and simple. A suede belt will complement casual wear, so why not knot a silk cord belt for dressy evening wear?

DIMENSIONS OF FINISHED PIECE

26 inches (66 cm) long, not including tying strands

YOU WILL NEED

24 feet (7.3 m) of brown suede lacing, approximately ⅛ inch (3 mm) wide

16 feet (4.9 m) of tan suede lacing, approximately ⅛ inch (3 mm) wide

Tape measure or ruler

Scissors

T-pins

Knotting board

KNOTS AND WORKING METHOD

Overhand knot (OK), square knot (SQKT)

Knotting from the midpoint

Preparing the Materials

Determine what size belt you want to make. For a longer belt, add length to the knotting strands in a 5-to-1 ratio. For example, if you need to add 6 inches (15.2 cm) to the length, add 30 inches to each strand you need.

Cut three pieces of brown lacing, each measuring 8 feet (2.4 m) long or to your measurement. Cut two pieces of tan leather lacing to the same measurement. Hold the five suede strands together, identify the midpoint, and tie an overhand knot using all five strands.

3 Repeat steps 1 and 2 six times. You've completed almost half of the belt.

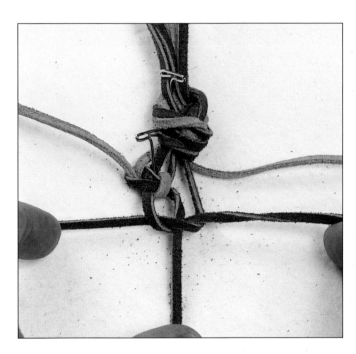

1 Use a T-pin to anchor the OK to the knotting board. Arrange the strands: tan on the outside, three brown in the middle. Pick up the tan cord on the left, combine with two brown to the right, and tie one SQKT using one knot-bearing cord. Lay the tan lace to the side. Tie one SQKT with three brown cords. Pull the knot up to and just below the first knot you tied.

4 Use the tan laces as knotting strands. Tie three SQKTs around the brown laces. Pull the last knot snug. Remove the T-pin from the OK and untie the knot. Anchor the belt to the board. Knot the second half of the belt as described in steps 1, 2, and 3. Repeat the design sequence of four knots a total of nine times.

2 Pick up the tan cord on the right, combine it with two brown cords, and tie one SQKT. Then tie one SQKT with three brown cords. Pull the knot up to and just below the first knot you tied.

5 Finish the ends of the leather cords with coil knots. Vary the position of the coil knots, if you wish to create different lengths for the cord ends.

Dinner Place Mat

This is a great introductory project for the novice knotter. The cords (and knots) are large and easy to manage. You'll be surprised just how quickly the project can be finished. Go ahead: knot a pair for tonight's dinner while the chicken is roasting in the oven.

YOU WILL NEED

85 yards (77.7 m) of braided cotton cord (per mat)

Ruler or tape measure

Scissors

T-pins

Knotting board marked with a 1-inch (2.5 cm) grid*

*If you don't wish to mark a grid on your fabric-covered knotting board, mark the grid on a piece of paper the same size as your board. Pin or tape the paper to the board.

DIMENSIONS OF FINISHED PIECE

12 × 21 inches (30.5 × 53.3 cm) including the fringe

KNOTS AND WORKING METHOD

Square knot (SQKT), overhand knot (OK)

Knotting from the midpoint

Preparing the Materials

For each place mat, measure and cut 36 pieces of cotton cord, each seven feet (2.1 m) long. Gather four strands at a time. Tie an overhand knot (OK) in each group at the midpoint. Repeat until you have nine groups.

1 Mark your knotting board with a 12 × 19-inch (30.5 × 48.3 cm) grid of 1-inch (2.5 cm) squares. This grid will help you keep the knots evenly spaced.

2 Anchor each group of cords to the midline of your grid with a T-pin through the OK.

3 Tie one SQKT in each group. Pull the first half of the knot up to the line. Pin it in place. Finish the second half of the knot, pulling it securely. Continue tying and pinning one SQKT in each of the nine groups.

4 Regroup the cords for the next row. Leave two threads inactive on the left side. Use the next four threads to tie one SQKT. Then tie one SQKT in each regrouped group of four across the row. On the right side you will end with two inactive threads. Regroup the cords again. Knot a total of eight rows of alternating SQKTs. As the work progresses, move the T-pins down to secure the next knotted row.

5 Knot a ninth row with two SQKTs in each group. Regroup and knot a 10th row with one SQKT in each group, pulling it up close to the previous row. Starting on the left, tie an OK with two cords together. Pull the knot snug. Repeat across the row, finishing this half of the mat. Trim the ends evenly.

6 Reverse the position of the knotting board. Remove the OKs. Knot the second half of the place mat with seven alternating rows of SQKTs. Rows eight and nine should be knotted and finished as described in step 5.

Red Rover Pet Leash

"Red Rover, Red Rover, send…" Fido (or Floyd or Spot!) right over into canine chic with this sturdy leash.

DIMENSIONS OF FINISHED PIECE

60 inches (1.5 m) from base of hand loop to swivel snap-hook

YOU WILL NEED

20 yards (18.2 m) of small twisted nylon cord, approximately ⅛ inch (3 mm) in diameter

Swivel snap-hook (available at hardware and home supply stores)

Ruler or measuring tape

Scissors

Knotting board

T-pins

Clear-drying white craft glue

KNOTS AND WORKING METHOD

Lark's head knot (LHK), overhand knot (OK), square knot (SQKT)

Knotting from one end

Preparing the Materials

Measure and cut two pieces of cord each 28 feet (8.5 m) long. Fold each cord in half at the midpoint. Mount each doubled cord on the swivel hook with an LHK.

1 Use the two inside cords as knot-bearing cords and the outer cords as knotting cords. Tie four SQKTs. Exchange the outside knotting cords with the inside knot-bearing cords.

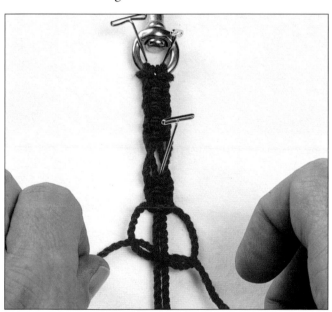

2 Create an opening one inch (2.54 cm) below the last SQKT. Position a T-pin in the board, below the four knots, to hold the space. Tie four SQKTs with the cords in the new positions. Repeat the pattern of tying four SQKTs, exchanging the cords and leaving a space, and tying four more SQKTs, until the sinnet measures 48 inches in length.

3 Exchange the position of the outside and inside strands, but leave only a ½-inch (1.3 cm) opening. With the new cord arrangement, tie 36 SQKTs.

4 Insert the two outside knotting strands in the ½-inch (1.3 cm) opening and pull them through. The 36 square knots have formed the hand loop. Place the longer knot-bearing strands at each side of the leash body.

5 Tie two SQKTs around the entire leash body and the free strands you pulled through earlier.

6 Tie one OK in each pair of two loose strands, and pull firmly into place against the leash. Trim the cord ends close to the OK. Coat the knot with clear-drying white craft glue to prevent fraying. Allow the glue to dry before you take Fido for a walk.

Beaded Napkin Rings

These napkin rings are such a breeze to make that you may end up with several sets in different colors for your family members and friends. If hemp is not your cup of tea, use a similarly sized cord for a different look.

YOU WILL NEED

22 yards (20.1 m) of hemp, or a similar natural-colored cord, approximately ⅛ inch (3 mm) in diameter (will make a set of 4)

4 glass beads*

Knotting board

T-pins

Scissors

Clear-drying white craft glue

Cardboard tube

*Remember to take your knotting material with you when you purchase your beads. You'll thread one bead onto two strands in this project.

DIMENSIONS OF FINISHED PIECE

1½ inches (3.8 cm) in diameter

KNOTS AND WORKING METHOD

Overhand knot (OK), square knot (SQKT), double half hitch (DHH)

Knotting from one end

Preparing the Materials

Cut six lengths of cord, each 32 inches (81.2 cm) long, for each napkin ring.

1 Tie an OK in a group of six strands about two inches (5 cm) from one end. Anchor the cords to your knotting board through the knot.

2 Divide the six strands into two groups of three. First row: Tie one SQKT using one group of three strands. Tie one SQKT in the second group of three strands.

Second row: Make a group of four. One cord will be inactive on either side. Tie one SQKT with the grouped cords.

Repeat these two rows of knotting three times.

3 You are now ready to tie two diagonal rows of DHHs. Think of the design in two parts: three cords on the left, and three cords on the right. Begin on either side.

Hold the outside cord across the two remaining cords and tie one row of DHHs. Pick up the outside cord again and tie a row of DHHs. Pull this row tightly against the first. Complete the design by tying two rows of DHHs on the opposite side.

Thread the two middle strands of cord through the bead and pull into place against the DHH row.

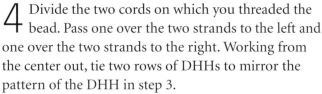

5 Remove the knotting from the board. Untie the OK and turn the knotting over. Smooth the cords, making sure that the cords are in order. Shape the work into a loose ring. Knot the cord ends in sequence with square knots—as you would in tying packages. There are no knot-bearing cords, so pull the knots evenly and securely. Tie six SQKTs in all.

4 Divide the two cords on which you threaded the bead. Pass one over the two strands to the left and one over the two strands to the right. Working from the center out, tie two rows of DHHs to mirror the pattern of the DHH in step 3.

Pick up the four strands in the middle (there will be one inactive cord on each side) and tie one SQKT. Regroup the cords into two groups of three and tie one SQKT in each group. Repeat these two rows three times to mirror the square knot pattern in step 2.

6 Slip the knotted ring onto a cardboard tube. Trim the cord ends ⅛ inches (3 mm) from each knot. Squeeze a bit of white craft glue on each SQKT. Allow the glue to dry.

True-Blue Trio of Bookmarks

Using only two colors of thread you can knot three very different-looking bookmarks. What's the secret? We're knot telling yet. This project is a great practice piece for some tricky (and not so tricky) knots.

DIMENSIONS OF FINISHED PIECE

11 inches (27.9 cm) including fringe

YOU WILL NEED

8 yards (7.3 m) of blue cotton crochet thread

8 yards (7.3 m) of grey cotton crochet thread

Ruler or measuring tape

Scissors

Knotting board

T-pins

Tapestry needle

KNOTS AND WORKING METHOD

Overhand knot (OK), double half hitch (DHH), square knot (SQKT), reverse double half hitch (RDHH)

Working from one end

Preparing the Materials

For each bookmark, you will need eight lengths of thread, four of each color. Measure and cut each thread 4 feet (12.2 m) long. Gather eight threads together with an OK tied 4 inches (10.2 cm) from one end. Anchor the eight strands to the knotting board through the OK.

Finishing the Bookmarks

After you have followed the directions for any of the three bookmarks, finish any bookmark by tying three SQKTs, using six strands as knot-bearing strands. Turn the bookmark over. Thread a tapestry needle with a knotting thread. Pull each knotting thread under the back of the SQKT. Trim the ends flush with the loop of the first SQKT. Trim the remaining six ends as desired. Remove the OK and repeat at the opposite end.

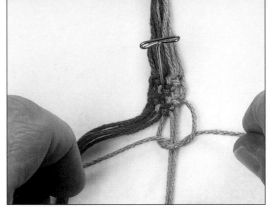

Alternating Square Knot Bookmark

2 Anchor the eight strands to the board with a T-pin through the OK. Arrange the strands into two groups: four blue on the left and four grey on the right. Tie one SQKT in each group using two strands as knot-bearing strands. Regroup the strands: two blue inactive on the left and two grey inactive on the right. Tie one SQKT with the blue and grey strands. Regroup the strands and tie two SQKTs. Repeat the alternating SQKT pattern until the knotting is about 8 inches (20.3 cm) in length.

Finish the bookmark as directed.

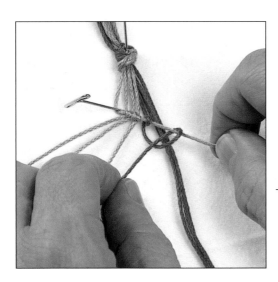

Double Half Hitch Bookmark

1 Anchor the strands to the knotting board with a T-pin. Arrange the eight strands: four grey on the left and four blue on the right. Pick up the outside strand on the left. Hold it diagonally across seven threads. Tie a row of DHHs, using all seven threads (see photo). Pick up the next outside strand on the left. Hold it across seven threads. Tie a row of DHHs. Continue to pick up a thread from the left and tie a row of DHHs until you have a total of 48 rows.

To finish this bookmark pick up the strand on the left and tie six DHHs (row 49). Tie rows 50 through 54 with DHHs, decreasing the number of DHHs in each row from five to one. Then finish the bookmark as directed.

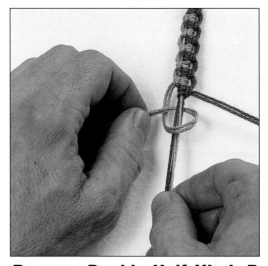

Reverse Double Half Hitch Bookmark

3 Anchor eight strands to the knotting board with a T-pin through the overhand knot. Arrange the strands: four blue on the left and four grey on the right. Hold the four middle strands taut (two blue and two grey). Tie one RDHH on the left using two blue strands. Holding the four middle strands taut, tie one RDHH on the right using the two grey strands. (Review tying RDHHs on page 240 if needed). Repeat this sequence until the knotting measures 8 inches (20.3 cm) in length.

Finish the bookmark as directed.

Leather Fob Key Ring

You won't be frantically patting your pockets for keys if they're attached to this handsome key ring. Dangle the end of the finely knotted fob from your pocket—you'll surely receive compliments from admirers.

YOU WILL NEED

8 feet (2.4 m) of rust-colored coated cotton cord, approximately $\frac{1}{16}$ inch (1.6 mm) in diameter

8 feet (2.4 m) of black-colored coated cotton cord, approximately $\frac{1}{16}$ inch (1.6 mm) in diameter

$\frac{5}{8}$-inch (1.6 cm) metal O-ring

Split ring

Scissors

Ruler or measuring tape

Knotting board

DIMENSIONS OF FINISHED PIECE

$1\frac{1}{2} \times 10$ inches (3.8 × 25.4 cm) including the fringe

KNOTS AND WORKING METHOD

Lark's head knot (LHK), double half hitch, (DHH), square knot (SQKT), reverse double half hitch (RDHH), alternating half hitch (AHH), overhand knot (OK), gathering double half hitch (GDHH), four-ply braid

Knotting from one end

Preparing the Materials

Measure and cut two pieces of rust cord, each 4 feet (1.2 m) long; cut two pieces of black cord, each four feet (1.2 m) long. Fold each cord in half. Mount the cords on the O-ring using an LHK. Mount both black cords, then mount a rust cord on either side of the black cords. Pin the ring to the knotting board.

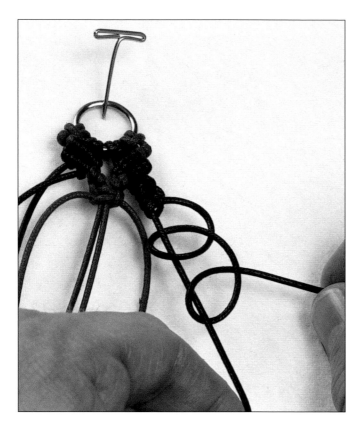

1 Pick up the outside strand on the left side. Bring it across the rust and two black strands. Tie three DHHs. Pick up the strand on the right side, hold it across the rust and two black strands toward the middle. Tie three DHHs. Pick up the rust cord on the left. Tie a second row of DHHs. Pick up the rust cord on the right. Tie a second a row of DHHs. The four rust-colored cords are now in the center. Tie an SQKT using the rust-colored cords (see photo).

2 Tie three RDHHs with each set of black cords on the left and right.

Pick up one of the two rust-colored cords in the center. Use it as a knot-bearing cord and tie one row of DHHs working outward to the left or right. Pick up the second center cord and tie one row of DHHs in the opposite direction. Tie a second row of DHHs, using the rust-colored cords as knot-bearing cords, to the left and right.

3 Four black cords are now together in the center. Use two cords as knot-bearing cords. Tie four SQKTs with the four black cords. With the two rust-colored cords on the left and right, tie seven AHHs.

Divide the eight cords into groups of four (each group will contain two rust and two black cords). Tie one SQKT in each group. Regroup the cords leaving two cords on the left and right inactive. Tie one SQKT in the four cords remaining. Repeat this regrouping sequence two times.

4 Complete the design with one row of DHHs worked diagonally on each side under the SQKTs.

5 Tie the next row in GDHHs. See page 241 to review this knotting process.

6 Finish the key ring with a long four-ply braid. Keep pairs of rust and black cords together when you braid them. When the braid is about 5 inches long (12.7 cm) long, secure it with an OK. Use scissors to trim the ends of the cords evenly or at a slight angle.

Western Hatband

What cowboy or cowgirl wouldn't be proud to be seen two-stepping or line dancing on a Saturday night sporting this knotted hatband?

YOU WILL NEED

32 feet (9.8 m) of fine hemp twine

20 black glass beads, approximately ⅜ inch (9.5 mm) in diameter

Scissors

Knotting board

T-pins

DIMENSIONS OF FINISHED PIECE

24 inches (61 cm) long

KNOTS AND WORKING METHOD

Overhand knot (OK), square knot (SQKT), double half hitch (DHH)

Knotting from the midpoint

Preparing the Materials

Measure and cut six strands of twine, each 64 inches (1.6 m) long. Tie an overhand knot at the midpoint with all six strands together. Anchor the twine to the knotting board with a T-pin through the OK.

1 Tie one SQKT with four cords used as the knot-bearing cords.

2 With the two outside cords inactive, tie two SQKTs, using the four remaining strands.

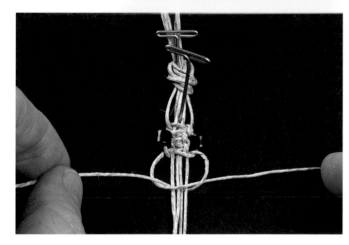

3 String one black glass bead on each of the inactive outside cords. Use these cords to tie one SQKT over four knot-bearing cords. The glass beads are held in place by the knot.

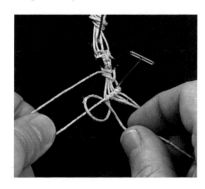

4 Anchor the outside cord on the right with a T-pin below the SQKT made in the previous step. Hold the cord diagonally across the remaining five cords. Tie one row of DHHs (see photo).

Tie one SQKT using the four cords on the right side. Tie one SQKT using the four cords on the left side. Tie one SQKT using four cords on the right side.

Anchor the outside cord on the left side with a T-pin. Hold the cord diagonally across and down over the remaining five cords. Tie a row of DHHs. This completes your first pattern.

Repeat steps 1 through 4 three times.

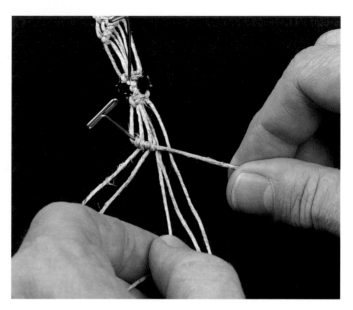

5 Remove the overhand knot, and anchor the knotting with a T-pin. Repeat steps 1 through 4 four times. To make the design units symmetrical, anchor the outside strand on the left for the first row of DHHs, working left to right. Also, tie the first SQKT using the four strands on the left.

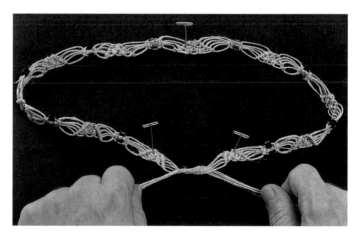

6 Wrap the knotting around the crown of the hat to estimate the needed length. Then join the two ends with a square knot. Trim the ends about 1 inch (2.5 cm) from the knot. If desired, secure the knot with a dab of clear-drying white craft glue.

Neo-Victorian Scarf Fringe

Victorian needlewomen knotted endless rows of delicate macrame edging for household articles and clothing. If you're feeling truly Victorian—edge a tablecloth—or fringe the parlor curtains—with this design.

DIMENSIONS OF FINISHED PIECE

The 6-inch (15.2 cm) fringe was designed for a 6-inch-wide (15.2 cm) scarf.*

*The simple design unit of this fringe is easy to increase for a wider scarf. Add a working unit of eight mounted cords (four blue and four green) to increase the width as needed.

KNOTS AND WORKING METHOD

Lark's head knot (LHK), square knot (SQKT), double half hitch (DHH), alternating half hitch (AHH), overhand knot (OK)

Knotting from one end

48 feet (14.6 m) of #3 mercerized-cotton crochet thread (navy blue)

50 feet (15.2 m) of #3 mercerized-cotton crochet thread (green)

Ruler or measuring tape

Scissors

Knotting board

T-pins

Tapestry needle

Sewing needle

Thread

Preparing the Materials

Measure and cut one piece of green thread two feet (60.9 cm) long. Measure and cut 32 pieces of blue and 32 pieces of green thread 3 feet (91 cm) long each. Fold the two-foot green thread in half. Tie an OK about two inches (5 cm) in from each end. Pin this strand through the OKs to the knotting board. This is your anchor cord.

Find the midpoint of one blue thread. Mount the doubled thread to the anchor cord with an LHK. Mount three more blue strands, then mount four green strands. Continue mounting strands across the holding thread (four blue, four green) until all the strands are used. You will have a total of 64 knotting strands.

1 Begin knotting with the left-hand group of blue strands. Tie one SQKT using two knot-bearing cords. Tie one SQKT with each group of four blue strands. You will have two blue SQKTs. Tie two SQKTs with the green strands.

Return to the previously knotted blue strands. Make two strands on the left inactive. Regroup the blue strands and tie one SQKT (see photo). Working from left to right, tie two more SQKTs. You will combine two blue strands and two green threads for one SQKT. Continue working to the right using the remaining green strands. Leave the last two green strands inactive.

Move back to the left and regroup threads for row three. Make four threads inactive. Tie a single SQKT in each group of four, leaving four threads inactive at the end of the row. You'll now have two knots in this row. Return to the left and regroup again. Make six threads inactive on the left. Tie one SQKT with the four remaining threads (two blue, two green). Leave six threads inactive on the right.

2 Anchor the outer blue strand on the left with a T-pin. Hold the strand diagonally below the bottom of the square knots. Tie one row of DHHs using the seven blue strands. Pick up the next outside blue strand and tie a second row of DHHs. Repeat this sequence from the right with the green strands.

Create the long, knotted fringe with groups of two threads. Tie 40 AHHs in each group of two threads (see photo). Tie one OK below the last AHH of each two-thread unit. Work from left to right until you have created the fringe for the first design unit.

Repeat steps 1 and 2 with each of the remaining units.

needle. Weave the threads of the anchor cords under the back side of the LHKs (see photo). Weave the threads approximately 1 inch (2.54 cm). Repeat on the opposite end of the anchor cord. Trim the thread ends closely with scissors.

4 Stitch the fringe to one end of your scarf. Make a second fringe for the opposite end of the scarf.

3 Remove the finished fringe from the board. Turn the fringe over. Untie the OK on one side, and thread the two ends of the anchor cords in the tapestry

Gossamer Pillow Overlay

Imagine coming home to one—or several—of these pillows. Lacy knotting
adds an elegant handcrafted touch to plain pillows.

DIMENSIONS OF FINISHED PIECE

12 × 12 inches (30.5 × 30.5 cm)

YOU WILL NEED

12-inch (30.5 cm) square pillow

132 feet (40.2 m) of nylon crochet cord

Scissors

Ruler or tape measure

Knotting board marked with a
12 × 12-inch (30.5 × 30.5 cm) grid of
1-inch (2.5 cm) squares*

T-pins

Straight pins

Sewing needle

Thread

*If you don't wish to mark a grid on your
fabric-covered knotting board, mark the
grid on a piece of paper the same size as
your board. Pin or tape the paper to the
board.

KNOTS AND WORKING METHOD

Square knot (SQKT), overhand
knot (OK)

Knotting from the midpoint

Preparing the Materials

Cut 44 pieces of cord, each three feet (.9 m) long. Gather four strands and tie an overhand knot at the midpoint of the strands. Prepare 11 groups. Anchor the overhand knots with T-pins equally spaced on the center line of the marked work board.

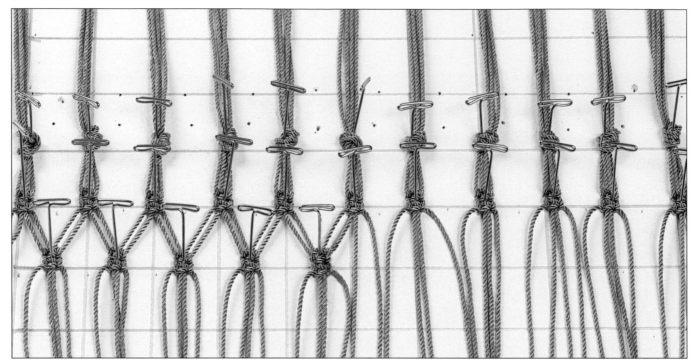

1 Tie two SQKTs in each group of four strands. Anchor each group of finished knots with a T-pin to the line on the grid. Regroup the strands into groups of four. Two strands will be inactive on the left and right. Tie two SQKTs in each of the new groups of four. There will be 10 groups of square knots in this second row (see photo).

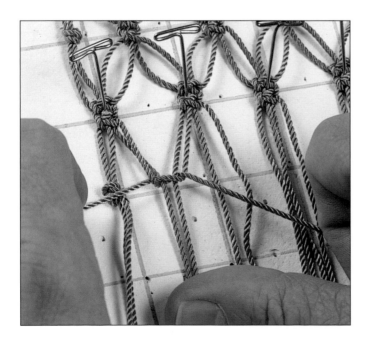

2 Tie an OK in each of the two unknotted, inactive strands on the left and right sides. Center each OK on the grid line and secure it with a T-pin.

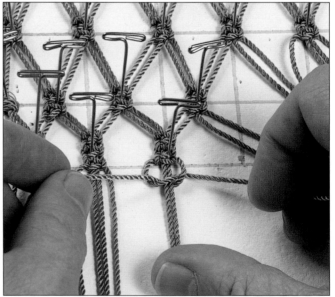

3 Work four more alternating rows made up of SQKTs and OKs for a total of six rows in all. Work a seventh row of SQKTs, this time with three SQKTs in each group of four.

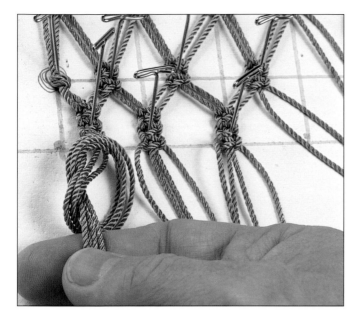

4 Tie an OK in each group, pulled snugly against the last square knot (see photo).

Turn the board around. Remove the T-pins above from the first row of pinned OKs. Move the pins to the first row of SQKTs. Untie the OKs. Follow the knotting directions in steps 1 through 3. Finish this end with OKs.

5 If the pillow has a removable cover, remove the pillow, otherwise, center the overlay directly on the pillow. Using straight pins, pin overlay on all sides to the cover or the pillow.

6 Thread a needle with thread to match the knotted overlay. Hand-stitch the knotted piece to the cover or pillow, catching each knotted end around the outer edge. Knots in the center of the pillow may also be anchor-stitched, if desired.

Classic Pendant Necklace

Veteran knotters already know the pleasures of working with linen thread—it's the Rolls Royce of knotting materials. This classic interpretation of a knotted necklace will introduce you to the pleasures of working with linen. But be forewarned: after finishing this piece you may never want to knot with any other fiber!

DIMENSIONS OF FINISHED PIECE

1⅞ inches (4.8 cm) at the widest point of the pendant; total necklace length is approximately 13 inches (33 cm)

YOU WILL NEED

54 feet (5.5 m) of medium-weight linen thread

⅜-inch (9.5 mm) black glass bead

12 black glass pony beads, approximately ³⁄₁₆ inch (5 mm) in diameter

5 frosted-glass beads, approximately ¼ inch (6 mm) in diameter

Ruler or measuring tape

Scissors

Knotting board

T-pins

KNOTS AND WORKING METHOD

Reverse double half hitch (RDHH), square knot (SQKT), slip-loop knot (SLK), double-half hitch (DHH), overhand knot (OK), three-ply braid

Knotting from one end

Preparing the Materials

Measure and cut six lengths of thread, each measuring 9 feet (2.7 m). Pick up three threads and align the cut ends. Thread all three strands through the ⅜-inch (9.5 mm) black bead. Slide the bead to the midpoint of the three strands. Set this group aside. Locate the midpoint of the three remaining strands. Tie an SLK about 4 inches (10.2 cm) above the midpoint of the remaining three strands.

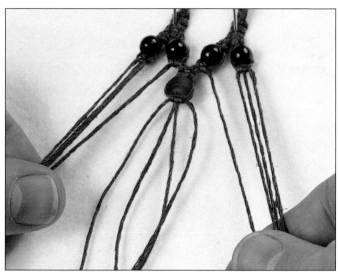

JOINING THE LOOP AND CLOSURE

2 Place the completed loop and closure about ½ inch (1.3 cm) apart on the knotting board. Anchor each with a T-pin. Divide the strands into four groups made up of three strands. Tie two SQKTs in each group. Thread a ³⁄₁₆-inch black bead on the knot-bearing strand of each group. Secure each bead in place with a SQKT.

CREATING THE LOOP AND CLOSURE

1 Use a T-pin to anchor the group of threads with the SLK to the knotting board. Pick up one strand to use as the knotting strand. Hold the two remaining strands taut with the other hand. Tie 10 RDHHs with the single strand. Remove the T-pin from the board and pull out the SLK. Shape the knotted section into an arc, creating a group of six cords underneath. Use two outside strands to tie three SQKTs around the remaining four threads. This creates the loop for the necklace. Divide the six threads into three groups with two strands in each. Make a 9-inch (22.9 cm) three-ply braid with the strands. Finish the braid with three SQKTs. Set this unit aside.

Pick up the three strands with the single bead. Anchor the bead and strands to the knotting board with a single T-pin. Bring the strands together under the bead. Use two outer strands to tie three SQKTs around four knot-bearing strands. This creates the closure for the necklace. Divide the six threads into three groups with two strands in each. Make a 9-inch (22.9 cm) three-ply braid with the strands. Finish the braid with three SQKTs. Set this unit aside.

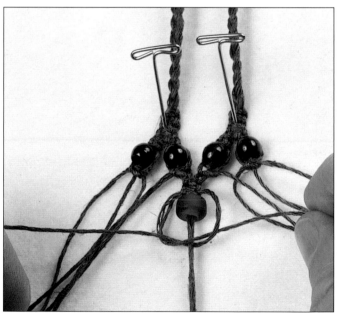

3 Divide the strands into three groups made up of four strands. Tie two SQKTs in each group. Thread one ¼-inch (6 mm) frosted-glass bead on the knot-bearing strand of each group. Secure each bead in place with one SQKT below the bead. Make the two outside strands inactive on the right and left side. Regroup the remaining eight strands into two groups

of four. Tie one SQKT in each group. Make four outside strands on the left and right inactive, and tie one SQKT in the four remaining strands.

Tie two rows of DHHs diagonally below the SQKTs. Hold the outside strand on the left diagonally across five strands. Tie a row of DHHs using the five strands. Pick up the outside strand on the left and tie a second row of DHHs across four cords. Repeat this knotting sequence with the right-hand cords.

second strand from the center unit. Repeat this sequence on the right-hand side.

Locate and pick up the four strands in the center. Tie three SQKTs (see photo).

Two rows of DHHs are now tied to mirror the DHH rows described above. This creates a diamond-like outline around the SQKTs. Divide the strands in the SQKT unit into two groups, and tie double rows of DHHs.

CREATING THE CENTRAL PENDANT

4 Begin working with the four strands in the center. Tie one SQKT. Thread a black glass pony bead onto the two knot-bearing strands. Secure the bead in place with one SQKT. Thread a frosted-glass bead on the two knot-bearing strands. Secure the bead with one SQKT. Thread a black glass pony bead on the knot-bearing strands and secure it in place with one SQKT.

Pick up two strands to the left of the unit you just tied. Tie 15 RDHHs. Pick up the next two strands and tie 18 RDHHs. Repeat this sequence with the four strands on the right.

Divide the strands used to tie the SQKT unit into two groups. Pick up the outermost strand in the left-hand group. Anchor the thread with a T-pin. Hold the strand diagonally over the threads in both RDHH units on the left. Tie a second row below the first using the

5 Finish the necklace with three beaded units. Locate the four center strands. Tie one SQKT, and thread a frosted plum bead on the knot-bearing strands. Secure the bead with one SQKT. Thread a black pony bead onto the knot-bearing strands. Slide it into place and secure with one SQKT. Add one more black pony bead and secure with an SQKT. Tie an OK, pulling it up against the SQKT (see photo).

Work with four strands on the left. Tie one SQKT, then thread a black pony bead and secure it in place with an SQKT. Add a second black pony bead and secure in place with an SQKT. Finish this unit with one an OK. Trim the thread ends as desired. Repeat with the right-hand group.

Eyeglass Case

Stylishly knotted in soft black and white cotton threads,
this eyeglass case is—dare we say it?—a fine piece of Optical Art.

YOU WILL NEED

3 × 12-inch (7.6 × 30.5 cm) piece of
heavy corrugated cardboard*

28 yards (25.6 m) of white, 4-ply, worsted weight
100% cotton yarn

28 yards (25.6 m) of black, 4-ply, worsted weight
100% cotton yarn

Decorative button, approximately ⅞ inch (2.2 cm)
in diameter

Ruler or measuring tape

Scissors

Knotting board

T-pins

2 short lengths of any color yarn, each about 6 inches
(15.2 cm) long

Tapestry or yarn needle

*Measure and cut this from a corrugated box that you're
planning to recycle.

DIMENSIONS OF FINISHED PIECE:

3⅝ × 7 inches (9.2 × 17.8 cm)

KNOTS AND WORKING METHOD

Lark's head knot (LHK), square knot (SQKT),
slip-loop knot (SLK), reverse double half hitch (RDHH),
overhand knot (OK)

Knotting in the round

Preparing the Materials

Measure and cut one 18-inch (45.7 cm) length of white yarn for a mounting cord. Measure and cut two pieces of black yarn 24 inches (70 cm) long for the closure. Set them aside.

Measure and cut 18 strands of white cotton yarn, each 54 inches (1.4 m) long. Measure and cut 18 strands of black cotton yarn, each 54 inches (1.4 m) long.

Center one 18-inch (45.7 cm) length of white cotton yarn across the short width of the cardboard strip. Bring the ends around the strip and back to the front. Tie the two ends together with a single SQKT. Position the tied cord approximately 3 inches (7.6 cm) from the top of the strip. This is your anchor cord. Pin the cardboard form to your knotting board with T-pins.

2 Pick up four white threads. Tie an SQKT, then tie another SQKT in the next group of threads. As you continue to knot the row around the form, you will need to remove the pins, turn the form over, and pin it again. Continue around the form.

1 Fold one 54-inch (1.4 m) length of white cotton yarn in half. Mount the yarn on the holding strand using an LHK. Mount a second length of white yarn in the same way. Mount two lengths of black cotton yarn on the holding strand with LHKs. Continue mounting yarn in pairs: two white and two black. Mount cords over the SQKT you tied in the anchor cord. Move the pins to turn the cardboard. Mount 18 units on each side. Clip the loose ends of the anchor cord as needed.

3 After you have completed the first row, you will need to regroup threads. Pick up two white and two black threads. Tie one SQKT. Continue around the form, regrouping and tying SQKTs. Tie eight rows of alternating single SQKTs.

Row 9 will be knotted with two SQKTs in each group of four threads. Row 10 is tied with single SQKTs. Repeat rows 9 and 10 two times.

The remainder of the case will be knotted in alternating rows of single SQKTs. Tie 28 rows of alternating SQKTs.

FINISHING THE CASE

4 Identify the four strands at each side of the case (two white and two black). Tie a short length of red yarn around each of the four strands of yarn. Bend the cardboard a bit, slide the case off the form, and turn it inside out. Slip the case back onto the form. Slide the case down until the last row of knotting is even with the edge of the form. Comb the threads with your fingers, letting them fall to the side of the pouch where they originated. Make sure that the cords you marked with the red yarn thread are on the side edges of the form. The bottom of the pouch will be tied off using SQKTs without a knot-bearing cord. The marked side strands will be tied last. Pick up a pair of threads from each side of the form next to one of the marked pairs. Tie one SQKT (see photo). Pull it securely against the cardboard edge. Pick up the next pair of threads and tie an SQKT. Continue across, picking up matching pairs in order until all are tied. Remove the red yarn and tie each pair in an SQKT. Trim the thread ends to ¼ inch (6mm) with scissors.

5 Turn the case inside out. This is best done by pushing against the bottom with your thumbs while you begin to pull down the sides. Be sure you push out the bottom corners with your fingers before the case is fully turned.

CREATING THE CLOSURE

6 Use a 6-inch (15.2 cm) length of black yarn to attach a button on the front of the case. Thread the yarn through the holes or shank of the button. Pull the ends even and center the button on the thread. Tie an SQKT. Locate the center knot on one side of the case. Thread one end of the yarn in the tapestry

needle. Bring the end through the case to one side of the center knot (see photo on page 273). Unthread the needle and repeat with the other yarn end. Tie one SQKT with the thread ends on the inside of the case. Finish with a tightly made OK. Trim the yarn ends.

7 Pick up two 24-inch (70 cm) black yarn strands. Secure both strands together at their midpoint with an SLK. Pin the knot to the knotting board. Tie 20 RDHHs.

9 Thread two of the strands in the needle. Identify the center knot in row 3 on the back of the case. Pull the strands to the inside of the case on one side of the knot. Repeat with the other two strands. Tie one SQKT with the four strands. Finish with one OK in each pair.

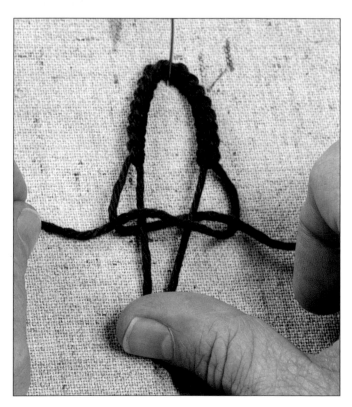

8 Remove the SLK. Bring the four strands together creating a loop. Pin the loop to the knotting board. Tie eight SQKTs.

Key Ring Pouch

Slip everything into this pouch and travel light. Keys on the ring, cash, and one or two important plastic cards stashed inside are all you'll need.

DIMENSIONS OF FINISHED PIECE

2½ × 3½ inches (6.4 × 8.9 cm)

YOU WILL NEED

2 × 7-inch (5 × 17.8 cm) piece of heavy corrugated cardboard*

Metal O-ring, approximately ½ inch (1.3 cm) in diameter

Metal split-ring

82 feet (24.9 m) of oatmeal-colored, cotton quick crochet thread

82 feet (24.9 m) of blue, cotton quick crochet thread

Ruler or measuring tape

Scissors

Knotting board

T-pins

Tapestry needle

*Measure and cut out a piece of a corrugated box that you're planning to recycle.

KNOTS AND WORKING METHOD

Lark's head knot (LHK), square knot (SQKT), double half hitch (DHH)

Knotting in the round

Preparing the materials

Measure and cut three pieces of oatmeal thread, each 3 feet (91 cm) long. Measure and cut 18 pieces of oatmeal thread, each 4 feet (1.2 m) long. Measure and cut 18 pieces of blue thread, each 4 feet (1.2 m) long.

Anchor the O-ring to the knotting board with a T-pin. Fold each 3-foot length of oatmeal thread in half. Mount each thread on the ring using LHKs. You will have six knotting strands. Tie four SQKTs around four knot-bearing threads.

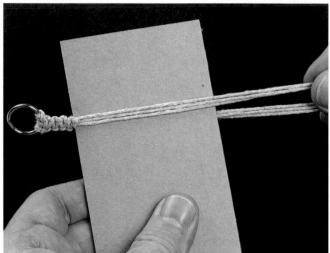

1 Remove the O-ring from the knotting board. Slip the cardboard strip between the oatmeal threads, as shown in the photo. Make sure you have three threads on each side. The cardboard strip becomes a form to separate the sides of the pouch as you knot. Wrap the thread ends back around to the SQKTs. These threads are your anchor strand.

2 Hold the cardboard form between your knees with the O-ring toward your body. Pick up single strands from each side and use them as knotting strands. Tie four SQKTs around all the strands including the first sinnet of SQKTs that you tied.

3 Thread the tapestry needle with one knotting thread end. Push the needle back under the SQKTs and pull the thread through. Repeat with the other thread. Trim the excess thread ends.

4 Lay the form down on your knotting board with the O-ring on the left. Pick up one of the long blue threads. Fold it in half at midpoint. Mount the folded thread onto the anchor strand with an LHK. Mount a second blue thread in the same way. Mount two oatmeal threads with LHKs. Continue mounting all of the long threads in alternating pairs of color around the

cardboard form. When all threads have been mounted, check your pattern. Do you have alternating pairs of color? If you don't, fix the pattern now! Move any misplaced colors as needed.

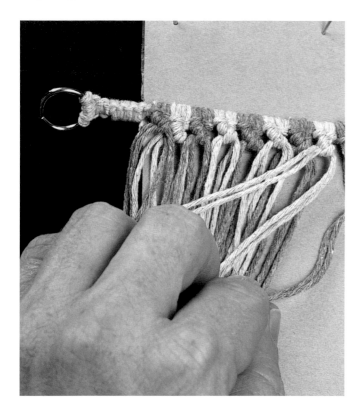

5 You'll work with two pairs of thread at a time to create this design. It looks complicated, but it isn't. If you pay attention to the pattern's color changes, any mistake you make will jump out at you and can be easily fixed. Start with the ring on the left and work to the right. Hold the first double blue strand across the adjacent double blue strand. Tie a DHH with the right strand around the left. Pick up the next double oatmeal strand, hold it across the next oatmeal strands and tie one DHH with the right strand around the left. Continue knotting around the form until you arrive back at the O-ring. All pairs of strands will have been knotted.

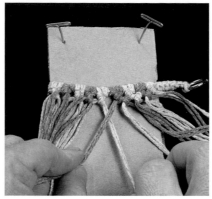

6 The O-ring is now on the right. Regroup the strands to begin the second row. Work toward the left, with the strand on the right held over the left. Use one pair of blue and one pair of oatmeal strands to tie one DHH. Work around the cardboard form.

You will tie 24 rows in all, regrouping as each row is completed, and working back toward where you started each time.

FINISHING THE POUCH

7 Tie a short length of a contrasting thread color around the double strands at each bottom corner of the cardboard form (see photo). Bend the cardboard a bit, and slide the pouch off the form. Turn the pouch inside out. Slip the pouch back onto the form. Slide the pouch down until the last row of knotting is even with the edge of the form.

Comb the threads with your fingers, letting them fall to the side of the pouch where they originated. Make sure that the cords you marked with contrasting thread are at the corners again. The bottom of the pouch will be finished with SQKTs tied without knot-bearing cords. The marked side strands will be the last to be tied.

Pick up a pair of threads from each side of the form starting at a marked double strand. Tie one SQKT. Pull it securely against the cardboard edge. Pick up the next pair of threads and tie another SQKT. Continue across, picking up matching pairs until all are tied. Remove the contrasting threads and tie each pair in an SQKT. Trim the thread ends with scissors. Turn the pouch inside out. Poke the corners out with your fingertips.

Slip the split-ring onto the O-ring.

Sands of Time Watchband

Timeless…that's how to describe the style of this finely knotted watchband. For him or for her!

Preparing the Materials

Measure and cut four strands, each 8 feet (2.4 m) long. Measure and cut two strands, each 2 feet (61 cm) long. Set the shorter strands to the side.

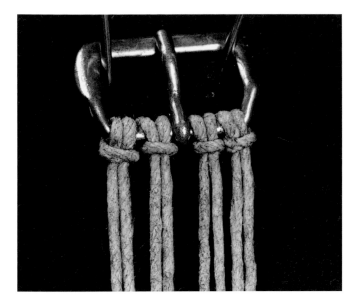

1 Find the midpoint of one long strand. Fold it in half and mount it on the buckle bar with an LHK. Mount the remaining long strands in the same way. Make sure you have two sets on either side of the tongue. Secure the buckle to the knotting board with T-pins.

Divide the strands into two groups. Tie one SQKT in each group. Make two strands inactive on each side. Tie an SQKT in the center group of four. Repeat this alternating SQKT pattern six times. You will have knotted 14 rows in all.

2 Pick up an outside strand from the left side. Tie two diagonal rows of DHHs below the square knots. Repeat this step on the opposite side.

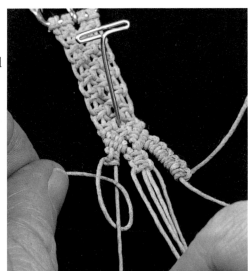

Pick up the four strands in the center and tie two SQKTs. Use the two outer strands on the right to tie six RDHHs. Tie six RDHHs on the left side (see photo).

Working with the fourth strand from the left side, hold it diagonally downward to the left across three strands and tie DHHs. Repeat, again using the fourth strand from the left. Repeat this pattern of DHHs on the right side.

3 Pick up the four strands in the middle, and tie one SQKT. Regroup all of the strands into two groups of four. Tie one SQKT in each group. Repeat the two rows of SQKTs twice.

Think of the strands (counting from the left) as numbers one through eight. Allow strands 1 and 2 to be inactive. Combine strands 3 and 4 with strands 5 and 6, and tie one SQKT. Allow strands 1, 2, 3, and 4 to be inactive. Combine strands 5 and 6 with strands 7 and 8, and tie one SQKT. Repeat this sequence in reverse order to the left, then back to the right.

Using the four middle strands tie one SQKT. Regroup eight strands into two groups of four; tie one SQKT in each group. Repeat this sequence twice. Tie one SQKT using the four center strands.

Water Bottle Tote

Life is a juggling act and you've only got two hands. Why should toting life's necessities—cell phone, briefcase, gym bag, and perhaps a toddler as well—be complicated with one more thing? When you knot this tote you'll give yourself an extra hand, and quick access to a refreshing swig of water!

DIMENSIONS OF FINISHED PIECE

22 inches (55.9 cm) in length

YOU WILL NEED

180 feet (54.9 m) of cotton cable cord

2 metal O-rings, each approximately 1 inch (2.54 cm) in diameter

Scissors

Ruler or measuring tape

T-pins

Rubber bands

Masking tape

Knotting board

Water bottle*

*You start the knotting for this project on the knotting board, and then move to knotting directly around your water bottle. Make sure your bottle is filled with water to provide a sturdy surface to work on.

KNOTS AND WORKING METHOD

Lark's head knot (LHK), square knot (SQKT), alternating half hitch (AHH), double half hitch (DHH), overhand knot (OK), gathering double half hitch (GDHH)

Knotting in the round and from one end

Preparing the Materials

Measure and cut 18 pieces of cotton cable cord, each 10 feet (3.1 m) long. Locate the midpoint of one strand, fold it in half, and mount it onto one of the O-rings with an LHK. Mount all 18 strands with LHKs. Anchor the O-ring to the knotting board with a few T-pins.

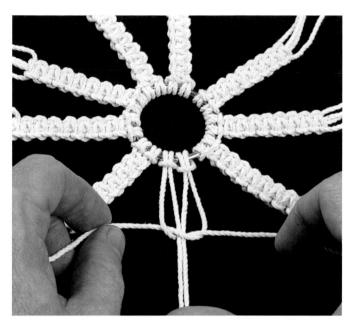

1 Fan out the cords on the knotting board. Separate the cords into groups of four. Tie a sinnet of eight SQKTs in each group. Remove the T-pins.

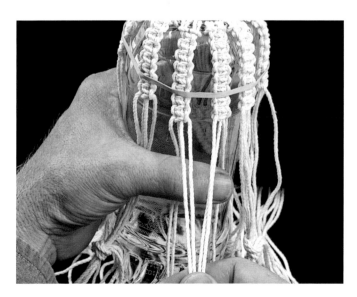

2 Turn your filled water bottle upside down. Center the O-ring on the bottom of the bottle. Secure the knotted sinnets to the bottle with a rubber band. Once the rubber band is in place, space the sinnets evenly around the bottle.

Divide the four cords in one sinnet into groups of two. Tie two AHHs in each set of two. Repeat with each group of cords around the bottle.

3 Regroup the cords into groups of four, using two cords from adjacent sinnets of AHHs. Tie two SQKTs. Tie the first half of an SQKT, but do not pull it tight. Leave approximately a ¾-inch (1.9 cm) space. Use a T-pin to hold the space open.

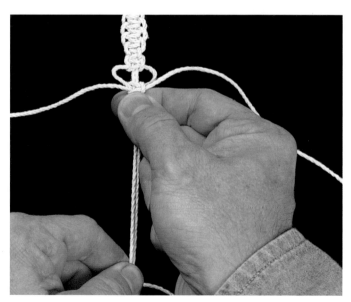

4 Complete the second half of the SQKT. Remove the T-pin and slide the knot-bearing cords up against the first half of the SQKT. This creates decorative loops. Finish the sinnet with an SQKT pulled tight against the previous SQKTs. Repeat this knotting sequence around the bottle.

Market Bag

Make your shopping stops with this stylishly knotted version of the classic string bag.

DIMENSIONS OF FINISHED PIECE

14 × 30 inches (35.6 × 76.2 cm)

YOU WILL NEED
192 yards (175.6 m) natural hemp cord
2 bamboo handbag rings, approximately 5 inches (12.7 cm) in diameter
16 × 24-inch (40.6 × 60.9 cm) knotting board*
T-pins
Scissors
Ruler or tape measure
Marking pen

*You will need to make a smaller knotting board specifically for this project. Wrap both sides of the board with a single length of fabric. Staple and tape the fabric to the board, as shown on page 233.

KNOTS AND WORKING METHOD

Lark's head knot (LHK), square knot (SQKT), double half hitch (DHH), overhand knot (OK), coil knot (CK), alternating half hitch (AHH)

Knotting from one end and in the round

Preparing the Materials

Measure and cut 6-yard (5.5 m) lengths of hemp. You will need 32 lengths in all. Find the midpoint of each strand and fold it in half. Use LHKs to mount 16 strands on each bamboo ring.

Use T-pins to secure one bamboo ring to each side of the knotting board. The top of each ring should be pinned approximately 1 inch (2.5 cm) from the top edge of the board. Comb and separate the cords with your fingers to place them in order.

1 You may start on either side of the board. Pick up two outer strands on the right. Tie 20 AHHs and place the unit aside. Pick up the adjacent unit of four strands. Tie three SQKTs (see photo).

Exchange the knotting strands with the knot-bearing strands. Exchanging strands will create an open space. With the strands in a new position, tie three SQKTs. Exchange the strands again, and tie three more SQKTs. Place this unit aside.

2 Pick up the next unit of four strands; tie three SQKTs. Exchange the knotting strands with the knot bearing strands. Tie three SQKTs, and place this unit aside. Pick up the next unit of four strands. Tie

three SQKTs, and place this unit aside. Pick up the next unit of four strands and tie two SQKTs. This becomes your center unit. Place this unit aside.

The cords remaining are knotted in reverse order from the center unit of two SQKTs. (You will have one unit of three SQKTs, a unit of SQKTs with one strand exchange, and a unit with two strand exchanges.) The last two strands will be tied with 20 AHHs.

Turn the knotting board over and knot the other side following steps 1 and 2.

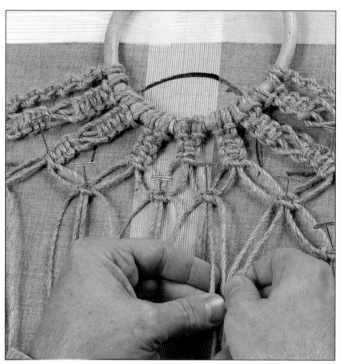

3 Use a marking pen to mark at the bottom of the center unit of two SQKTs. Measure from the mark to the top of the board. Use this measurement to mark two points on each side of the board. Draw a parallel line across the board using a ruler to make a straight line. Spread the strands evenly across the width of the board. Anchor the end of the knotted portion of the strands with T-pins close to the marked line (see photo).

The body of the shopping bag is created with a simple pattern of alternating SQKTs. Knots will be spaced approximately 1 inch (2.54 cm) apart. Begin knotting on either side of the board. Regroup the strands across the row and tie a single SQKT in each group. Secure each knot with a T-pin to maintain spacing. Turn the board over, and knot the opposite side in the same way. Regroup the strands again. This time the two outer strands on each side of the board will be grouped with two strands from the other side. Tie one SQKT in each side group. Secure the SQKT to the edge of the board with a T-pin. Now, tie one SQKT in each group of four strands across the board. Repeat on the opposite side. As you work down the board, move your T-pins from one knot to the next. Otherwise, you'll need a lot of T-pins

Knot 18 rows of alternating SQKTs on each side. Your last row should occur near the bottom of the board.

CLOSING THE BAG

4 Locate the SQKT pinned to the side of the board in the last row. Divide the four strands into two groups of two. Tie six AHHs in each group of two. Start from the left and hold the first strand from the AHH across the four strands of the adjacent SQKT. Tie DHHs using all four strands.

5 Hold the second strand from the AHH unit across the four strands just used and tie a second row of DHHs.

Repeat steps 4 and 5 with the cords on the right side. Then, turn the board over and repeat on the left and right as just described.

6 The remainder of the bag bottom will be tied off with a combination of SQKTs and OKs. Work from either the left or the right. Pick up two corresponding strands from each side of the bag. Tie one SQKT without a knot-bearing strand. Continue tying SQKTs across the bottom of the bag until all strands have been used and the bottom is joined.

7 Tie one OK using the four strands that you used to tie an SQKT. Pull the knot up snugly against the SQKT.

8 Tie a CK about 2 inches (5 cm) below the OK in each strand. Use scissors to trim the strands as desired.

Seafarer's Sampler

Ahoy, matey! Macrame projects don't always have to be functional. Inspired by the knot samplers tied by nineteenth century seafarers, which are eagerly collected as folk art today, this project will show off your knotting prowess.

DIMENSIONS OF FINISHED PIECE

5 × 6 inches (12.7 × 15.2 cm)

YOU WILL NEED

90 feet (27.4 m) of medium cotton cable cord

Ruler or measuring tape

Scissors

Knotting board

T-pins

Paper clamps

Clear-drying white craft glue

KNOTS AND WORKING METHOD

Slip-loop knot (SLK),
lark's head knot (LHK),
square knot (SQKT), half knot (HK),
reverse double half hitch (RDHH),
double half hitch (DHH),
overhand knot (OK)

Knotting from one end

Preparing the Materials

Measure and cut two cords each 8 feet (2.4 m) long. Measure and cut 16 pieces of cord each 5 feet (1.5 m) long.

1 Grasp the two 8-foot (2.4 m) pieces at the midpoint. Tie an SLK about 4 inches (10.2 cm) from each side of the midpoint. This becomes your anchor strand. Place T-pins through each SLK to hold the anchor strand to the knotting board. Double each 5-foot (1.5 m) cord at the midpoint. Mount each cord with an LHK to the holding strand. Wind the cord ends of the anchor strand and secure them with paper clamps.

2 Divide the cords into two groups of 16 cords. Divide the left group into four groups of four cords. Tie one SQKT with each group. Regroup with two inactive cords on the left and right. Tie one SQKT in each group of four. Knot five rows of alternating SQKTs in all.

Divide the 16 strands on the right into groups of four. Tie a sinnet of five SQKTs with the four strands on the right and left side of this half. Tie HKs in each of the two middle groups of four.

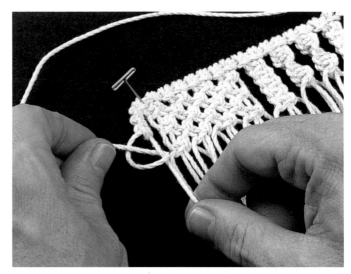

3 Remove the T-pin on the left side of the anchor cord. Pin the upper left SQKT. Remove the paper clamp and the SLK in the anchor strand. Use the left strand as the knotting strand, the right one as the knot-bearing strand. Tie five RDHHs. Place a T-pin in the fifth RDHH.

4 Lay the outside strand (below the RDHHs) across 17 strands as a knot-bearing cord. Tie DHHs with the 17 strands. Place a T-pin in the last DHH and turn the knot-bearing cord back to the left. Tie a second row of DHHs using all 17 strands around the knot-bearing cord. You will have two strands hanging on the

Wired-Up Bracelet

Forget traditional knotting materials! This project lets you explore new knotting dimensions using colored wires. Yes, wires. It's a little tricky, but the result is well worth the effort. When you've practiced with craft wires, move on to fine-gauge sterling silver or gold wires.

DIMENSIONS OF FINISHED PIECE

9 inches (22.9 cm) in length

YOU WILL NEED

8 feet (2.4 m) of 22-gauge colored craft wire in the color of your choice*

10 feet (3 m) of 24-gauge gold-colored craft wire

2 large pony beads

16 small pony beads

2 round focus beads, about $\frac{3}{8}$ inch (9.5 mm) in diameter

4 round opaque beads, $\frac{3}{16}$ inch (5 mm) in diameter

8 gold-plated E beads

Ruler or tape measure

Wire cutters or scissors

Knotting board

T-pins

Jewelry pliers (flat or round-nose)

*Craft stores now stock a wide selection of colored craft wire. This bracelet is knotted with a powder blue wire; the beads were chosen to complement it. Let yourself be seduced (but not over-whelmed) by the variety of colors you'll find. Choose two fabulous focus beads for the central portion of the design before you select the rest of the beads for the bracelet.

KNOTS AND WORKING METHOD

Square knot (SQKT), half hitch (HH), alternating half hitch (AHH)

Knotting from one end

Preparing the Materials

Measure and cut two pieces of colored wire, each 4 feet (1.2 m) long. Measure and cut two pieces of gold-colored wire, each 5 feet (1.5 m) long.

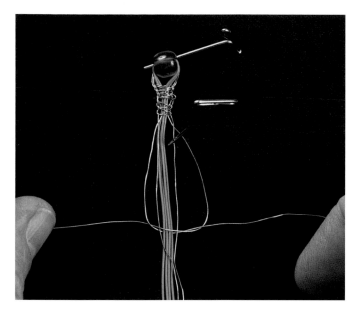

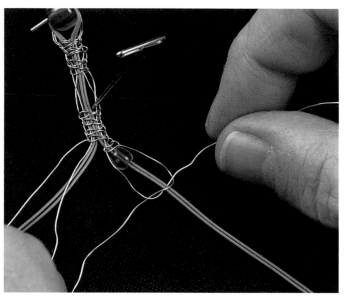

1 Thread one large pony bead onto all four wire strands. Slide the bead to the midpoint of the strands. Bend the wires down around the bead. Use a T-pin to secure the bead and wires to the knotting board. Use two gold-colored wires to tie four SQKTs around the remaining wires. Pick up the gold wires used as knot-bearing wires. Move them to the outside. Place the knotting wires (just used) parallel to the colored wires.

Place a T-pin about ¼ inch (6 mm) below the first group of SQKTs. Tie four SQKTs. Bring the first knot up to the T-pin. This will form a space between the groups of knots.

2 Divide the wires into two groups with two colored and two gold wires in each group. Tie one SQKT with the gold wires in each group. Thread one small pony bead onto both colored wires of each group. Tie one SQKT below the bead with the gold strands. Add two more beads to each group, securing each bead with an SQKT. You will have added six small pony beads in all.

3 Knot one group with eight AHHs using the gold wires around the colored wire. Knot the opposite group. Tie one SQKT below the series of AHHs. Thread a ³⁄₁₆-inch (5 mm) bead onto the colored wires of each unit. Secure each bead with one SQKT. Thread all four colored wires through a ³⁄₈-inch (9.5 mm) focus bead.

INTRODUCTION

I remember, as a teenager, trying to convince my mother to let me paint my bedroom black. We argued back and forth for months until finally we reached a settlement: she would let me paint the doors and woodwork black, but the walls had to remain off-white. Although I felt insulted and artistically compromised, I had to give in; she, after all, paid the bills. But when it was my turn to own the house, you may be certain there was no off-white. Red, orange, purple, even chartreuse, but no off-white. I won't say my rooms were always tasteful, or even bearable, but they were colorful.

I've always been a believer in the power of color. Color does more to transform the atmosphere of a room than any other component—more than furniture, rugs, window treatments, or accessories. Color sets a mood and lets you express yourself. Often overlooked, but just as important as color, is texture. And a good, subtle decorative finish is the perfect way to combine the powers of color and texture, unifying a look and helping everything in the room to make sense.

What is a decorative finish? More than just a paint treatment, a decorative finish takes a surface beyond a flat layer and adds another dimension, making it richer, deeper, and more textured. A faux finish (in which a surface such as marble or wood is simulated with paint and glaze) is one kind of decorative finish, but that's just the beginning. You can use glaze, plaster, stencils, imprints, and embossed borders and more to create an infinite variety of textures.

A good decorative finish makes a room warmer and more personal, or more elegant. It can also take the place of a rug or wallpaper, giving you the flexibility to change your mind and the freedom to choose your own colors and patterns. But decorative finishing isn't just for walls and floors. You can transform unfinished furniture, home accents and accessories, or painted wooden pieces. You aren't limited to working with wooden or plaster surfaces, either. With a little chemistry, you can create a stunning finish on metallic surfaces.

Achieving the sophisticated look you want can seem intimidating. In fact, my first attempt at a decorative finish was an unmitigated disaster. I was trying to replicate a beautiful leathery brown, antiqued finish I had seen in an English pub. My walls ended up looking like chocolate and vanilla swirl pudding rather than leather. After consulting books, taking courses, practicing, and experimenting, I finally got the hang of it. The trick, it turns out, is to know your materials and start small. That's what this book is about.

In the Basics section, we begin by discussing the materials and tools you need to create basic finishes. You'll learn about the different products that are made especially for decorative painting, and discover how easy it is to use everyday household items like plastic bags to create beautiful, subtle finishes. Next, you'll learn how to prepare surfaces, from walls to painted furniture, for finishing. I'll introduce you to six basic techniques that can easily be applied to a variety of surfaces. Finally, we'll review some basic facts about color that will help you combine paints and glazes to achieve the best results. The Glossary contains terms that you'll refer to over and over again as you work on the projects.

In the next section of the book, you'll find 20 attractive and functional projects that introduce a variety of techniques and let you practice your skills on a small scale, maximizing your chances for success before moving on to larger projects, like walls. Every finish you'll learn to create can be reproduced on either a wall or an object.

You may not achieve a perfect finish your first time out, but with just a little patience and practice, you can create a professional look. Relax. Remember: it's only paint—you can always paint over it!

DECORATIVE FINISHES BASICS

Materials

There are hundreds of specialty products available for decorative painting, ranging from expensive single-purpose brushes to metallic glazing powders. Before you sink a lot of money into advanced tools and materials, it's important to familiarize yourself with the basics. To create most simple finishes, all you really need is a base coat of paint, glazing medium and tint, and a simple tool for manipulating the glaze. The following section of the book will introduce you to these materials and others you'll need for a variety of projects. Most of these supplies can be purchased at paint or home improvement stores, although you may find better quality products through online sources. To search online, try using the keywords *faux finish, faux effects, faux finishing schools, faux finish products, glazing medium,* or *Venetian plaster,* and see what you find.

PAINTS AND GLAZES

For years, I worked only with oil-based paints and glazes because they were the best on the market. Despite the mess and difficult cleanup involved in working with these products, oil-based glazes stayed "open" (that is, remained wet and easy to manipulate) longer than any water-based products. Also, oil-based glazes are easily colored using *universal tints* (a highly concentrated type of liquid pigment used by professionals), which are available at any paint store.

Tints.

Now I only use water-based products. In the last 10 years, paint manufacturers have developed new water-based paints and glazes which surpass even the best oil-based products in quality. These new products are completely nontoxic, they don't smell bad, and you don't need as much ventilation in the rooms where you use them. Water-based paints and glazes can be manipulated as easily as oil-based products, and best of all, you can clean up your tools and work space with soap and water after you're done, saving you time and hassle.

Almost any paint store carries a line of water-based decorative finishing products, and you can also find them at many big home improvement stores. My favorite products, however, are those developed and sold by faux and decorative finishing schools. There are several excellent product lines out there, and most of them can be found online with a little research.

Primer

If you work with water-based products, primers usually aren't necessary. For example, if you're using a base coat product (see the following description) developed specifically to go under a glazing medium, you won't need to use one. You may need a primer, though, if you want to cover up a particularly grimy wall that's been painted with oil-based paint, or if you're trying to paint a very light color over a dark one. If you're painting a wall with red or a dark color, for example, you might want to use a water-based primer tinted as closely as possible to the base coat color you'll be using. This may save you a little money (primer can be cheaper than base coats). Ask the staff at your paint store for advice and guidance on whether or not your particular project needs a primer.

Base Coat or Undercoat

As the name suggests, a *base coat* or undercoat is the first color of paint you'll use in a decorative finish. Depending on what you're painting, you may use more than one coat of base coat before adding a glaze.

You can create a base coat with regular interior latex house paint in an eggshell finish. For the best results, however, use a product called "base coat" made especially for decorative painting. Base coat looks like regular house paint, and is applied in the same manner, but it's not paint. It's manufactured specifically to work under a glaze, holding the glaze open for 30 minutes or more. Base coats come in a range of ready-mixed colors, or you

Base coat in a variety of colors.

can buy them clear, or ready-to-tint (your paint store can custom tint them for you). I recommend using base coat rather than latex paint for particularly large projects, such as painting a whole room. You can usually find base coat at paint or home improvement stores, but again, the best quality products are made by faux and decorative finishing schools, and can be ordered online.

Glazing Medium and Tint

Glazing medium is the material that makes all those marvelous decorative finishes possible. It's the transparent liquid that's mixed with tint and applied over your base coat, then manipulated with any number of creative techniques (see pages 318-320). Oil-based glazing medium has a yellowing effect, but water-based medium goes on clear, even though it appears white in the container.

Adding Tint to Glazing Medium

No matter what products you choose to use, the recipe for mixing a glaze remains the same. Always begin by mixing a small amount of glazing medium with a small amount of tint (I use a disposable container as a mixing bowl). Start with about 2 tablespoons (30 mL) of glazing medium. Add a very small amount of tint to the medium and test the result on white paper or poster board. Remember: when making a glaze you can add tint, but you can't subtract it. If you put in the wrong color or too much of the one you want, you'll have to start over. Always experiment with less color first. Add more tint until you achieve the result you want.

Adding tint.

to start with smaller projects and work up to a wall glazing. If you *only* want to do a wall project, go ahead and give it a try. After all, it's only paint—you can always start over.

Mixing a glaze.

The best way to learn about glazing medium is to use it. You may not create a masterpiece the first time out, but once you're familiar with your product, you'll be able to glaze like a pro. It's best

Pouring glazing medium.

You *must* keep careful notes about the glazes you mix, the base coats you use, the preparation for the project, and any special problems you encounter. I always record on white paper a brush stroke sample of any glaze, along with the formula for the color. These records are *essential* should you ever need to patch and repair a project.

CLEAR FINISHING COAT OR TOPCOAT

A clear finishing coat, often called a *topcoat,* is a coat of varnish or polyurethane applied after the base coat and glaze have been applied and dried to seal the finish and protect it from nicks and scuffs. I rarely use a topcoat on walls that have been treated with a decorative finish. Glazing a wall adds durability to its finish, so there's no need for varnish or polyurethane.

Rag for removing glaze, spray topcoat, brush-on topcoat, bristle brush, roller.

Smaller projects, such as furniture, candleholders, floorcloths—anything that will be handled frequently—do need a protective clear finish like polyurethane.

There are many good clear topcoat products available. They often look milky when wet, but they all dry clear (some oil-based products will leave a yellowish tinge). I generally use a water-based polyurethane coat applied with a brush or roller, depending on the size of the project. You can also use a spray polyurethane finish, either water or oil-based. If I'm brushing on a topcoat, I always use a water-based product. It's easier to clean up and just as durable as oil-based topcoat. If I'm spraying a small pro-

ject, I use spray polyurethane—it doesn't make a difference whether it's water or oil-based because there's no cleanup involved.

When using a clear topcoat, always apply two or three light coats rather than one heavy coat. Polyurethane runs and sags just like paint, so thin coats work best. You may need to sand the surface of your project lightly after the first coat, particularly if you're working with a water-based product.

Clear topcoats come in four sheens, so you'll need to choose a "gloss" that suits your project. A *matte* finish has no gloss at all and is used for finish protection only. A *satin* finish has a light gloss, very little shine, and is perfect for most projects. A *semi-gloss* finish has more shine, and a *gloss* finish is ultra-shiny for when you want a very reflective surface. When it comes right down to it, the topcoat you use is just a matter of personal preference.

CRACKLE MEDIUM

A crackle finish is one of the most popular decorative finishes, especially for furniture. To create an old-paint look, *crackle medium* is applied between two coats of water-based paint. The second coat reacts to the medium, and cracks develop on the surface. In the past, achieving a good crackle finish was unpredictable, quite difficult, and better left to professionals. Many decorators craved the aged, cracked-paint look a crackle finish gives, but ended up with a messy, muddied surface instead. New crackle mediums available today are easy to use. I've had good experiences with just about all the crackle mediums on the market, so I buy the least expensive one. Paint stores, art supply stores, and some home improvement stores carry crackle medium.

Even though it's easier than ever to create a crackle finish, it's better to experiment first on small projects, like boxes or furniture. If you want to tackle a large project, such as a wall or a large piece of furniture, or if you want a perfectly consistent crackle, use a sprayer—there simply is no other way to crackle a large surface. Sprayers are available at paint and hardware stores. They're quite expensive, so you'll only want to make the investment if you think you'll be doing lots of spraying in the future.

You should be able to apply a crackle finish successfully by following the manufacturer's instructions, especially regarding drying time between coats. Practice a few times on sample boards before applying the finish to your project. A crackle finish takes some time to master, but is well worth the effort.

ANILINE DYES

Aniline dyes are powdered, synthetic, colorfast dyes that you can mix with either water or rubbing alcohol to use. They're more like stains than paint, and offer great depth of color and absorption. You can find these dyes at art supply and some paint specialty stores. They come in a wide variety of colors and have many applications. In this section, they are used on unfinished candleholders (see pages 326-327), but they would also work beautifully on cabinetry, furniture, trim, or paneling.

You'll need to keep a few things in mind when using aniline dyes. First, it takes very little dye to create a deep, rich stain. Don't add too much powder to your mix. Aniline dyes will stain your hands, clothes, or anything they touch, so wear gloves and protect your work surface.

Aniline dyes and paint pens.

Stains from aniline dyes bleed, or seep across and under a surface. If you're using more than one color of aniline dye on a project, don't apply the dyes too close together, as they will bleed into one another.

Always spray on a clear coat of polyurethane if your project uses more than one color of aniline dye. A brush-on clear finish will pick up the dye, and your colors will mix together and become indistinguishable.

DISTRESSING CHEMICALS

Decorative finishes are most often associated with painting on walls or wooden surfaces, but if you want to achieve an interesting effect on a metallic surface, you can use chemicals instead of paint and glaze. Copper, sil-

ver, gold, or dutch metal leaf all react to chemical compounds such as sodium sulfate and cupric nitrate, creating unique distressed features. These chemicals are available through chemical supply companies, and most

Sodium sulfate and cupric nitrate.

can be purchased online or through catalogues. Buy the smallest quantities available of these chemicals. It only takes about 1 tablespoon (15 mL) of chemicals to create ½ cup (120 mL) of liquid.

When using chemicals, follow all manufacturer's instructions carefully. Protect your skin, hands, and eyes against any contact, and always wear chemical-resistant gloves. Experiment before using this technique on a valuable item, as it's not altogether predictable.

METALLIC PAINTS, FOILS, AND LEAF

I use metallic paints and glazes a lot. They're a perfect way to add subtle interest to a finish—they shimmer and shift in different kinds of light. Gilding with gold, silver, or other metallic leafing can create a rich antique look on a surface, turning a plain or unpainted piece into a treasure.

To add metallic highlights to a finish, especially on small projects, I use a paint pen (available at art and craft supply stores) whenever possible. It gives me more control over application than a paintbrush would. For larger pieces, or when broad bands of gold or silver are needed, I use a flat artist's brush to apply water-based metallic paint. You can find this product at almost all art supply stores and some paint stores.

Oil-based gold and silver leafing paint is also quite versatile, and appropriate for smaller projects such as

Hole filler, putty knife, tack cloth, trowel, sandpaper, razor.

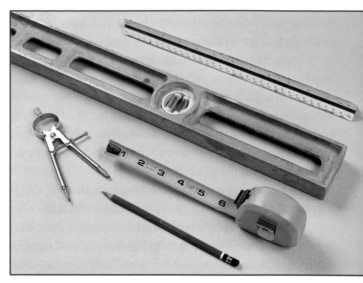

Hard lead pencil, steel measuring tape, compass, level, ruler.

Sandpaper (150- and 220-grit)

I use 150-grit sandpaper to smooth out rough spots, and fine-grit (220) to create a perfectly smooth, soft "final" finish. Using a coarser grain may damage a project.

Painter's Tape

You'll need low-tack painter's tape for protecting ceilings, baseboards, or trim from drips and splashes. Low-tack tape doesn't tear the plaster or paint off the walls when you remove it. For some projects, such as the mirror on pages 342-343, use high-tack painter's tape. High-tack tape is stickier, helps prevent seepage, and helps you create a hard boundary—just burnish the edges of the tape to the surface by rubbing them with a coin, or very fine sandpaper.

Steel Tape Measure

A measuring tape is essential, especially for big projects where you're creating patterns on a wall or floor and need to be precise.

Ladder

Get a good sturdy ladder that locks into place. A 5-to-6-foot (1.5 to 1.8 m) ladder is ideal. Try to get a painter's ladder—it has a place for your bucket or roller tray.

Tack Cloth

Tack cloth is just cheesecloth that's been treated with a sticky substance so that it collects and traps dust, dirt, lint, and any other residue that might be lurking on your surface. You'll use tack cloth after sanding to clean dust off your surface before you paint. It's important to have a clean surface before you begin to glaze, because any dirt or dust *will* show up.

Lightweight Hole Filler

You'll often need filler to plug holes and indentations in a wall or other surfaces. Get a quick-drying variety to reduce the time between prepping your walls and starting a finishing project.

Caulk and a Caulk Gun

Caulk is a semisoft vinyl or rubber product used to seal off the spaces between walls and trim or baseboards, or along windows. A well-caulked seam gives you a smoother surface to work with. Caulking is easy to apply with a caulk gun. Drying times vary between projects, so read your manufacturer's instructions to find out how much time you need.

Bucket of Clean Water

Keep plenty of water on hand for rinsing brushes, cleaning up, and a host of other uses.

Hard Lead Pencils

You'll use hard lead pencils for marking stripes on a wall, creating grids on a surface, tracing templates, or marking off areas that need to be painted. Use number 3 or 4 pencils so your marks will be light and you won't need to erase them. A darker pencil mark is difficult to remove and usually shows through the paint or glaze.

PAINTING TOOLS AND EQUIPMENT

Brushes

You could spend a fortune on brushes for decorative painting. There are dozens of different kinds available, some made only for one specific, limited purpose. I have about 75 paintbrushes, some of which I use frequently, some rarely. Try buying multipurpose brushes to start out with—you'll be able to use them for most finishes in this book. As you become more interested in and skilled at creating finishes, you can add more brushes to your collection.

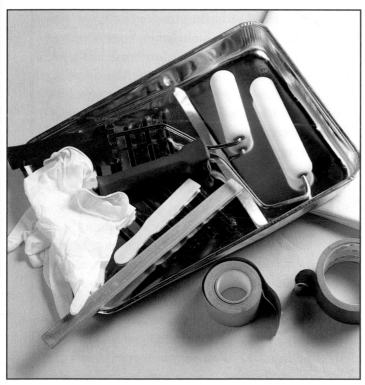

Standard painting supplies.

Always buy the best brush you can afford (except where indicated). There really is a substantial difference between a cheap brush and a good one. Cheap brushes lose their bristles, and you'll spend a lot of time picking bristles out of your glaze. The more expensive the brush, the better it will be. Ask your paint or hardware store person for advice. Of course you can use cheap bristle brushes for the smaller projects, but when working on walls, get the good ones.

You don't need to go out and buy a new specialty brush for each project, but there are some basic brushes you'll definitely want to have on hand. Invest in a couple of good brushes for applying glazes, creating *dragged* or *strié* finishes (see page 318), and applying *colorwashes* (see

page 318). These specialty brushes are available at online stores, art stores, and some paint stores.

Bristle Brushes and Synthetic Brushes

I always have one of the following brushes on hand: a 2-inch (5.1 cm) angled synthetic brush for "*cutting in*" (see page 317) and a 4-inch (10.2 cm) synthetic brush for applying glazes and colorwashing.

A *bristle brush* is made from real animal hair or natural fibers. Bristle brushes absorb more paint and hold it longer than synthetic brushes, which are made from acrylic materials. Bristle brushes are great for applying base coat, for pouncing (applying paint with an up-and-down motion for a mottled effect) small areas, for rough blending, and even for mixing glazes. They are available everywhere and are really inexpensive. I keep a supply of all

Brushes, left to right: bristle brush, softening or blending brush, angled trim brush, badger blending brush, large bristle brush, dragging brush. Bottom to top: stencil brush, artist's brush, round brush, flat artist's brushes.

sizes on hand. While synthetic brushes are good for applying water-based products, they do not work well with oil-based media. Bristle brushes work with all products, which is why I have so many of them (but I always have a good synthetic angled brush on hand as well).

Glossary

Angled or angular brush. A flat brush with bristles that are cut at an angle to make getting into corners easier.

Badger blending brush. A specialty decorative painting brush made from soft badger hair. Used for a final touch to blend brush strokes from a glaze.

Bagging. Manipulating a wet glaze with a plastic bag. See also ragging and padded finish.

Base coat. The first coat of paint applied in a finish. A glaze is applied over a base coat.

Blending. A soft or gradual transition from one color or tone to another. Also, a softening technique to reduce brushstrokes.

Burnishing. Rubbing vigorously to smooth a surface or transfer an image.

Cheesecloth. A lightweight cotton gauze material used to manipulate glazes.

Clear coat. See topcoat.

Colorwashing. A translucent "washed" effect achieved when a thin glaze is brushed over a painted surface, then blended with a brush or cloth.

Combing. Using a rubber comb, dragged across a just-painted surface to create stripes, plaids, waves, or squares.

Crackle medium. An antiquing medium used between two layers of paint. The top paint layer reacts with the crackle glaze and forms cracks, revealing the base color to create an aged paint look.

Curing time. The amount of time it takes for paint to "set," or reach its most stable state.

Cutting in. Applying paint around doors, ceilings, and trim carefully before applying it to a whole wall.

Distressing. Any technique that simulates the effects of wear and tear on newly painted surfaces.

Dragging. Using a paintbrush pulled in a straight "drag" across a wet surface to create a grained effect. See also strié.

Drybrushing. See blending.

Eggshell finish. See satin finish.

Faux finish. Decorative painting that imitates the look of wood, marble, etc. Faux means false.

Finishing coat. See topcoat.

Finishing plaster. See also Venetian plaster. A recently developed plaster product that can be applied to almost any surface to create a textured look.

Flat brush. A brush with squared-off bristles with a sharp edge.

Glazing. Applying glaze to a previously painted area.

Glazing medium. Transparent liquid that's combined with paint or tint to create a glaze that is then worked up into a decorative finish.

Gloss finish. Shiny finish with a reflective quality.

Graining. See Dragging

Hole filler. Lightweight plasterlike product used to patch holes in preparation for painting.

Imprint bonding agent. Liquid used to activate the transfer of an image from a specially-treated paper to a surface.

Matte finish. Flat finish with no gloss.

Open time. The period of time when a glaze is still wet and easy to manipulate.

Padded finish. See also bagging and ragging.

Pouncing. Giving a textured appearance by lightly loading a small amount of paint onto a brush and "pouncing" up and down on the painted surface, allowing some background color to show through.

Primer. A product designed to go under a coat of paint to prepare a surface to accept paint.

Ragging. Giving a textured effect by bouncing or dabbing a rag up and down on freshly applied glaze. See also bagging and padded finish.

Random edge. Glaze applied not in squares, but in loose organic patterns.

Rubber comb. A toothed implement developed for woodgraining and now used for other decorative finishing techniques.

Satin finish. Finish with a light gloss.

Semigloss finish. Somewhat shiny, durable finish.

Sponging. Using sea sponges to apply or remove paint from a surface.

Strié. A dragged paint or woodgrain finish.

Softening. See blending.

Tack cloth. Cheesecloth treated with a sticky substance so that it collects and traps dust and dirt.

Topcoat. Clear coat of varnish or polyurethane applied after a glaze to protect a finish from scuffing or chipping.

Undercoat. See base coat. Preliminary color over which other colors or glazes are applied.

Universal tints. Highly concentrated liquid pigment for coloring oil or water-based paints. Used by professional house painters and decorative painters.

Venetian plaster. A recently developed plaster product that can be applied to almost any surface to create a textured look.

Wet edge. Keeping a portion of a glaze unmodified and wet so that there is a gradual, rather than a harsh, transition between areas of glaze application.

Tuscan Flowerpots

These aged-finish flower pots would look right at home on the steps of an Italian villa. You could spend a bundle to buy a planter for this gorgeous old-world look, or you could make one yourself with a little finishing plaster, glaze, and an ordinary terra-cotta pot. This finish also looks great on other home furnishings, such as ceramic bowls, vases, or candleholders.

Terra-cotta flowerpot

Disposable gloves

White base coat

2-inch (5.1 cm) bristle brush

Putty knife

Finishing plaster

Aluminum foil

Oven

Mixing bowl or tray

Glazing medium

Dark brown or black tint

Stiff bristle brush

Paper towels or rags

Additional tint colors (optional)

2 Using a putty knife or even your hands (wearing gloves), apply a generous coat of finishing plaster to the outside of your pot. Smooth the surface somewhat with the putty knife, but make sure that the texture is still generally rough and uneven. Apply a layer of plaster inside the rim of the pot, starting about 2 inches (5.1 cm) down, and smooth it somewhat with your putty knife.

4 Mix a glaze (1:1 medium-to-tint ratio) using dark brown or black tint, and apply it to the surface of the pot with a stiff bristle brush, working the glaze into all the cracks.

5 Use a paper towel or rag to remove most of the glaze from the surface. Since this plaster is so sturdy, you won't need a topcoat of polyurethane.

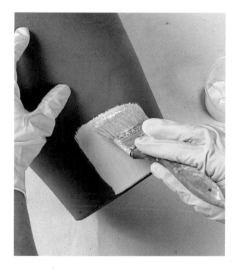

1 Wearing gloves, apply two coats of white base coat to the inside and outside of your terra-cotta pot with a 2-inch (5.1 cm) bristle brush. Allow to dry.

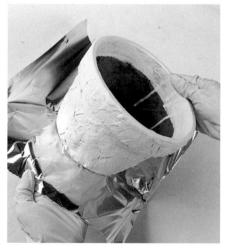

3 Place the pot on a piece of aluminum foil, and place it in an oven set to 175°F (79°C) until the pot is dry, about one hour. Large cracks will appear in the surface because of forced drying time. Allow the pot to cool completely.

■ TO INCREASE COLOR DEPTH ON YOUR POT, REPEAT STEP 4, USING ADDITIONAL TINT COLORS.

Whimsical Candleholders

When dreaming up a new decorative finish, don't limit yourself to paints. Try these versatile materials—aniline dyes and paint pens. Aniline dyes are powders that, when mixed with water, are applied like any wood stain. You can buy them in art supply or paint stores. Paint pens are easy to find at most stationery or craft supply stores. Try using them on any unfinished wood projects—a stool, a chest of drawers, or even kitchen cabinets!

3 Test your colors on a scrap of wood. Observe how the stains penetrate the grain. Add more powder or water until you get the desired colors.

5 Apply the next color to the next section, again making sure the colors don't bleed into each other. It's helpful to leave a small unpainted area between each color. Let each section dry for about one hour before beginning the next.

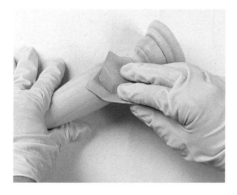

1 Sand your candleholder using 220-grit sandpaper. Remove all dust with tack cloth.

2 Mix the aniline dyes using about ¼ teaspoon (1.2 mL) powdered stain to 1 ounce (30 mL) of water. The more powder you use, the stronger your color will be.

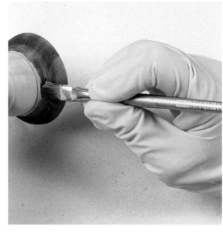

4 Using a small artist's brush, apply the first color to the base of the candleholder, being very careful not to let it seep into the next section. Stains will bleed a bit, and you don't want your colors to mix with each other. Allow the first section to dry for about one hour.

6 Using a metallic paint pen, fill in the unpainted areas and embellish with lines, stripes, dots, circles, and patterns of your own design. Seal your finish with a clear coat of polyurethane spray. Do not use brushed-on clear coat, as the colors will still bleed until sealed.

Distressed Copper Leaf Frame

YOU WILL NEED

Newspaper

Empty wooden frame

Low-tack painter's tape (optional)

Latex paint (optional)

Disposable gloves

Leaf adhesive*

Small artist's brush

8 to 10 copper leaf squares,* each 4 × 4 inches (10.2 × 10.2 cm)

Soft bristle brush

Cheesecloth or soft rag

Heavy-duty, chemical-resistant gloves

Old glass dish for mixing chemical solution

Water

Sodium sulfate**

Stir stick (or craft stick) for mixing solution

Small sea sponge

Garbage bag

Paper towels

Water-based, clear, spray polyurethane in a satin finish

*available at art supply stores

**available through chemical supply companies

Paints and dyes can create fascinating distressed finishes on wood or plaster, but if you're working on a metallic surface, you'll need chemicals to achieve that weather-worn look. This unusual finish is created with a chemical compound applied to copper leaf, but the process also works on silver, aluminum, or dutch leaf. You'll need to be extra cautious and read your manufacturer's instructions carefully when attempting this finish. Most importantly— wear chemical-resistant gloves and make sure you have proper ventilation.

NOTE: BEFORE YOU BEGIN, EITHER TAPE OFF THE GLASS OR MIRROR IN YOUR FRAME OR REMOVE IT COMPLETELY. COVER YOUR WORKSPACE WITH SEVERAL LAYERS OF NEWSPAPER. PAINT THE FRAME IF IT'S UNFINISHED OR YOU DON'T LIKE THE BASE COLOR.

1 Cover your work surface with newspapers. Wearing disposable gloves, brush the leaf adhesive onto the whole frame in even strokes. Allow the mixture to set for about 45 minutes (leaf adhesive will keep its tack for several hours).

2 Apply the copper leaf by laying it on the surface of the frame. Leave small unleafed areas to allow the base color to show through.

3 Brush over the leaf with a soft bristle brush.

4 Smooth the surface with a soft rag or cheesecloth. Remove any excess leaf from the frame.

5 You must work over newspaper and wear chemical-resistant gloves for the next steps—rubber or latex gloves won't protect your hands. In an old glass dish, dissolve about 1 tablespoon (15 mL) of sodium sulfate in a small amount of water. If the granules don't completely dissolve, that's okay. They will still do the job. This solution will smell very sulfuric; make sure your workspace is well ventilated!

6 Dab a small sea sponge into the solution, then apply it to the frame, leaving some areas untouched. You can also "puddle" the solution in places for interesting effects. Allow the solution to set for several hours or overnight. When finished, dispose of the sponge, the solution, and the bowl by wrapping them in newspaper and placing them in a plastic garbage bag. Do **not** pour the leftover solution down your sink.

NOTE: IF THE CHEMICAL REACTION STARTS HEADING TOWARD "TOO MUCH," RINSE THE PIECE WITH WATER AND PAT IT DRY (I USE A GARDEN HOSE AND AN OLD UTILITY SINK). THAT WILL STOP THE REACTION.

7 Spray the frame with clear polyurethane, preferably in a satin finish.

Aluminum Finish Curtain Rod

Why spend a fortune on fancy curtain rods when you can get the same elegant look from an inexpensive wooden pole and a simple decorative finish? Aluminum paint over a black base is a quick way to achieve a metallic-look curtain rod that will dress up any window treatment. If aluminum doesn't match your décor, try the same technique with a gold or copper paint. You can use this finish on any raw wood piece, from a picture frame to a chair.

3 Dip a small sea sponge into aluminum paint, and dab the sponge over the black paint in a random pattern. Don't aim for full coverage; you want a good deal of black to show through under the aluminum paint. Let the paint dry overnight.

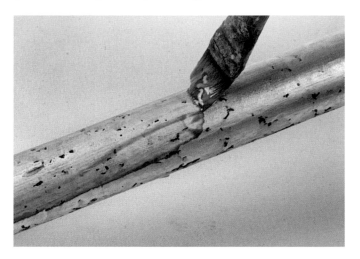

4 Mix a glaze with a raw umber (dark brown) tint using a 3:1 medium-to-tint ratio, and brush the glaze over the entire surface of the pole. Allow to dry. Spray with two coats of polyurethane to seal the finish, if desired. Attach the end finials (you can apply the same finish to the finials, paint them, or leave them as is for a contrast).

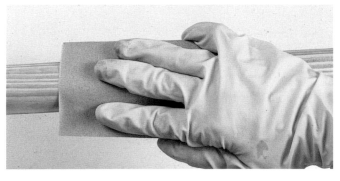

1 Sand the pole with 220-grit sandpaper; remove all dust with tack cloth.

2 Wearing gloves and working over a protected surface, use a small flat artist's brush to paint the pole with two coats of black latex paint in eggshell or semigloss finish. Allow to dry.

Checkerboard Breakfast Tray

Combing is one of the most popular and versatile decorative finishes. It can be used to create a woodgrain effect or any number of patterns on a wall or decorative object. Dragging a comb through wet glaze creates the attractive texture. In this project, the flat bottom of the tray is painted in a checkerboard pattern, and then glazed in a different shade of blue. Once you've mastered the technique on a small project like this, try it on a wall to create a beautiful textile look.

2 Paint the inside bottom of the tray with the bright blue base coat. Use two coats. Tape off the angled interior sides of the tray if it helps you to paint more neatly. Let dry.

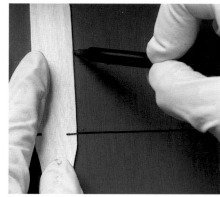

3 Using a straightedge (I used a paint mixing stick) and a hard lead pencil or marker, draw a checkerboard pattern on the inside bottom of the tray. This tray is a 12-inch (30.5 cm) square, so I marked off 3-inch (7.6 cm) squares.

1 Using a 2-inch (5.1 cm) bristle brush, paint the entire tray with the warm yellow base coat. Use two coats if necessary. Let dry.

4 Mix a small amount of white base coat into your bright blue base coat to lighten it. Add enough to ensure there's a contrast between your new lighter blue color and the bright blue coat you've already painted. Paint every other square in the checkerboard pattern with your new mix of blue using a 1-inch (2.5 cm) flat artist's brush. Your coverage should look hand-painted—it doesn't have to be perfect. Let dry.

5 Mix a bright blue glaze (3:1 medium-to-tint ratio) and apply over all the squares with the artist's brush.

6 While the glaze is still wet, pull your rubber combing tool across each square in the manner seen in the photo.

8 Once the bottom of the tray is dry, mix a warm sienna glaze with a 1:1 ratio of glazing medium to tint. Starting on the angled interior sides, use the artist's brush to apply the glaze in fairly wide vertical stripes. You can measure the space in between the stripes and mark them with a pencil if you like, or paint them in a less regimented, handpainted style, as seen here. When you're finished painting the interior stripes, start painting stripes along the outside. Match them up with the interior stripes, so that they look continuous from inside to outside.

9 When the stripes are dry, glaze the interior and exterior angled sides with a warm sienna glaze (using about a 3:1 medium-to-tint ratio).

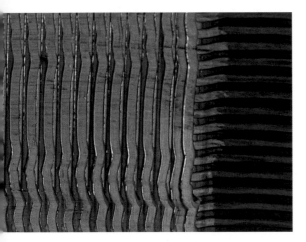

7 Alternate the pattern, using different sides of the comb to pull different patterns in adjacent squares. A vertical pull next to a horizonal pull is a nice contrast. To effectively fit the comb into the corners, you can cut off some of its teeth.

10 Using a small artist's brush, paint the inside of the tray handles with a contrasting color latex paint, such as warm brown. Spray the entire tray with a clear coat of polyurethane in a matte or satin finish.

Ginger Jar Lamp

You had about 10 of these lamps in the 1980s, and now they look tired and out-dated. Give your ginger jar a long-overdue facelift. For this project, you'll apply a simple sponging finish to the ginger jar. The sponge is used to dab on several layers of paint in different colors to create a mottled texture. For the shade, you'll create a coordinating strié finish using a blending brush. These are great techniques to learn on a small-scale, unintimidating project.

FOR THE GINGER JAR

1 Using a small bristle brush, apply two coats of warm yellow base coat or latex paint to the ginger jar, allowing drying time between coats.

2 Using a small piece of a sea sponge, pick up some of the black paint or base coat and apply it to the ginger jar. Coverage should be uniform, in small specks rather than big patches.

3 Repeat step 2 with the red paint.

4 Repeat the same process with the light brown paint.

5 Add the dark green paint in the same manner. Use a light hand. For each additional color you add, you should still be able to distinguish the other colors.

6 Add the white paint, mixed with a touch of black, in the same way.

7 Finally, add the dark brown paint with the sea sponge. Dab a little dark brown on with the sponge, but not as much as you did with the other colors.

FOR THE SHADE

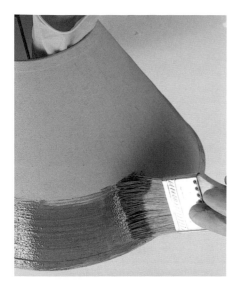

8   Mix the glazing medium and the warm sienna tint in a 1:1 ratio. Apply the glaze around the bottom edge of the shade with a bristle brush.

10   Blend the glaze with a badger brush or any very soft brush. Allow to dry.

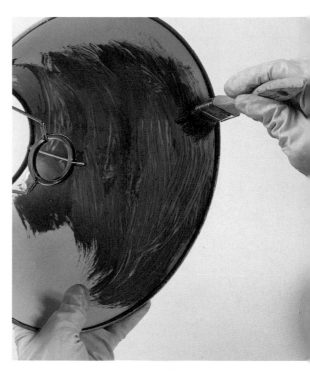

12   Using a small brush, apply gold metallic paint to the inside of the shade. Blend or soften the look with cheesecloth, and allow to dry.

9   Using a dry bristle brush, push the glaze up into the unglazed areas, lessening the amount as you go.

11   Use a metallic paint pen to highlight the bands of the shade.

Metallic Highlight Mirror

A mirror can be an important focal point for a room, especially if you don't have much artwork on your walls. A mirror frame is a perfect place to try out new decorative finishes and add interest to a wall. This Egyptian-inspired look is easy to create, thanks to metallic paint pens. Painting directly on the mirror helps extend the decorative effect and gives you more room for creativity.

YOU WILL NEED

Mirror mounted in a wooden frame

Ruler

Soft lead pencil

High-tack painter's tape

Coin or credit card for burnishing

Black latex paint or base coat

Dark brown latex paint or base coat

Mixing bowl or tray

½-inch (1.3 cm) small, flat artist's brush

Metallic silver paint pen

Metallic gold paint pen

Water-based clear brush-on polyurethane

Single-edged razor blade

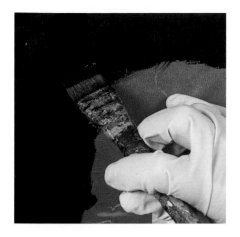

1 Measure in 2 inches (5.1 cm) from the mirror frame, and apply high-tack painter's tape all around the mirror. Burnish the edge of the tape by rubbing with a hard edge, such as a coin or credit card. This will help minimize paint seepage. Pour a small amount of the black and brown paint into a mixing bowl or tray. Using a ½-inch (1.3 cm) artist's brush, pick up some of each color and apply randomly to the entire frame and to the glass inside the tape line. *Do not* mix the brown and black; it should appear splotchy. Allow to dry.

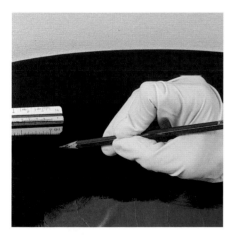

2 Decide how big each design area will be. Use a pencil to mark off each section.

3 Paint over the pencil lines with a metallic silver paint pen.

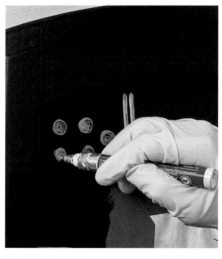

4 Create the rest of your patterns using gold and silver paint pens. You may need to pencil in the designs first. I like a symmetrical look, so I created the same designs on each side of the mirror, but reversed the orientation of the patterns.

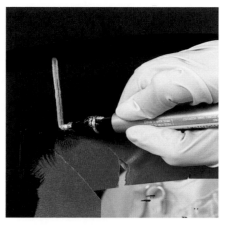

5 After the paint is thoroughly dry, apply two coats of clear, high-gloss polyurethane using the small, flat artist's brush.

6 Remove the tape carefully and slowly.

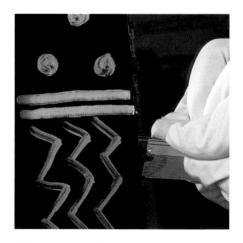

7 Scrape off any seepage with a single-edged razor blade.

Animal-Print Folding Table

You don't have to be an artist or have advanced painting skills to create this wildly attractive look. The secret is all in the imprint. Imprints transfer a preprinted pattern from a coated paper to the surface of your project. All you need for the transfer is an activating liquid, called imprint medium, and a flat utensil for rubbing the back of the imprint. The result is a fantastic finish that looks like it was done by a pro.

YOU WILL NEED

TV trays or folding table, any color or finish

Disposable gloves

Warm red base coat

White base coat

Mixing bowl or tray

4-inch (10.2 cm) polyester bristle brush

Imprints of zebra, giraffe, and ocelot*

Scissors

Small foam brush

Imprint bonding gel*

Low-tack painter's tape

Flat stick, such as a paint mixer, for rubbing the imprint

Hard lead pencil

Drafting compass

Small artist's brush

Gold metallic pen

Glazing medium

Dark brown tint

Mixing bowl

Cheesecloth

Water-based, clear spray-on or brush-on polyurethane in satin or matte finish

*available online from decorative finishing sources

1 Using your 4-inch (10.2 cm) polyester bristle brush, apply two coats of warm red base coat to the legs and underside of the folding table. Paint the tabletop with a white base coat.

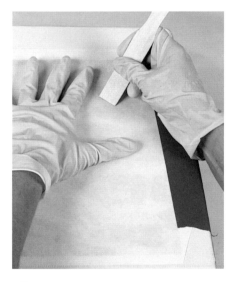

2 Cut the animal imprint to the correct size. For this project, I cut the imprint to fit on the tabletop with a 2-inch (5.1 cm) border all around. Using a foam brush, apply imprint bonding gel to the tabletop. Allow it to set for about one hour, until tacky. Place the imprint facedown on the table. Secure it to the tabletop with painter's tape. Rub the back of the imprint to transfer the color. A paint-mixing stick works well. So does a credit card!

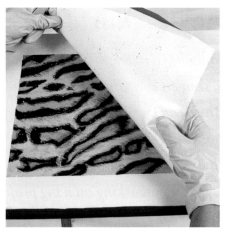

3 Carefully lift the imprint to make sure all color has been transferred. If not, place it back down and rub it again.

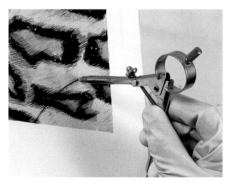

4 Position your drafting compass at the edge of the table, and draw a semicircle on each corner of the imprint.

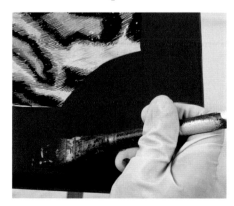

5 Paint the border of the tabletop in the same warm red you used for the rest of the table. Paint over the semicircles at each corner of the imprint in the same color. This adds interest to the border.

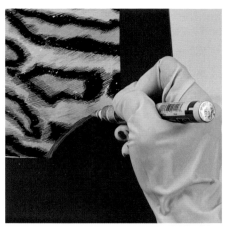

6 Highlight the border of the imprint with a gold metallic paint pen.

7 Mix a dark brown glaze (3:1 medium-to-tint ratio), and apply it to the entire table.

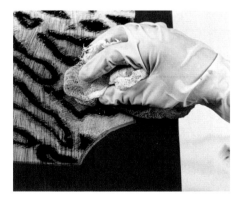

8 While it's still wet, blend the glaze with cheesecloth, removing some glaze. Allow the piece to dry overnight. Apply two coats of clear polyurethane in a satin or matte finish to the top of the table. Use more clear coats if the table will get a lot of use.

Venetian Plaster Wall Finish

This project uses the same material as the Domed Treasure Box (pages 340-341) and the Tuscan Flowerpots (pages 324-325), but on a much larger, more ambitious scale. If you've never plastered a wall, you might want to practice in a small area before tackling a whole room. Once you've gotten the hang of it, try creating this worn, aged look in a kitchen or bathroom.

YOU WILL NEED

Low-tack painter's tape

Drop cloths

Disposable gloves

Off-white base coat

10-inch (25.4 cm) foam roller

Roller pan or tray

Finishing plaster*

Putty knife

10-inch (25.4 cm) plastering trowel

Bucket of hot water

Synthetic closed-celled sponge

Glazing medium

Orange tint

Dark brown tint

Black tint

4-inch (10.2 cm) synthetic brush

Soft rags or paper towels (optional)

Utility knife

*Finishing plaster is available through decorative finishing sources or home improvement stores. It's sold by the gallon. Each gallon covers approximately 300 square feet (27m²).

1 Tape off ceiling, windows, doors, and baseboards and put down drop cloths. Apply two coats of the off-white base coat, allowing two to three hours of drying time between coats.

4 If you prefer a smoother look, wet the closed-cell sponge and skim over the plaster while the plaster is still somewhat wet (within 15 minutes of application). Allow the walls to dry overnight.

6 Apply the glaze to the walls using the 4-inch (10.2 cm) synthetic brush. Work the glaze into the cracks and depressions created by the plaster. Distribute the glaze over the walls with the brush in a random fashion, criss-crossing your strokes.

2 Use the putty knife to load the trowel with plaster.

5 Prepare a glaze using orange and dark brown tint. For a terra-cotta effect, mix a 3:1 medium-to-tint ratio with the orange tint, and add about ½ of one part black.

3 Using the trowel, skim across the wall, making several passes until you get the look you want. The plaster should vary in thickness. Leave some places unplastered. For tight corners, use your putty knife as a trowel. Wipe any plaster off trim or baseboards immediately.

7 Brush over the same areas again and again, removing hard brush strokes and creating a washed look. You may wish to remove some of the glaze using a soft cloth. You want to achieve a washed and worn look, not a uniform color throughout. Allow to dry. Remove the tape by cutting through the finish to the tape with a utility knife and then lifting off the tape. Do not simply pull the tape off, as that will pull the plaster off the wall as well.

Harlequin *Faux Bois* Floor

Beautiful wood floors can make *a room, but what do you do if your floors have lost their luster? Try this wood-look finish, called* faux bois, *and a harlequin or diamond-shaped pattern. It's perfect for hiding flaws and imperfections in a wooden floor, drawing attention away from defects in the wood, and focusing it on the bigger picture—the diamond-shaped pattern. The warm brown glaze mimics a real wood finish—only the most discerning eye will be able to tell the difference.*

1 Vacuum and clean your floor with a trisodium phosphate substitute, and let it dry. Wearing disposable gloves, apply two or three coats of warm yellow base coat to the floor with a roller, and let it dry.

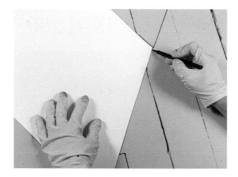

2 Photocopy the harlequin template on page 370, and enlarge it to the desired size for your floor pattern (the pattern for this project was approximately 2 ½-feet long × 12 inches wide (76.2 × 30.5 cm). Copy the template onto cardboard or stiff poster paper. Find the center point of two adjoining walls in your room. Using a straightedge and a pencil, draw a line from each wall to this point. This is the center against which you line up your first row of diamonds. Set your template on the floor with the center of the diamond over the center point. Trace around it with a soft pencil. Move the top point of the template to the bottom point of the drawn diamond, and trace another diamond. Continue this process going down the floor and then across until the pattern extends across the whole floor.

3 Mix a glaze using dark brown, warm brown, and a touch of red, to suit your desired outcome. Using a 4-inch (10.2 cm) stiff bristle brush, apply the glaze to every other diamond, moving from the left to the right, from the top to the bottom of the floor. Apply the glaze in straight stokes to achieve a natural wood-grain look. Allow to dry overnight.

4 Add a little more color to the glaze you created in step 3. Using a soft bristle brush, apply the glaze across the entire floor, over the diamonds that are already glazed and those that are unglazed. Again, pull down in straight lines to create a strié (striped) effect that resembles wood graining. Allow to dry overnight.

5 Apply several coats of satin water-based polyurethane topcoat across the whole floor with a roller.

Aged Chinese Newspaper Wall Finish

Chinese characters have a simple graphic quality that looks impressive even if you don't understand their meaning. On a wall, Chinese newspapers can create a striking pattern.

Use them like wallpaper to camouflage a dull or damaged section of the wall.

You can also use this finish on small decorative items, such as boxes, canisters, or trays.

Once you've mastered this technique, you can turn any paper into distinctive wallpaper.

2 Repeat the process until the entire wall is covered. It's okay to overlap the pieces in a random pattern. Allow to dry overnight.

4 Mix a glaze using dark brown tint, adding tint until you reach the depth of color you want (a light orange glaze also looks good on Chinese newspaper). Apply the glaze using a 4-inch (10.2 cm) bristle brush.

1 Using a foam roller and clear polyurethane base coat, paint a section of your wall. Place a sheet of Chinese newspaper on top of the wet clear coat, and roll over it until it's thoroughly soaked and adheres firmly to the wall. (Briefly soak the newspaper first so it's damp, not wet; if you apply it to the wall dry, it will wrinkle.)

3 As the newspaper dries, add more polyurethane if there are places where the paper didn't adhere, and let these additional coats dry.

5 Use a badger brush to smooth the brush strokes. Let dry. If you want, apply another coat of polyurethane for durability, using your roller to create even coverage and avoid brush strokes.

Colorwash Wall with Antiqued Border

A colorwash is one of the simplest and most attractive of wall finishes. It can add texture and depth to a wall without overwhelming the surroundings, and it's easy to do. Add a wallpaper border to a wall that's been antiqued with glaze, and you'll add an elegant tone to any room in the house.

YOU WILL NEED

Disposable gloves

Low-tack painter's tape

Base coat in warm yellow

Roller pan

Foam roller

4-inch (10.2 cm) bristle brush

Glazing medium

Mixing bowl or tray

Orange tint

Dark brown tint

Black tint

Cheesecloth

1- to 2-inch (2.5 to 5.1 cm) bristle brush

Badger blending brush

Prepasted embossed wallpaper border

Rag or paper towel

Tape measure

Hard lead pencil

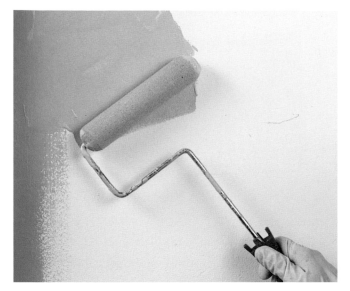

1 Prep and patch your walls as needed, and tape off your ceiling, windows, doors, and baseboards. Apply two coats of the warm yellow base coat: first, cut in around the trim, using a roller or brush as needed, then paint the rest of the surface. Allow three to four hours' drying time between coats. After the second coat, allow the wall to cure overnight.

2 Mix a glaze with orange tint mixed at about a 3:1 medium-to-tint ratio. Add dark brown tint and a touch of black. Add the black tint a drop at a time, mixing well after each addition. Keep going until you achieve the depth of color you want—you're going for a rich terra-cotta.

3 Apply the glaze to the wall using a 4-inch (10.2 cm) brush or foam roller. Always leave a wet, unworked edge.

4 Gather the cheesecloth into a ball, folding in all raw edges so stray threads won't land in the glaze. Softly dab the walls with the cheesecloth, turning cloth back and forth as you work. Your application should be random, not even.

5 Brush over the entire surface of the wall with a badger blending brush to soften the texture. Softly blend the finish, moving the brush up and down, back and forth.

6 Mix a dark brown glaze using a 1:1 medium-to-tint ratio. Apply the glaze to your embossed wallpaper border with a 1 to 2-inch (2.5 to 5.1 cm) bristle brush.

7 Use a rag or paper towel to remove most of the glaze from the border.

8 Measure and mark on your wall the horizontal line that you'll use as the top of your border. Measure and mark the height of your border (it can be used as a chair rail or wall border). Hang the border according to the manufacturer's instructions.

African Mudcloth Floorcloth

The striking, simple patterns of African mudcloth are recreated in this functional painted floorcloth. Painted to echo the warm, handloomed texture of real mudcloth, this floorcloth adds interest to a floor without tying you down to a permanent paint job. You don't need stencils or templates for this one—you can mark off different sections with just a pencil and ruler. The designs are done freehand, so you can paint as loosely as you like. If you're using this floorcloth over a bare floor in a high traffic area, buy a very thin rug pad to use underneath.

Preprimed canvas measuring 46 × 64 inches
(116.8 × 162.5 cm)

White latex house paint or artist's acrylic paint

Roller pan

4-inch (10.2 cm) foam roller

Duct tape or two-sided carpet tape

Soft lead pencil

Tape measure

3-foot (91.4 cm) straightedge

Disposable gloves

Black flat latex paint

2-inch (5.1 cm) angled synthetic brush

1-inch (2.5 cm) flat artist's brush

Gold metallic paint pen

Mixing tray or bowl

Glazing medium

Dark brown tint

4-inch (10.2 cm) stiff bristle brush

Cheesecloth

Water-based clear polyurethane finish

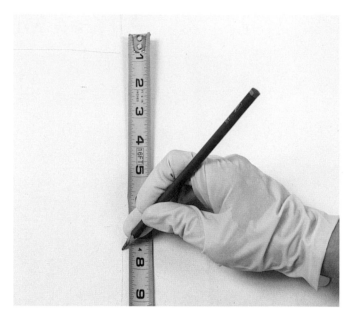

2 Create a checkerboard pattern on your canvas by drawing a series of 9-inch (22.9 cm) squares inside the rectangle. The easiest way to do this is to set a tape measure along each edge, and mark every 9 inches (22.9 cm). Connect the hash marks using a straightedge.

3 With the 2-inch (5.1 cm) angled brush, paint the outside border and every other square with the black paint. One coat should be enough. Use your pencil marks as guidelines only. You don't need to paint perfect squares—you're striving for a hand-painted fabric effect. Erase any unwanted pencil marks after the black paint has dried.

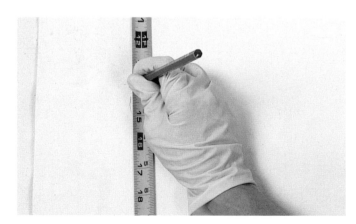

1 Paint your canvas with the white latex paint using a roller or a brush. Let dry. Hem it by turning under 2 inches (5.1 cm) on all four sides and taping the hem to the back with duct tape or two-sided carpet tape. Your canvas will now measure 42 × 60 inches (106.7 × 152.4 cm). Measure and mark a 3-inch (7.6 cm) border on all four sides of the canvas. You should now have a rectangle that measures 36 × 54 inches (91.4 × 137.2 cm).

4 Using a 1-inch (2.5 cm) flat artist's brush, paint a white, freestyle wavy design on each black square. Repeat this design on the white squares using black paint.

5 Outline each square with a gold paint pen. Again, imperfections are good. Draw circles at the intersections of the squares.

6 Let dry. Mix a dark brown glaze (1:1 medium-to-tint ratio.) Brush the glaze over each square with a 4-inch (10.2 cm) bristle brush.

7 With cheesecloth, dab the surface, softening and blending the glaze. Continue to dab with cheesecloth until you've removed a lot of the glaze and have achieved a soft effect. Allow to dry.

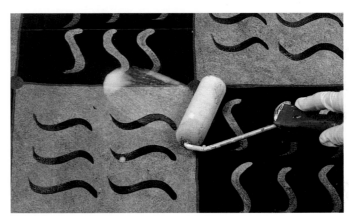

8 Using the foam roller, coat the floorcloth with a clear acrylic finish. Apply at least two coats, using more if the floorcloth will be used in a high traffic area, such as a bathroom.

Moroccan Souk Folding Screen

Folding screens are great for dividing a space or hiding a room's less attractive features, but many of them come with plain, dull canvas panels. Why not use the blank canvas to create an evocative decorative finish? Using simple stencils and templates, you can create an exotic Moroccan mood for your room. This project is a great solution when you don't want to commit to a permanent wall finish—when you're ready for a change, just pick up your screen and move it, or paint another finish over it.

Disposable gloves

Dark blue latex paint

Light blue latex paint

Mixing tray

Small foam roller

Canvas folding screen

Masking tape or other sturdy tape

Moorish stencil or other decorative stencil

Yellow-gold latex paint

Minaret template on page 370

Heavy poster board or cardboard

Scissors or craft knife

Felt-tip marker

1-inch (2.5 cm) flat artist's brush

Gold water-based paint

Warm red latex paint

Bronze water-based paint

½-inch (1.3 cm) flat artist's brush

Glazing medium

Brown tint

Gold metallic water-based paint

Small flat artist's brush

2 Using the roller, apply the paint to the screen's canvas panels in a random pattern. Move the roller back and forth, mixing the two colors together. Paint the front of each panel in the screen to about two-thirds of the way down the screen, leaving the bottom third of the screen unpainted. You don't have to paint the panels evenly—the irregularities in the color are part of the appeal of this finish. Allow to dry.

3 Tape your stencil in place at the top of the first canvas panel. Using the foam roller, paint over the stencil with the yellow-gold paint. Don't overload the roller, or paint will seep under the stencil—use a light touch.

1 Pour a small amount each of dark and light blue paint into a mixing tray or plate. The pools of paint should be near enough to each other to touch without mixing too much. With a small foam roller, pick up some of both colors on opposite sides of the roller.

2 On a soft work surface, rub the section to be raised from the back of the foil. Use a blending stump for aluminum. On brass and copper foil, use a broad pencil stylus for small areas and a blending stump for large sections. Stroke gently to form the desired shape and height of relief. Apply more pressure to areas where higher relief is desired. Gradually lessen the pressure when you sweep across areas of lower relief.

NOTE

If there are several convex relief areas in a design, fully emboss and define the foreground item first, completing steps 2 and 3; then, finish the item on the next level using the same process; and so on until all convex forms are created.

3 Working from the front side of the foil on a very hard work surface (glass pane), use the flat of a screwdriver stylus for aluminum or a small ball stylus for brass and copper to define the edges and emphasize the relief of the convex form. Apply enough pressure to sharply define the shape at its perimeter.

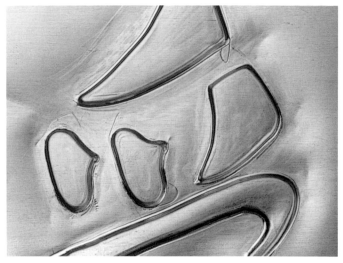

Flat relief

FLAT RELIEF

Like convex relief, flat relief is characterized by a broad, elevated surface. However, the raised surface is flat and parallel to the work surface, not curved or domed. The vertical "walls" of a flat relief are at a 90° angle to both the upper and lower surfaces of the foil.

YOU WILL NEED

Basic tool kit, page 377

Metal tooling foil with transferred pattern, such as the Asian character from Basket of Love, page 444

1 Retrace the pattern from the back side of the tooling foil over a soft work surface (computer mouse pad). Use a pencil stylus for aluminum and a ball stylus for brass or copper. Apply enough pressure to emboss the foil.

2 Working from the back side of the foil on the soft work surface, uniformly increase the amount of relief throughout the pattern area. Use a blending stump or screwdriver stylus for aluminum or an extra-broad pencil or screwdriver stylus for brass and copper.

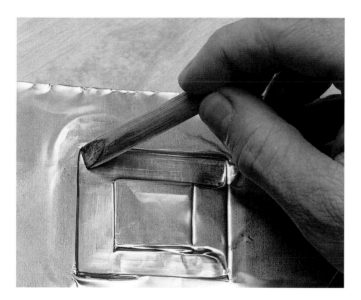

3 Working on the back side of the foil on a very hard work surface (glass pane), "iron" the design from the center, or *floor*, to the raised sides, or *walls*. This process removes bubbles and imperfections and creates greater contrast between the high- and low-relief areas. Slide a screwdriver stylus to form sharp corners between the walls and the floor. (Remember to hold the screwdriver stylus at a 45° angle to the foil.)

4 Repeat the ironing process—this time on the background of the design—from the front side of the foil. Begin away from the flat relief area, and iron toward its walls. Use a screwdriver stylus to define the corners. Repeat steps 2 through 4 until you have achieved the desired amount of relief.

HINTS

- Placing a light source directly above the embossed foil causes the flat relief to cast shadows. Narrow shadows cast by the walls indicate that 90° angles have been achieved.

- The more tooling foil is worked, the thinner it becomes. Take care to avoid tearing the foil. If a tear does occur on the edge of a relief form, simply close the gap; it probably will not show once the filler and patina are added.

BACKGROUND RELIEF

You can add texture to the background of a metal embossing either before or after filling in its hollows. Select any background you enjoy, a very simple linework or an ornate decorative pattern. Working on a softer surface produces a background texture with a higher and more pronounced relief. A harder work surface results in lower relief and a more subtle texture.

1 Select a background design from page 433, or create your own motif. Place the foil face up on a medium (foam place mat) or hard (cardboard) work surface. (Most background designs are embossed from the front side of the foil.)

2 Emboss the background design on a medium (foam place mat) or hard (cardboard) work surface.

3 Working on the front side of the foil on a very hard work surface (glass pane), outline the boundary between the background texture and the embossed image. Use a pencil stylus for aluminum and a ball stylus for brass and copper.

FILLING IN THE HOLLOWS

After embossing the foil, you will fill in the hollows on the back side of the artwork with wood filler to give support to the raised areas. Carefully and cleanly filling the hollows results in a higher quality embossing. On some occasions, however, thick brass and copper foil designs will not require filling. Always refer to the project instructions.

1 Place the embossed foil face down on a very soft (foam rubber) or soft (computer mouse pad) work surface or hold it in your hand. Use a small plastic palette knife, spatula, or butter knife to fill the hollows with the wood filler as shown. It may be helpful to use the wall of the hollow to scrape the filler off the spatula, and then fill the center. (If the background design is in low relief, it will not need filling. A background in high relief, especially on aluminum, may require support.) Do not fill in embossed areas that will be cut out. Remove all excess wood filler by scraping with the side of the spatula and/or wiping it off with a damp cloth. Rub off small amounts of dry filler with a blending stump.

2 Use the spatula to level the wood filler to the height of the background. Sprinkle the surface of the filler with an absorbent powder such as baby powder, talc, or flour. Pat the filler to remove air bubbles. Cover the filled area with a layer of tissue paper. Roll a dowel over the paper to level the filler (see photo above). Remove the paper. If more filler is needed, repeat steps 1 and 2. (Don't worry if the filler shows your fingerprints.)

3 Use the blending stump to remove any filler that overflowed its borders. Once the overflow is removed, the outline of each raised design will be clearly visible. Clean the borders with a damp cloth.

4 Set work aside to dry on a soft surface. Drying time will vary depending upon air temperature, humidity, and the depth of the hollows. You can speed the drying time by using a hair dryer or by placing the embossing near a heating vent or outdoors (weather permitting). The filler is dry when it becomes hard. Test for hardness at the point with the deepest filler. Repeat steps 1 through 4 to refill any shrunken or cracked areas in the dried wood filler (see photo just above).

APPLYING A PAINT PATINA

Use a paint patina when you want to create a more dramatic embossing. The addition of a color that contrasts with the metallic tooling foil enhances the depth of the relief.

YOU WILL NEED

Basic tool kit, page 377

Metal tooling foil with any embossed design (hollows filled in)

1 Working outdoors or in a well-ventilated area, prepare the black lacquer or enamel paint for use following the manufacturer's instructions. Brush or spray the paint on the foil to cover all the downfolds and the embossed background of the design. (Painting beyond these areas is not a problem.) Allow the paint to dry only to the touch; a longer drying time makes the removal of excess paint more difficult.

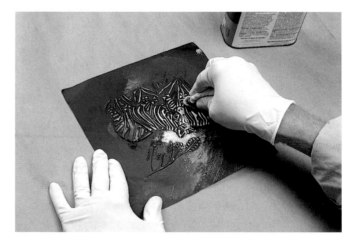

2 To remove the excess lacquer or enamel paint, first wad a soft cotton cloth into a tight bundle, or wrap the cloth around your index finger. (A taut cloth ensures that the paint is removed only from the high relief areas.) Dab a small amount of the lacquer or paint thinner onto the cloth. Using long strokes, rub across the entire painted metal embossing as shown. Remove as little or as much of the paint as you desire.

Switch Covers

Add a unique touch to your interior design with these embossed switch and socket covers. Whether you choose the floral, animal, or graphic motif, many embossing techniques will come into play. These small projects can be created in an afternoon, and make great gifts.

Design: Spring

YOU WILL NEED

Basic tool kit, page 377

Aluminum or thin brass tooling foil, 3 1/2 × 5 1/2 inches (8.9 × 14 cm)

Traced base template, decorator or toggle, page 436

Light switch plate

Traced pattern of your choice, pages 436 and 437

Paring knife (Lace design only)

TECHNIQUES

Cutting, page 378

Transferring, page 379

Line relief, page 380 (Desert Friends, Spring, Lace, Harvest, Hunter's Pride)

Convex relief, page 381 (Desert Friends, Spring, Harvest, Hunter's Pride)

Flat relief, page 382 (Harvest, Hunter's Pride)

Background relief, page 384

Filling in the hollows, page 384

Applying a paint patina, page 385

Designs, left to right: Hunter's Pride, Harvest, Lace

BEFORE YOU BEGIN

Please note the following symbols and their meanings when working with the templates on page 436 and 437.

Dotted lines indicate the location
of the switch opening.

Dashed lines indicate the fold line of the foil.

Circles with intersecting lines indicate
the location of the plate's screw holes.

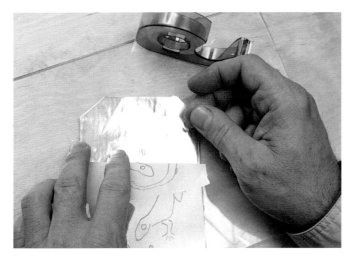

1 Cut the foil as the base template and mark the
screw hole locations from the light switch plate.
Match the screw symbols on the pattern to those
marked on the foil (see photo). Transfer the pattern
onto the foil.

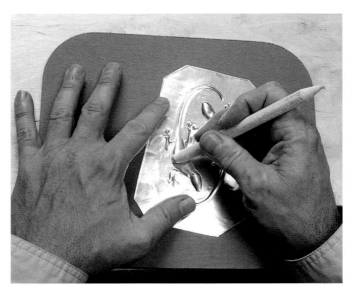

2 Emboss the foil using the techniques described
for your selected pattern.

Desert Friends

Emboss the lizard bodies in convex relief as shown.
Emboss the lizard toes in line relief.

Spring

Emboss the flower petals and round flower centers
in convex relief. Retrace the petal lines with a pencil
stylus from the front side of the foil.

Lace

Emboss the stems in line relief. To create the small
leaves, use a pencil stylus on the back side of the
foil over a medium work surface (foam place mat).
Emboss a 1/4-inch (6 mm) line, and then curve the
line back to the beginning point without raising the
stylus. Outline the small leaves from the front side
of the foil on a very hard work surface (glass pane).
To imprint a leaf vein, lower the point of the paring
knife on the pointed end of the leaf.

Harvest

Emboss the small wheat centers in convex relief.
Emboss the wheat bristles in line relief. To create the
flat leaves at the top and sides of the pattern, emboss
the shapes in flat relief. Draw the leaf veins from the
front side of the foil with an empty ballpoint pen.

Hunter's Pride

Emboss all pointed and rounded shapes in convex
relief, all square shapes in flat relief, and all narrow
lines in line relief.

3 From the front side of the foil, add a low background texture of your choice as shown, but keep the foil at the plate openings flat. Fill in the hollows. Add a patina if desired.

4 Brush the glue onto the plate and adhere the embossed foil. Perforate the foil over the screw holes. Swivel a pencil stylus into the perforations to mold the foil to the plate as shown. Smooth down the foil background with a blending stump to remove air pockets and to locate the switch openings. As needed outline the design again with a ball stylus.

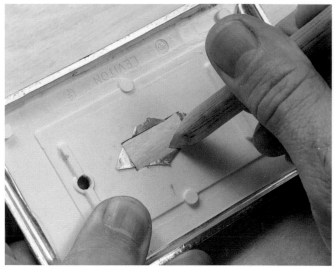

5 Use a craft knife to slit the foil over the switch opening from corner to corner. Fold the sections of slit foil to the back side of the plate and trim. Smooth down the foil-covered openings with a screwdriver stylus (see photo).

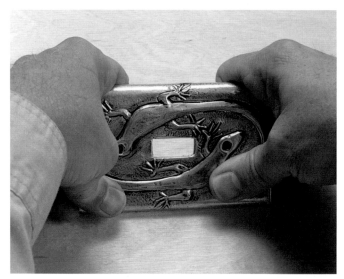

6 Firmly hold the foil and plate combination face down and neatly fold the edges of the foil. On a very hard work surface, slowly drag and turn the plate around to the back as shown. Wrap and mold the excess foil with a stump or stylus to fit the contour of the back of the plate. Repeat this process on the opposite side of the plate, and then on all remaining sides. Trim and tap the foil-covered corners of the plate on a very hard work surface (glass pane) to make them smooth.

Catch-of-the-Day Panel

Fish species are found from the Polar regions through the tropics, in deep oceans and tiny brooks. Nearly as ubiquitous, this template can be used in many different ways. The two fish can be embossed onto a single piece of foil, paired on separate sheets, or featured individually. You can arrange them vertically as shown, or set them swimming horizontally in an underwater scene.

YOU WILL NEED

Basic tool kit, page 377

Traced pattern, page 435

Aluminum tooling foil, 5 ³/₄ × 3 ¹/₄ inches (14.6 × 8.3 cm) plus 1-inch-wide (2.5 cm) margins for each fish

TECHNIQUES

Cutting, page 378

Transferring, page 379

Line relief, page 380

Convex relief, page 381

Filling in the hollows, page 384

Applying a paint patina, page 385

Mounting, page 386

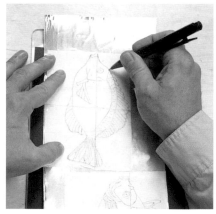

1 Position the pattern on the foil in a pleasing way, and transfer the design.

2 Emboss the fishing line, and then the fins, eyes, and mouths, in line relief. Use the same technique to outline the spots of Fish 1 (see photo) and the gill-tail line on Fish 2. Emboss the remaining fins and both fish tails.

4 Work from the back side of the foil on a soft work surface (computer mouse pad). Hold the pencil stylus at a very low angle to make the scales on Fish 2 (see above photo). The placement and size of the scales are up to you. Outline the curve of each scale from the front of the foil with a small ball stylus.

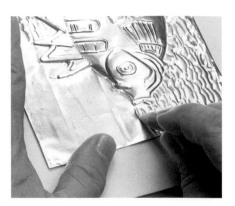

6 From the front side of the foil use a fine-point pencil stylus to draw a background pattern of closely packed waves or any other texture you wish.

3 From the back side of the foil, use blending stumps to form the layers of the fish faces in convex relief as shown. Working on a very hard work surface (glass pane), define the layers of the faces from the front side of the foil with a fine-point pencil stylus.

5 Contour each fish body in convex relief from the back side of the foil. Use a broad blending stump or a wadded cloth over a very soft work surface (foam rubber) as shown. Use a pencil stylus to outline the entire fish from the front side of the foil over a very hard work surface (glass pane). Repeat this process until you achieve the desired amount of relief.

7 Fill the hollows. Refill them to the level of the background after the application dries (see above photo). Apply a paint patina. Mount or frame the panel as you wish. (I chose a wooden frame with an antique blue finish, hammered a rusty nail on each side, from which I hung two coordinating fishing bobs to enhance the rustic style.)

Chili Pepper Bottle

Many people are making their own flavored oils and vinegars and storing them in bottles. Decorating these bottles and their caps is a great way for the conscientious crafter to refashion and recycle. The cutout chili peppers in this design let the bottle's colorful contents show through the embossed foil.

YOU WILL NEED

Basic tool kit, page 377

Traced patterns A, B, and C, page 435

2 aluminum tooling foil strips, each 1 × 5 inches (2.5 × 12.7 cm)

Aluminum tooling foil strip, 3 × 11 inches (7.6 × 27.9 cm)

Aluminum tooling foil square, 2 × 2 inches (5.1 × 5.1 cm) for cap top

Glass bottle with cap

Pinking shears

Measuring tape

TECHNIQUES

Cutting, page 378

Transferring, page 379

Line relief, page 380

Convex relief, page 381

Filling in the hollows, page 384

Applying a paint patina, page 385

NOTE:
Pattern B, repeated once, fits a bottle with a 3-inch (7.6 cm) diameter. The circumference of the bottle is approximately 10 inches (25.4 cm).

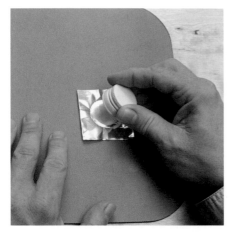

1 Transfer pattern A onto the two 1 × 5-inch (2.5 × 12.7 cm) strips of aluminum tooling foil. Transfer pattern B onto the 3 × 11-inch (7.6 × 27.9 cm) foil strip, repeating the pattern at the dots. Imprint the bottle cap opening in the center of the 2 × 2-inch (5.1 × 5.1 cm) square as shown, and then transfer pattern C onto the foil.

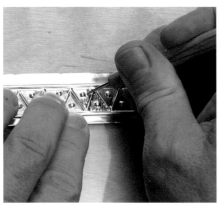

2 Emboss the narrow foil strips in line relief. Tool the dots. Draw closely packed lines on a very hard work surface (glass pane) to lower the background as shown.

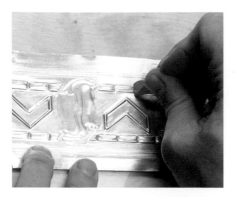

3 Outline the V-shapes on the wide foil strip in line relief. Emboss each horizontal bar as one piece. On a very hard work surface (glass pane), greatly press a screwdriver stylus on the vertical pattern lines to divide the bars (see photo above). Emboss the pepper stems in line relief. Fill the background with dots tooled from both the front and back sides.

4 Use convex relief to form the chili pepper in the center of the cap foil square (see above photo). Emboss the pepper's stem and lines. Lower the background as in step 2.

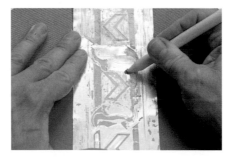

5 Fill all hollows of the embossed foil, let dry, and then clean off any excess filler as shown. Apply a paint patina.

6 Cut out the foil areas as indicated by the shading on pattern B. Trim the wide strip with pinking shears. Measure the height of the cap and trim one of the narrow strips to fit this dimension. Cut the margins off the other narrow strip. Use pinking shears to trim off about 1/8 inch (3 mm) from the outer edge of the embossed bottle cap as shown.

7 Apply glue to the wide embossed strip, and then smooth the strip onto the bottle with a blending stump. Trim the length of the strip as needed. Use rubber bands to hold the strip in place while the glue dries. Mount and trim the neck band. Clip the round piece between the points to the circle, and adhere the foil to the bottle cap. Holding them firmly together over a very hard work surface (glass pane), drag and turn the points around to mold the foil edges to the cap wall. Mount and trim the narrow band around the bottle cap as shown. After the glue dries, scrape any excess off the glass with a craft knife.

Bear Tracks Panel

This pattern is taken from real bear tracks indented into the ground.
The paw prints are done using concave relief with convex shapes at the center.
Adding a strong black patina inside the prints enhances their graphic character.

YOU WILL NEED

Basic tool kit, page 377

Aluminum tooling foil, 3 1/2 × 10 1/4 inches (8.9 × 26 cm) plus 1-inch-wide (2.5 cm) margins

Yard or meter ruler

Traced pattern, page 438

Wood plaque, painted if desired

Hot-glue gun and glue stick

Decorative metal studs (optional)

Hammer (optional)

Large turquoise beads (optional)

TECHNIQUES

Cutting, page 378

Transferring, page 379

Line relief, page 380

Convex relief, page 381

Concave relief, page 381

Filling in the hollows, page 384

Applying a paint patina, page 385

Mounting, page 386

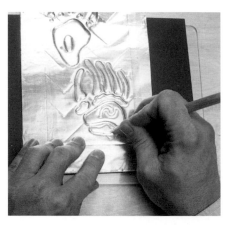

1 Find the center of the aluminum tooling foil with a yard or meter ruler. Transfer the pattern onto the tooling foil. Working from the front side of the foil on a hard work surface (cardboard), use a pencil stylus to outline the outer boundary of each section of the paw prints as shown above.

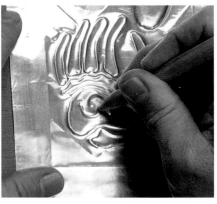

2 From the back side of the foil, emboss the center sections of each paw print in convex relief, but do not outline these center sections. Emboss the remainder of the paw print from the front for a concave relief (see above photo) so the foil curves down instead of up.

3 From the back side of the foil, smooth every other chevron stripe with a blending stump over a very hard work surface (glass pane). Repeat this process on the other stripes from the front side of the foil as shown. To keep the background subtle, do not sharpen the edges of the chevrons.

4 From the back side of the foil on a soft work surface (computer mouse pad), use a pencil stylus and a ruler to score the straight line border of the design. Hold the ruler on a scored edge, and fold the foil edge up to form one side of a box as shown. (The fold will not be perfectly straight.) Repeat this process on the other scored edges. Pinch together the corners of the folded edges to join the sides of the box. Define the edges around the inside of the box with a pencil stylus.

5 Slowly add water to the wood filler and stir until it reaches the consistency of cake batter. Pour the wood filler into the foil box to cover the bear tracks (see above photo). To remove air bubbles from the filler, carefully drop the artwork from a height of about 6 inches (15.2 cm) onto a level, padded surface. Repeat this action several times. Allow the wood filler to dry thoroughly.

6 Fold the side edges of the foil box over the dried filler as shown. Cut the corners as needed to make the folding neater and easier. Apply a paint patina to the embossed surface, and then hot glue the artwork to a wood plaque. Hammer decorative metal studs to the board if desired. Use hot glue to adhere turquoise beads between the studs if you wish.

Beautiful Book Trimming

By enhancing your plain photo albums and scrapbooks with an elegant embossed medallion and book corners, you can remember and honor your loved ones in style. Any hardback book, even one with a padded cover, can be embellished. Using copper and brass gives the design an antique look, making the book an instant heirloom.

Candle Rings

Forget-Me-Not Design

Let this candle ring embossed with flowers and ribbons add even more romance to your candlelit occasions. Its well-defined convex relief and background textures are heightened by applying a black patina.

YOU WILL NEED

Basic tool kit, page 377

Traced pattern, page 440

Aluminum tooling foil, 2 3/4 × 9 inches (7 × 22.9 cm) plus 1-inch-wide (2.5 cm) margins

Food can or jar, 3 inches (7.6 cm) in diameter

String, elastic, or strip of cloth

Candle, 3 inches (7.6 cm) in diameter

TECHNIQUES

Cutting, page 378

Transferring, page 379

Line relief, page 380

Convex relief, page 381

Background relief, page 384

Filling in the hollows, page 384

Applying a paint patina, page 385

Forget-Me-Not Candle Ring (left);
Simple Grace Candle Ring (right)

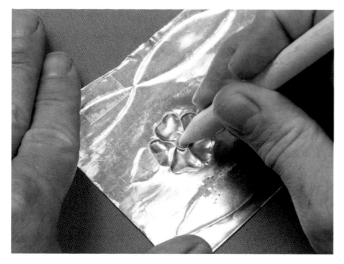

1 Transfer the pattern onto the aluminum tooling foil twice in a row, matching the pattern dots to begin the second transfer. Emboss the flower petals in convex relief. From the front side of the foil, firmly stand the point of the pencil stylus at the base of a petal. Slowly lower the pencil stylus onto the embossed petal to form a crease in the foil. Repeat this technique for each petal in the design. Using a soft work surface (computer mouse pad) and a blending stump, tap and raise the flower centers from the back side of the foil (see photo).

3 Emboss the ribbon edges in line relief. On the front side of the foil, over a hard work surface (cardboard), draw lines across the ribbon with an empty ballpoint pen as shown. Add a background of your choice to the area between the flowers and the ribbon. Fill the hollows. Add a paint patina. Trim the embossed foil at the outer margin of the ribbon.

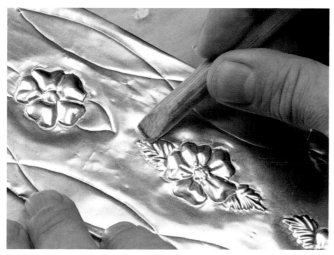

2 From the back side of the foil over a soft work surface (computer mouse pad), emboss lines from the leaf centers to the leaf edges. Working over a very hard work surface (glass pane), define the leaf edges from the front side of the foil. To form a serrated leaf edge, use the corner of a screwdriver stylus and push toward the leaf as you outline (see above photo). For a smooth-edged leaf, define the edges with the flat of the screwdriver stylus in a single stroke.

4 Form the embossed foil strip into a ring by smoothing it around the jar or can. Rub the background with a blending stump (see photo). Glue or tape the ends of the ring around a candle. If gluing, wrap a string, elastic, or cloth strip around the ring until dry.

On-the-Vine Wine Basket

This handy and attractive tote will let you carry picnic supplies or present party gifts in style. Four copper foil pieces are individually embossed, separately cut out, and then artfully arranged. A patina solution provides the perfect finish for the leaves, and copper wire makes lovely spiral tendrils.

YOU WILL NEED

Basic tool kit, page 377

Thick copper tooling foil, 4 × 3 inches (10.2 × 7.6 cm) plus 1-inch-wide (2.5 cm) margins

3 thick copper tooling foil pieces, each 3 ½ × 2 ½ inches (8.9 × 6.4 cm) plus 1-inch-wide (2.5 cm) margins

Traced patterns, page 441

Plastic circle template

Liquid patina solution, green

Small paintbrush

3 pieces 20-gauge copper wire, each 4 inches (10.2 cm)

Wire cutters

Hot-glue gun and hot glue

Basket of your choice

TECHNIQUES

Cutting, page 378

Transferring, page 379

Line relief, page 380

Convex relief, page 381

Filling in the hollows, page 384

Applying a paint patina, page 385

Mounting, page 386

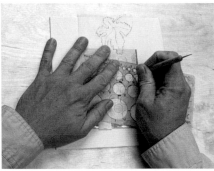

1 Transfer the patterns onto the tooling foil, using a circle template as needed (see photo above). Use the back and front sides of the pattern to transfer the three leaves.

2 Form the major veins of the leaves in line relief. Emboss the leaf edges from the back side of the foil over a soft work surface (computer mouse pad) as shown. Use one corner of the screwdriver stylus as you keep the other corner off and over the leaf image.

3 Work on the front side of each leaf over a very hard work surface (glass pane) with a ball stylus. Firmly push in the leaf outline at random points to create unique edges and creases (see photo). Return to the back side of the foil, and lightly emboss angled lines from the vein to the tip of each leaf.

4 Emboss the back of each grape in a circular as well as a rocking motion on a soft work surface (computer mouse pad). Work with an extra-broad pencil

stylus, and then a broad blending stump. Turn the foil over and use a very hard work surface (glass pane). Select a circle template that is large enough to allow a small ball stylus to retrace the grape outline and define the edge (see photo, bottom left). Repeat this step for each grape until the desired relief is obtained.

5 Place the embossed grape cluster on a very soft work surface (foam rubber) or in your hand. Use a wide blending stump or soft cloth to curve the cluster (see photo). On the front side of the foil, over a very hard work surface (glass pane), flatten the outer edge of the cluster with a screwdriver stylus, and then outline it with a ball stylus. Following the manufacturer's instructions, color the leaves by applying the green liquid patina solution.

6 To make the wire tendrils, form a small ¼-inch (6 mm) triangle at one end of a 4-inch (10.2 cm) piece of the copper wire. Coil the rest of the wire around a pencil or stylus as shown. Remove the wire and slightly stretch it to separate the coils. Repeat this process to create additional tendrils.

7 Fill the grape cluster's hollows to maintain and support its curved form. Keep in mind that the outer edges of the cluster will need to come in contact with the mounting surface. Fill the hollows of the leaves (see photo above). For more dimension when mounted, add more filler in any one area of each leaf.

8 Cut out the embossed pieces as shown. Place each one face up on a hard work surface (cardboard), and push their edges slightly under with an upright ball stylus. Arrange the pieces in an artful manner and adhere them to the basket with hot glue. Sections of the leaves may be mounted under the grape cluster. Insert the triangle end of the copper-wire tendrils under any embossed piece.

Splendor-of-the-Season Watering Can

The blooming tulips of spring look especially elegant in high relief. This thick copper gardenscape design transforms an ordinary aluminum watering can into a work of art. The background texture is a prominent basket weave, and the green patina is achieved by applying a liquid solution.

YOU WILL NEED

Basic tool kit, page 377

Thick copper tooling foil, 5 × 5 ¾ inches (12.7 × 14.6 cm) plus 1-inch-wide (2.5 cm) margins

Traced pattern, page 441

Liquid patina solution, green

Small paintbrush

Aluminum watering can

TECHNIQUES

Cutting, page 378

Transferring, page 379

Line relief, page 380

Convex relief, page 381

Filling in the hollows, page 384

Background relief, page 384

Applying a paint patina, page 385

Mounting, page 386

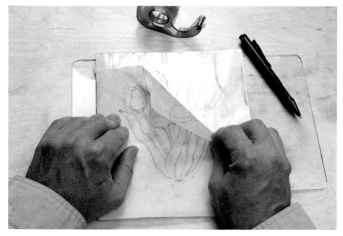

1 Transfer the pattern onto the thick copper tooling foil as shown above.

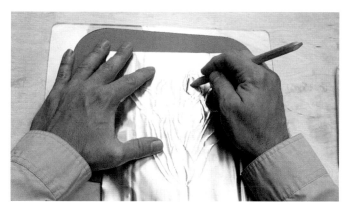

2 Use convex relief to emboss each tulip, fully completing one petal at a time.

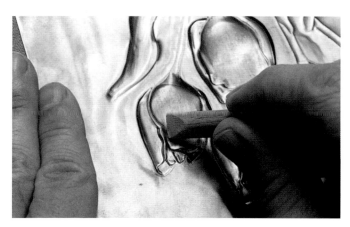

3 Working from the back side of the foil on a soft work surface (computer mouse pad), use a screwdriver stylus to retrace only the upper part of the petals (see photo). Apply pressure only on the corner of the screwdriver stylus that is outlining the petal. This gives each flower a more natural appearance. Working from the front side of the foil, finish each petal's outline with the ball stylus.

4 Emboss the stems and leaves in convex relief to create a natural appearance as shown. Fill in the hollows.

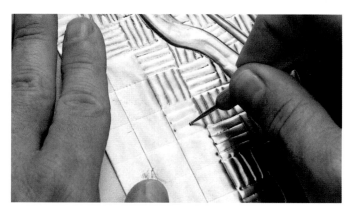

5 From the front side of the foil on a very hard work surface (glass pane) use a blending stump to smooth the background flat. Use a ball stylus on the front side of the foil to add vertical and horizontal lines to the background at ½-inch (1.3 cm) intervals. Draw closely packed lines within the squares to form a basket weave pattern (see photo above).

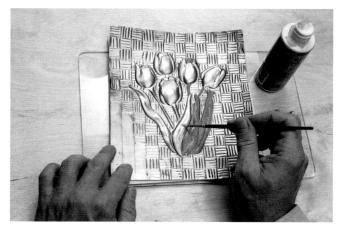

6 Add a paint patina. Following the manufacturer's instructions, add the liquid patina solution to the stems and leaves of the tulips. The solution gives the copper its green color. Use a hot-glue gun to mount the embossed metal onto an aluminum watering can.

Macrame Mirror Frame

The distinctive brass embossings applied to this mirror feature an intricate knot motif representing the unity that binds together friends and family. As you create numerous sweeping curves, you will gain plenty of experience embossing in flat relief. The frame is a solid sheet of foil cleverly slit at the corners to hold a photograph.

YOU WILL NEED

Basic tool kit, page 377

Mirror, 8 × 10 inches (20.3 × 25.4 cm)

Tempered hardwood, 8 × 10 inches (20.3 × 25.4 cm)

Clothespins

Traced patterns A and B, page 444

Plastic circle template or two coins (one 1 inch [2.5 cm] and one ³⁄₄ inch [1.9 cm] in diameter)

Thin brass tooling foil, 6 × 7 ¹⁄₂ inches (15.2 × 19 cm) plus 1-inch-wide (2.5 cm) margins

4 thin brass tooling foil strips, each 1 ³⁄₄ × 5 inches (4.4 × 12.7 cm) plus 1-inch-wide (2.5 cm) margins

4 thin brass tooling foil strips, each 1 × 7 inches (2.5 × 17.8 cm) plus 1-inch-wide (2.5 cm) margins

Transparent drafting ruler

Transparent acetate sheet, 3 × 5 inches (7.6 × 12.7 cm)

TECHNIQUES

Cutting, page 378

Transferring, page 379

Flat relief, page 382

Background relief, page 384

Filling in the hollows, page 384

Applying a paint patina, page 385

Mounting, page 386

BEFORE YOU BEGIN

Use circle templates or coins to guide the stylus along the curves. Use the large coin to steer the stylus around the outside curves and the small one for the inside curves. These circle guides are not the exact size, so you will need to frequently adjust their position. A plastic card will be handy for creating the short straight lines.

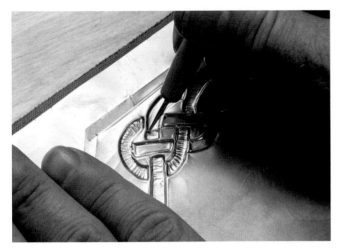

1 Glue the tempered hardwood to the back side of the mirror. Secure the pieces together with clothespins and let dry. Transfer pattern A (the frame centerpiece) onto the large piece of thin brass tooling foil. Transfer pattern B (the corner design) onto four of the small brass tooling foil strips. Emboss all the pieces in flat relief. Add lines across the ribbon images from the back side of the foil to add background texture as shown above.

3 Use a craft knife to make slits at the four dashed lines shown on the inside corners of pattern A. Insert the knife into the slits and widen the space (see photo above) to hold the corners of a photograph and the protective sheet of acetate.

2 Add a low relief background from the edges to the center of the frame centerpiece, covering about 1 1/2 inches (3.8 cm) on all sides (see photo above).

4 Fill in the hollows of all the embossed pieces. Add a paint patina. Cut out the four foil corners and the frame centerpiece as shown just above. Place the embossed pieces face up on a hard work surface (cardboard). Rub the sharp edges under with an upright ball stylus.

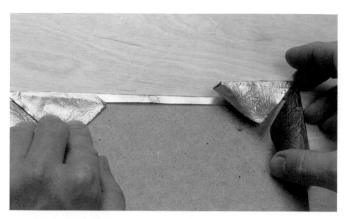

5 Center an embossed foil corner on a corner of the board-backed mirror. Fold back the edges of the foil to cover the mirror corner. Use the side of a stylus to shape the foil to fit around the mirror corner, as shown. Remove the foil corner, and then shape the other three foil corners using the same technique.

7 On a medium work surface (foam place mat) use a ball stylus and a drafting ruler to draw a line along the length of one thin foil strip, 1/4 inch (6 mm) in from its edge. Continue to hold the ruler on the line and run the point of a pencil stylus under the foil edge until it folds upward. Place the mirror edge along the 1/4-inch (6 mm) fold. Use the side of a stylus to mold the folded foil strip to the mirror (see photo). Remove this folded foil edge wrap, and then form the other three.

6 With two adjacent foil corners temporarily in place, measure the distance of the uncovered mirror edge between them as shown, and add 1/2 inch (1.3 cm). Cut a strip of thin brass tooling foil to fit this measurement. Repeat this process for the other edges of the mirror.

8 Apply glue to all the embossed pieces and edge wraps except the areas near the photo slits. Adhere the edge wraps, the corners, and then the centerpiece to the mirror. Position rubber bands along the edges to hold the corners in place while they dry. Place a piece of soft foam rubber and a heavy book over the centerpiece. After the glue dries, insert a 3 × 5-inch (7.6 × 12.7 cm) photo and acetate sheet into the slits, as shown.

Aztec Sun Tile

The sun, revered in ancient cultures, is a powerful symbol of life and growth. In this embossing, the warm tones of brass convey the sun's heat, and the broad, convex relief lets the metallic surface reflect an abundance of light. Golden paint, specifically designed for use on metal, provides additional highlights.

Daisy Chain Frame

Embossing this frame petal by petal and leaf by leaf is like watching your garden bloom. The dramatic relief radiates incredible luster. A black patina worked deep into the frame's recesses provides strong contrast, and a border of decorative aluminum strips sets off the composition.

1 Transfer the pattern onto the large piece of aluminum tooling foil. Working from the back side of the foil on a soft work surface (computer mouse pad), use a pencil stylus to give each petal a ruffled contour. Emboss long freehand strokes from the base to the edges as shown. Define the boundary of each petal from the front side of the foil using a pencil stylus and a very hard work surface (glass pane).

3 Emboss a leaf section so it appears to curl up as shown. From the back side of the foil, outline the upper part of this section with the corner of the screwdriver stylus. Outline the rest of the leaf from the back side of the foil. With a pencil stylus, further define the whole leaf from the front side of the foil. Draw the leaf veins from the front side of the foil. Use this technique to emboss the other leaves.

2 Work the flower bud and stem structures in convex relief. Working on a soft surface (computer mouse pad), tap randomly at the center of each flower with a pencil stylus from the back side of the foil. From the front side of the foil, using a very hard work surface (glass pane), outline the center of the flowers with a pencil stylus as shown.

4 On the front side of the foil, over a very hard work surface (glass pane), use a small ball stylus to draw tight scribbles in the spaces between the foliage (see photo).

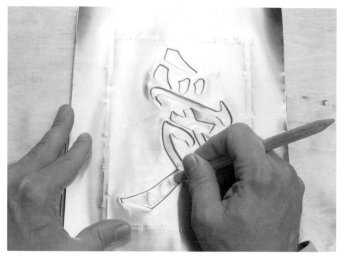

1 Transfer the pattern onto the center of the tooling foil. Emboss the central character in flat relief.

2 From the back side of the foil, apply a subtle fabric texture to the central character by drawing very close vertical and horizontal lines with an empty ballpoint pen on a very hard work surface (glass pane).

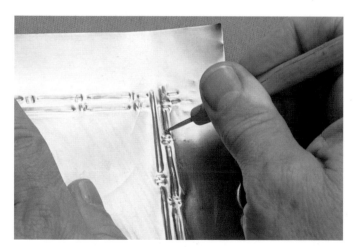

3 Emboss the long and short lines that form the bamboo frame with a wide ball stylus from the back side of the foil over a soft work surface (computer mouse pad).

4 From the front side of the foil on a very hard work surface (glass pane), use a small ball stylus to define only the outer edges of the bamboo sticks (see photo). Make the centers of the longer bamboo sections slightly narrower. Fill in the hollows of the embossing.

5 Add a background pattern that resembles a bamboo mat. From the front side of the foil, over a soft work surface (computer mouse pad), use a medium ball stylus and a transparent drafting ruler to draw closely packed lines as shown. From the back side of the foil, draw lines perpendicular to those previously drawn at 1/2-inch (1.3 cm) intervals.

6 Apply a paint patina to the embossing. If desired, mount it to the basket with brass brads at the corners (see photo).

BACKGROUND TEXTURES

1. Flying Commas

2. Dancing Crosses

3. Baby Locks

4. Thatch

5. Rose

6. Basket Weave

7. Snow Fall

8. Lattice

9. Linen

10. Drizzle

11. Mosaic

12. Bubbles

13. Cobweb

14. Loopty Loop

15. Spiral

PATTERN TEMPLATES

Sampler, page 388 (enlarge 150%)

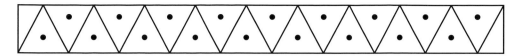

Chili Pepper Bottle, page 395, Pattern A

Chili Pepper Bottle, page 395
Pattern C

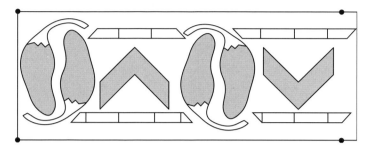

Chili Pepper Bottle, page 395
Pattern B (enlarge 150%)

Catch-of-the-Day Panel, page 393
Fish 2 (enlarge 125%)

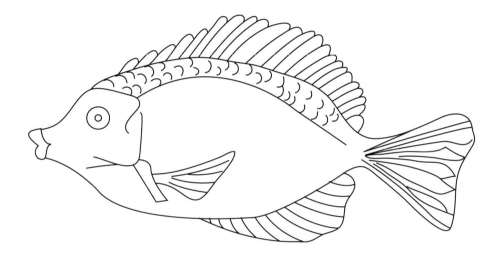

Catch-of-the-Day Panel, page 393
Fish 1 (enlarge 125%)

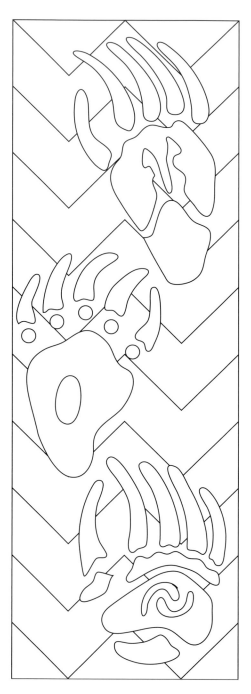

Bear Tracks Panel, page 397
(enlarge 150%)

Butterfly Basket, page 402
(enlarge 150%)

Beautiful Book Trimming, page 399
Pattern A, medallion design
(enlarge 125%)

Beautiful Book Trimming, page 399
Pattern B, single flower design

Moroccan Medallion, page 404 (enlarge 200%)

Bird-of-Peace Plaque, page 409 (enlarge 200%)

Simple Grace Candle Ring, page 408 (enlarge 125%)

Renaissance Box, page 411
Embossing Template
(enlarge 125%)

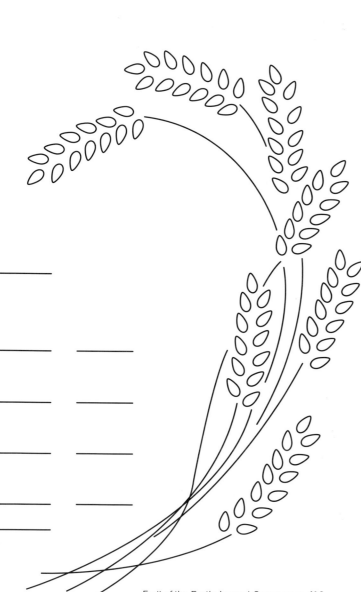

Fruit-of-the-Earth Journal Cover, page 416
Design pattern

Forget-Me-Not Candle Ring, page 406 (enlarge 150%)

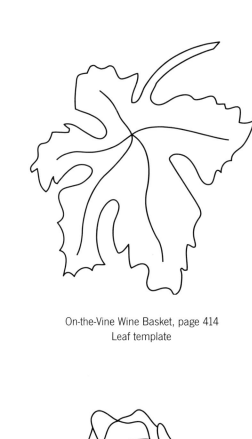

On-the-Vine Wine Basket, page 414
Leaf template

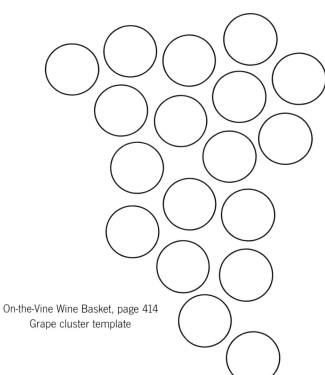

On-the-Vine Wine Basket, page 414
Grape cluster template

Splendor-of-the-Season
Watering Can, page 418